MICK BROWN
Professional Pike Angler

Happy 40th Lee!

Keep piking.

Tight Lines.

Mick Brown

MICK BROWN

Professional Pike Angler

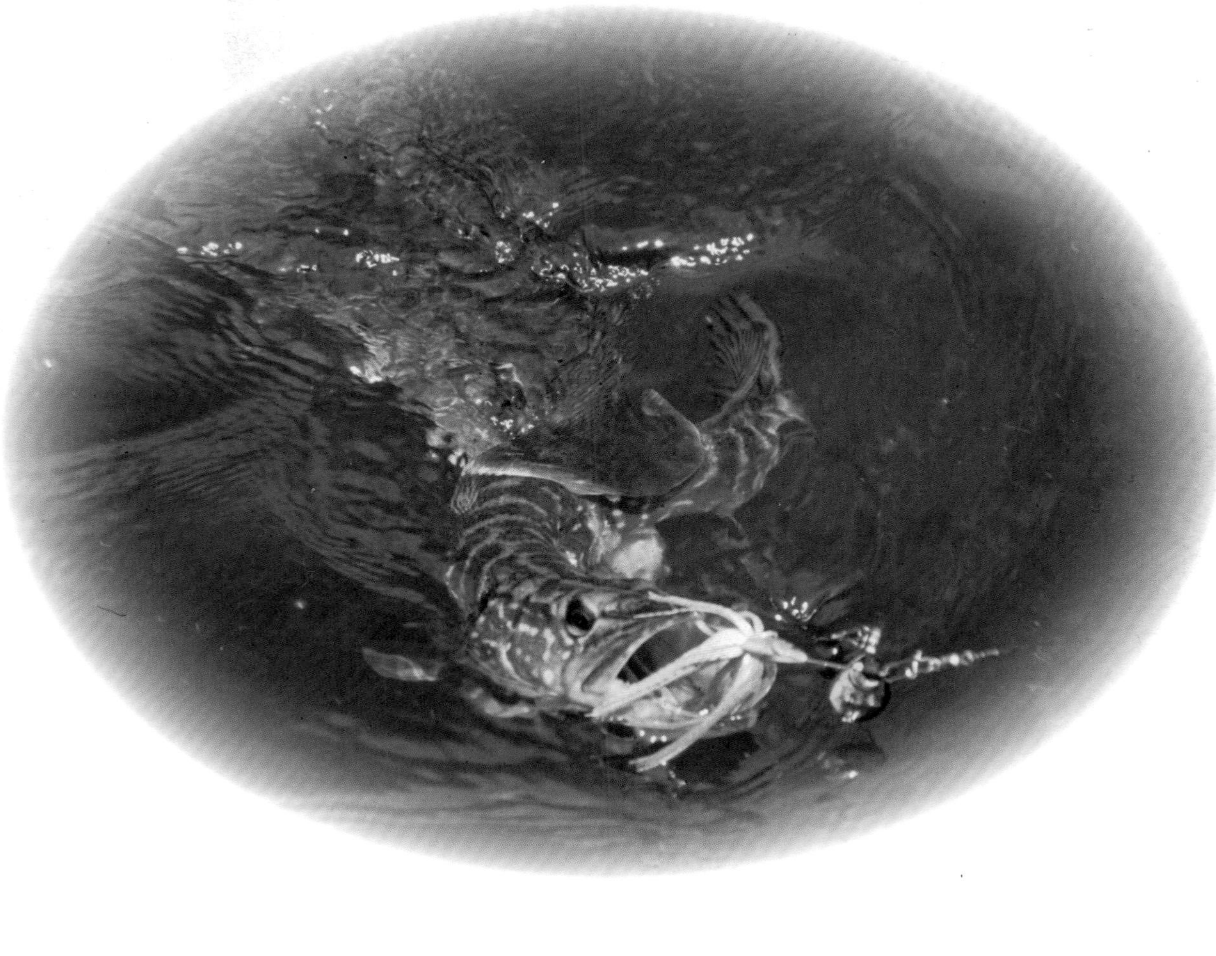

Dedicated to Jan

'THE WIND BENEATH MY WINGS'

Most of the unacknowledged pictures were taken by either Jan or myself

Acknowledgements

I would like to offer my thanks to everyone I have worked with who has made my working life in the tackle and media industries so rewarding. I hope I haven't missed anyone as there are so many but special thanks to all the management and staff at:

Bruce and Walker
Rapala
Shimano UK
Fox International
Dynamite Baits
Bauer Media
Metrocrest
David Hall Publishing
Blinker Germany
Anglers World Holidays

Special thanks to my friends and colleagues;
Matt Hayes, Dave Kelbrick, Max Cottis and Mick Rouse

ISBN 978-0-9569852-0-0
First edition 2011

Designed by **Ricci Cox**
Printed in the UK by **Butler Tanner and Dennis**, Frome, Somerset
Mick Brown Publishing

Contents

Introduction

MY FASCINATION FOR PIKE STARTED IN MY TEENAGE YEARS. A VERY YOUNG MICK WITH A PIKE CAUGHT ON A LIVEBAIT AT SLAPTON LEY LAKE IN SOUTH DEVON, OVER 200 MILES FROM HIS HOME IN BIRMINGHAM.

I have a lot to thank the pike for. They have featured in my life from 'day one' when my father laid one beside me on the kitchen table, just hours after I was born! The pike was eaten by my parents, and indirectly I suppose, I was nourished in my first days by the essence of the pike! Such tales, told in later years by my family, made me feel very aware of pike right from my infancy!

In my teenage years, seeing pike persecuted by match anglers who would often throw them into the bushes behind them if they accidentally caught one, drew me closer to pike as I felt I could see something in them that the ignorant all around me could not. When specimen fishing became popular in the sixties, I was drawn into the 'big fish' scene and fishing for pike became my passion, leading me to travel further afield in search of specimen pike and pike fishing adventures. My first specimen, one which topped the bench mark of 20 lbs, came from the Hampshire Avon River, 140 miles to the south of my midland home.

As the years rolled by, my wanderlust led me to travel far and wide and my pastime quickly grew into an obsession, which gradually led to a modest part time income derived from writing about pike. With each passing season, this little 'sideline' became more lucrative until it occurred to me that I had the basis for a small business – a business which could fund the lifestyle that I yearned for. As it developed, inevitably commercialism entered the scene and I had many financial offers pushed in my direction, all based around my pike fishing. I became well aware that if I continued to follow that route, then everything that I wanted from life would depend upon catching pike. I would have to put everything into it and putting big pike in my landing net would be the basis of my business! That sounded pretty good to me!

I call it a 'business', but it was not a business as most would know one to be. I was getting rewarded for doing what I wanted to be doing anyway, following my passion, and yet paying my way. In the years that followed, it gradually came together in a variety of unexpected ways, and eventually I was able to call myself a full time professional pike angler. This not only enabled me to make a living from pike fishing, but also to deepen my knowledge of pike in such a way that I could never have done on a part time basis.

Learning more about pike from my own first hand experiences became an important aspect of my fishing, as apart from anything else it enabled me to catch them more easily. With my livelihood depending upon catching pike, this deeper knowledge became vital as I became called upon to catch pike 'to order' from every situation imaginable to satisfy the demands of those who paid me for my various services, ranging from producing features for magazines to making films for television.

If I wanted to stay in business, I knew instinctively that I would have to move on from enjoying the simple pleasure that catching pike with rod and line can bring. 'Fun' had always been the keyword in my fishing and I loved the surprise element of luck when it smiled on me, but in order to offer my services at a higher level, I would have to build on my experience of catching pike and the many different ways of doing so. I tried to fish every different type of water that I could, in several countries and with a wide range of methods. It would be impossible to become a master of everything, but I have gradually built up enough experience to feel confident about tackling pike anywhere.

This new found outlook was a long way from the innocent and naïve days of simply trying to catch as many big pike as possible. I didn't let this trouble me too much as, beyond a certain point, it seemed meaningless and self indulgent to keep repeating what I had already done many times without it leading anywhere. Developing my skill and knowledge became much more interesting, and elevated my pike fishing passion to a higher level. Nowadays, I realise that catching lots of pike is not too difficult, but understanding them is very complex, and unravelling the mysteries of the pike's world is much more rewarding.

We will all have a different view of the pike's world, and I can only relate the pike's world as I see it and present the facts as I see them. I do understand the importance of counter argument though and I'm constantly testing my own theories against the findings and opinions of others, and any counter evidence enables me to re consider and adjust my own views if necessary. Writing articles for other pike anglers to read helps me to think things through. It keeps me sharp!

I can appreciate that the reader may only be interested in catching pike as a pastime. Its great fun and that may be enough for you. It was for me at one time, but something that I can't explain has taken over my life which now revolves around pike fishing. It has been beneficial to me though as I've kept things in perspective and used it to my advantage to provide a good life for my family. This book is about those days, the places they took me to and the characters and companies I was involved with. It details how I have pursued my interest of catching pike and learnt about them, and then used all the knowledge gained to pay for my unusual lifestyle. For the uninitiated, let me first of all introduce you to the fish which has brought so much to my life.

The Pike

The Northern Pike *(esox lucius)* is an awesome predatory freshwater fish which is widely distributed in the colder parts of the Northern Hemisphere. It is found in the northern reaches of the North American continent, all over Scandinavia and in most of the Northern European countries. Where the water temperature is suitably low enough, and particularly at higher altitudes, the pike can be found in some of the southern European countries and has been noted as far south as Morocco in North Africa. Fortunately, the British climate is perfect for pike to thrive if allowed to do so, and this offers widespread opportunities for British anglers to fish for them. As we enter the 21st century, anglers are enjoying pike fishing sport of the highest quality. Many are also taking advantage of cheap travel and the abundance of knowledge available through modern communication technology in order to travel far and wide in search of pike fishing adventures which were never thought possible just a few decades ago. In other words, there as never been a better time to become a pike angler! Pike anglers have become increasingly hungry for information and inspiration, and through my business I have tried to provide this. There was never a better time for me to become a professional pike angler!

The pike is a cold water creature but can tolerate our summer temperatures, albeit feeding spasmodically and somewhat unpredictably at this time. They become more active when falling autumn temperatures chill the water, now entering their 'comfort zone', feeding more consistently and building themselves up into top condition in order to be fit and ready for spawning. After spawning, during the early spring months, pike feed voraciously to get themselves back into condition before slipping back into their summer malaise.

Between autumn and spring lies the coldest part of the year and this is the period in which I really enjoy fishing for pike more than any other. The quality of pike fishing sport depends upon how low the water temperature falls and how long any bitterly cold spells last. Most winters in recent times have been quite mild, which has resulted in excellent pike fishing throughout most of the winter period. We had probably not appreciated how mild our winters have become until the last two winters (2009/10 and 2010/11) became the exception and were much colder than we had got used to. Our 'normal' winters are usually punctuated by very short cold spells which freeze the waters surface and stop us from fishing very briefly. Prolonged surface freezing is quite rare in the UK although in other parts of the world, long freeze ups are the norm. We are very lucky in the UK to have a climate which is as good as it gets for pike fishing in winter in terms of productive fishing and angler comfort. This means that, from a business point of view, I have plenty of opportunity to carry out pike fishing work related projects.

It's not all about winter fishing though. In parts of the UK, particularly in the more northerly regions which are slightly colder or anywhere where the water is very deep, good pike fishing is possible through the summer months too. On some such waters, the pike fishing is often at its best at this time. There was a time when I pursued pike around the calendar, but from lessons learnt, I fish less and less in the warmer months as I become more aware of the problems associated with fishing for them at this time.

In fact, most serious lowland pike anglers prefer to give the pike a rest from their attention during the summer months, from early June through to the end of September, having realised that we do them no favours by catching them when water oxygen levels are low. Being 'lean and mean' at this time of year, they fight very hard, often to exhaustion, and there is a risk that there may be insufficient dissolved oxygen in the water to revive them. I nowadays concede that there are times and places when the pike must be given a rest. When and where depends upon prevailing conditions and it is always wise to consider at any time, summer or winter, whether you should temper your enthusiasm if it is likely to endanger the pike's welfare. My rule of thumb is not to fish for pike when the water's surface temperature exceeds 15 degrees centigrade, and whenever pike fight really hard I go to extremes to handle them with care. Lessons learnt over a lifetime!

A NORWEGIAN PIKE TAKEN IN THE SUMMER FROM A HUGE LAKE WHERE THE WATER TEMPERATURE WAS LOW ENOUGH FOR SAFE PIKE FISHING.

A Way of Life

Why we fish for pike or any other fish for that matter, I really haven't a clue! It's something that some of us become excited by and others, like myself, can become quite fanatical about, driven to fish for them for no logical reason. It's relatively harmless though and has many benefits. It teaches us about nature and to respect it, and it takes us into the fresh air and to beautiful places. There are many other positive things I could say but these alone are, to me, enough reasons to go pike fishing. This gives me plenty of scope to pass on my knowledge to the many thousands of like minded individuals who share my interest.

FISHING IS MY WAY OF LIFE. MY CAMPER VAN HAS BEEN LIKE A SECOND HOME.

For me, it's gone even further than just an interest. It's become a way of life, eventually leading on to a full time career in which I have been very happy. When I published my first book – *'Pike Fishing: The Practice and the Passion'* (Crowood Press) in 1993, I felt that I had served my apprenticeship, and this book detailed more than 20 years of my earliest adventures and achievements in pike fishing. These were innocent days when I worked in engineering and pike fishing was just a weekend and holiday pursuit, and looking at it now the book seems very dated. So much has subsequently changed in technical terms and attitudes towards the sport, and indeed I have changed in my outlook and ability too. The book was of it's time though, and I look back at that era with fond memories and see the futility of making comparisons with pike fishing as it is today. Then was then, and now is now! At the time of its publication, my life was going through an enforced change when the tragic death of my first wife led me to re-evaluate my life and career, and make decisions which would change my life. This, my second book, records where this has taken me over the two decades that followed.

During that time, I have managed to make a reasonable living from my pike fishing activities, even though they produced a meagre return at first. I have always felt content with my lifestyle though and have never really wanted all the trappings of luxury that some might yearn for. Initially, my income was from my writing and photography sales to various angling publications, and with two small mouths to feed, we did live in relative poverty for a couple of years, but this did not stop us from being very happy, with great support from family and friends. How things progressed, I will detail in the next chapter and from a difficult starting point, of how things were about to change for the better!

Later chapters enter into aspects of pike fishing which I feel are important for any newcomer to the subject to look into. I have purposely not gone into great detail about pike fishing tackle and methods, as this sort of technical information can be obtained elsewhere quite easily. In the Fox International publication *'Mick Browns Guide to Pike and Predators'* (2009), I wrote in depth about every pike rig I can think of, and this includes the rigs mentioned in this book. It would be a very useful companion guide for anyone reading this book who wishes to learn more about the practicalities of catching pike.

Writing this book has been a trip down Memory Lane, and the stories told are just a sample of hundreds of similar stories I could tell. Selecting them has been the biggest headache as space is limited, but I hope that other pike anglers may be able to relate them to similar experiences of their own. We all have different stories to tell – these are some of mine!

My engineering background has given me the skills I need to carry out maintenance on my equipment.

CHAPTER 1

My Career

When asked what I do for a living, I usually find myself searching for an answer as my business is rather odd to say the least, if not unique. In the end I call myself a professional pike angler, which although sounding a bit pompous is all I can think of to describe what I do. In other words, I make most of my living from my pike fishing activities and have done so for the last twenty years.

Get it out of your mind that this means I spend all of my time watching floats! No one would pay me for that! My income is mainly generated from providing services to tackle and bait manufacturers in the form of developing their products and promoting them through various media outlets. The financial return from the printed media is quite minimal, but television has been more lucrative. This mainly revolves around pike fishing, but this is gradually changing as I am now using my knowledge and experience of other styles of angling to widen the scope of my work. There are a few other ways I top up my income, as any other self employed person would need to, and I can turn my hand to most practical work when required.

Catching fish is only a small part of my business, which might surprise you somewhat! It's the easiest part and takes up about a third of my working week. The rest of my time is divided between practical work and office work, and my technical background in engineering has given me the skills I need to deal with these demands. My engineering training and time spent later working on production engineering and building projects, has given me the practical skills I need to carry out the regular maintenance necessary on my equipment. This ranges from my vehicles to my boats (five of them plus engines and trailers) which always seem to need attention, and all the little bits and pieces that need fixing and repairing from time to time, such as bait boats, alarms and reels. Making such cost savings can make a big difference to your business profits if you have the ability. There is also a degree of practical work required in product development and testing for my sponsors, which is carried out either on the bank or in my workshop.

In my office, where I spend a lot of time, I am fortunate to have had extensive experience in technical report writing and basic business administration. This means that producing technical reports for my sponsors, and magazine features for the media, is quite simple compared to the work I used to do. It's a lot more interesting too!

It might be a revelation that I cannot go fishing where and when I like, but I can't just do as I please if I want to stay in business, and most of my fishing sessions are arranged with the predefined purpose of meeting the obligations of sponsors and clients. They are frequently at short notice and I can never really plan in detail too far ahead. I have to be ready to act rapidly to tackle any style of fishing, so my tackle and equipment needs to be well organised through endless tedious preparation, and doing this takes up further time. The trick is to organise everything so that you are out fishing at prime times and try to do the office and practical chores when the weather is bad! It's not always that straight forward though as I can never be sure what the next phone call might bring.

I mostly work alone and that probably wouldn't suit a lot of people. To do what I do, you need to be happy with your own company for long periods of time, and I prefer to work in this way rather than be restricted by others. I don't mean this in an unkind way, but I rarely come across another angler who fishes with a similar philosophy to my own. In fact, whether professional or not, most other serious pike anglers I know also prefer to fish alone for similar reasons. This doesn't seem a bad thing to me as long as this attitude does not spill over into other aspects of life. For me it doesn't, and when I get back home, Mick Brown the 'loner' is put away until the next session and I try to live a normal family life. I will admit though that the next session is never far from my thoughts!

Although my business is centred around pike fishing, this would not provide enough income on its own, so I am also involved in many other styles of fishing ranging from fly fishing for trout to feeder

'To do what I do, you need to be happy with your own company for long periods of time...'

fishing for barbel (it's not a bad life!). This really does result in a huge amount of tackle to sort out, but as most is supplied by sponsors, I'm not complaining! In fact, this wider involvement has been very useful in generating ideas which I feed back into my pike fishing tactics.

As for pressure to perform, it's no more than the responsibility you would find in any other line of work and I've found it's not a bad idea to push yourself hard rather than take it easy. It feels much better being slightly in front rather than struggling to catch up. I'm always busy, as would anyone be who is running a business, but that's how I like it, and my idea of hell is to have nothing to do! I do dread the nightmare scenario of entering a run of bad luck, which happens from time to time when everything goes wrong, and in particular when I just cannot catch much of any note, no matter how hard I try. This worries me less nowadays because I have learnt that life in general is like this, where most of the time you carry on at your own level of ability, with occasional ups and downs thrown in. It's nothing more than that, and over a period of time, provided that I don't give up, the job eventually gets done, whether it be magazine work, TV work or tackle development. The most important thing is to remain calm and focused, even if it can be a hard slog at times. These facts might come as a surprise to any budding young angler wishing to enter the trade, but I hope I have illustrated the importance of gaining a good education and a solid grounding in basic skills, and being positive. If you don't do so, you will not go very far in this business!

Geographical location can make a big difference to a business like mine. Travelling is costly and time consuming so living where I do, in the South Lincolnshire Fens, is very useful as it is probably one of the best places a pike angler can live. Within ten miles of my home in Market Deeping, I have lost track of the thousands of pike I have caught. There are more than 100 gravel pits, drains and rivers within this area and most have pike. It has been a pike anglers dream, but you will not have heard me mention this much in my media work. Good pike fishing thrives on neglect and I have been very careful not to draw attention to my local fishing. In fact I'm careful not to mention any pike venues at all if I can help it, just the household names and the huge waters that cannot be easily ruined by overfishing. It's a lesson that took a while to learn, but an important one!

Finding myself living in this perfect location was not just good fortune. I moved there from Birmingham in 1987 simply to be amongst good pike fishing and to make pike fishing a part of my lifestyle rather than a weekend hobby. At that time I had no agenda to become a professional angler, but events unfolded slowly whereby this happened. The death of my first wife in 1988, mentioned in the introductory chapter, led me to leave my work in engineering and become a full time single parent. It's not in my nature to be idle, so I started a part time business as an angling writer supplying material to the angling press, and this proved to be a great way of combining my family duties with a small, but useful, supplementary income. To progress in this business it is vital to get yourself noticed, and that's exactly what my writing started to do, although I had no idea where, if anywhere, it would lead to at the time.

When writing on a regular basis, it can become progressively more difficult to come up with articles which are interesting and varied. Anyone can write a few good articles, and many can do so for a short while, but to keep them coming month after month and year after year, takes a dedication that is very challenging. Such material can only come from experience, so it is vital to keep fishing new venues and using new tactics. To be accepted at a European level is even harder, and it's only by travelling and fishing in other countries that enables you to write for foreign publications with a degree of credibility through an understanding of how anglers in other countries view and approach their fishing. Philosophies and attitudes are different in each country and you have to reflect this in the style of your articles.

Whoever you write for, you must be reliable, accurate, and be able to keep to strict deadlines. If you can't, then you will have to make way for someone who can! Very few stay the course, and names come and go. You need to have a reputation for honesty and integrity, and if you blot your copy book, the angling public can be very cruel and unforgiving. Strangely enough this is often out of all proportion, and certain 'rouges' get away with it whilst other lesser offenders are finished for minor misdemeanours. It's a funny old world so you do need to keep your wits sharpened and watch your back at all times!

My business started to grow at a painfully slow pace at first until I had my first break in 1990 when Bruce and Walker, the world famous rod builders from Huntingdonshire, contacted me to see whether I would help them develop a range of pike rods on a commission basis. My features in the monthly angling magazines had obviously done the trick and got me noticed!

The 'Waterwolf' range which we came up with were terrific rods for their time, but far too expensive compared to the cheap imports starting to flood in from the Far East. They were happy days though as it was all new to me, and although I didn't earn much from this work, I did catch pike to 34lbs 7oz using the prototype rods during testing! That was worth more than money to me at the time, but I was always mindful of the fact that I did need to earn more. These were extremely tough times for me, and I had very little money to spend on tackle and bait and nothing was wasted. In fact, at one stage, the only trebles I owned were the ones I had on my three rigs in the water, and all of my pike 'end tackle' could be carried in a small Tupperware lunch box!

Other lucrative projects were later taken on in that era for various com-

PIC: MICK ROUSE

'I DID CATCH PIKE TO 34LBS 7OZ USING THE PROTOTYPE RODS DURING TESTING!'

panies and the most memorable was to be asked by Rapala, the biggest lure manufacturer in the world at that time, to compile and edit an English version of their world famous publication – *Rapala - How to Catch by the Book*. I was paid very handsomely to do so, flown over to Finland to visit the Rapala factory and then taken pike fishing on the Baltic Sea for three days. Coming home with a hundred lures in my suitcase and Scandinavian pike captures to 26 lbs under my belt was extremely satisfying, not to mention getting to fish with top lure anglers like Gord Burton, the 'Piking Pirate', who I'd worked with on the project.

In the early nineties, pike fishing videos were almost non existent, so I decided to have a go at making my own. The results by today's standards are quite laughable, but I've never been afraid to have a go. Two films were made, with my brother Ralph shooting behind an old VHS camera. The first film was made on a fen river and my old mate Carl Allen, then from Spalding, caught a twenty pounder for the camera. The second film would have been amazing if made professionally as I caught a pike of over 28 lbs for the camera from a local gravel pit using a Rapala minnow style lure. The technology we used was not exactly state of the art and editing of took place on my brother's kitchen table using two old VHS video players! The wind noise on the fenland film was really awful, so we dubbed on sound effects and a voiceover afterwards. I still smile when I watch it as the sounds of the pike thrashing in the water were actually made in my kitchen sink and it is pretty obvious too! Nevertheless, we sold several hundred copies of each film, probably because there was little else available on film about pike fishing.

During this period, I had the responsibility of bringing up two small children on my own, but a perk of this was that I had a few hours to myself each day while they were at school. I never wasted a minute, and when I could afford the fuel for my van I'd nip out fishing for a couple of hours. Having so many new waters on my doorstep I did a lot of exploration, and in a few years caught a huge number of pike from my local waters including six different thirty pounders. This gave me a lot to write about!

I HAD MANY AFTER SCHOOL FISHING SESSIONS WITH DANIEL AND NICOLA.

Before too long, I started to realise just how good my local area was and the more I explored it, the more it became apparent that very few other local anglers were aware of its pike fishing potential. They were hardly exploiting it at all, and the few who were had the sense to keep it low key as I did. It did require a lot of effort and determination to get results as few waters were easy to access, many being private and others leased by trout syndicates or water sports clubs. One way or another though, I found a way to fish them all! Maybe I'm being a little unfair to the local anglers as I was pushing myself beyond normal or sensible limits, but for whatever reason I was catching more pike, and plenty of big ones too, than I could ever have dreamed of.

I have now caught 11 different 30 pounders from my local waters and had a few recaptures too, which was inevitable as I will not walk away from waters that I suspect have more potential to come. I don't have a problem with recaptures of large pike. Recaptures happen with fish of all species and sizes, and I find it interesting to follow the progress of individual pike and reassuring to know that they are still alive. Believe me, outsize pike are never any easier to catch again than they were the first time. Ask anyone who has fished for a 'known' thirty and failed!!

'Flooding the press with articles...' Pic: Matt Hayes

Flooding the press with articles about some of these catches started to work for me, and this prompted Crowood Press to approach me to write my first book. The royalty payments are quite low from publishing in this way, but even to this day, I receive a steady trickle of income from it, which I believe has sold around 15000 copies to date. Showing that you can write and take good photos is a useful starting point in this industry, and it gradually became clear to me that all other opportunities are based upon ones ability to communicate with other anglers.

Opportunities started to develop more quickly after the exposure of my fishing adventures through the book, and this led Kevin Maddocks of Clean River Fishing Videos to approach me to make two films, one on river pike and another on stillwater pike. Apparently, the success of my book had been the reason he had approached me, and no sooner were they finished, I was then asked to make two more, this time about summer pike fishing. This was a real boost to my income, not to mention my ego!

I am quite amazed to see that these old VHS titles are now available in DVD format, even though the technical content is well out of date. Such titles get passed on to new owners who have no regard for this fact and have only seen an opportunity to make money from my later reputation, and there's nothing I can do about it. This has happened to me and others in a similar position, signing away rights to future income by not studying contracts closely enough. I made the same mistake with my later television work, proving that I am a much better angler than I am a businessman and have to suffer the financial consequences of rushing into things!

A phenomenon of the current age is for individuals to put clips from their favourite angling films on internet sites such as You Tube. I suspect that there is some financial gain to them somewhere along the way, although it's not always obvious. My old films frequently appear on these sites, and once again, I have no control over content or context. At least it's publicity, and when you have something to sell, any publicity is useful, especially when it's free!

I've talked about lucky breaks, but my biggest of all came in 1993 when I was fishing one day with John 'Watto' Watson from Norwich, when we went to the assistance of a young lady angler who needed help to unhook a pike that had taken her bait down quite deep. I can now happily report that 'love at first sight' does actually happen, but as this is a fishing book and not a romance novel, I will leave it there! Jan and I are now married, and she has also worked as my business partner for several years and taught me a great deal about business administration, not to mention doing a lot of my photography over the ensuing years. We have since enjoyed endless fishing adventures together, at home and abroad, and still do so to this very day. Isn't life strange? I have a pike to thank for bringing us together!

Things improved considerably for me when I joined the tackle giant Shimano in 1994 through a chance meeting with Matt Hayes when I was fishing a pike event at Ringstead Grange trout fishery in Northamptonshire. I didn't have a boat partner on that day, and neither did Matt who was not the 'high profile' star he is today. We struck up a conversation, and as we are both 'Brummies' we soon found that

'...LOVE AT FIRST SIGHT ACTUALLY HAPPENS...! JAN AND I AT PITSFORD RESERVOIR IN 1998.

we had a lot in common and decided to share a boat. Matt was already with Shimano, and at a later date, he contacted me to find out if I would also like to join them as their pike consultant. Of course I jumped at the chance as it meant earning much needed income and would obviously open up a few more doors for me. Shortly afterwards, I also joined Fox International as their pike tackle consultant too, which was possible as there were no product conflicts of interest as Fox did not make rods and reels at that time. It was actually me who approached Fox and offered my services as I was getting increasingly more confident that my business was viable, realising that if you don't ask, you don't get anything! It didn't take a very long conversation with Max Cottis, their Technical Director, to persuade him to take me on, albeit on a very modest starting rate. Neither company had previously had such consultancy positions for pike anglers prior to this, but paid consultants were starting to become fashionable with larger tackle manufacturers.

In 1998 Fox surprised everyone by moving into the rod market which created a conflict of interests with Shimano and at which point I left Shimano under an exclusive deal with Fox. The Shimano experience had been very valuable though and had given me a good grounding into what the tackle industry was all about. My life was made much simpler with just one company to promote rather than two, and the Fox products had much more range and diversity.

When enlisted by larger tackle companies to help them promote their equipment, there is usually a financial arrangement involved. This can be quite rewarding, but don't expect anything like the return of a full time 'normal' job. If such a sponsorship deal can provide you with a quarter of your required income, you are doing very well indeed!

Once your 'notoriety' grows, whether you are a professional or not, you will be requested to make public appearances such as talks and shows. Few of us are natural and confident public speakers, and for most it takes a lot of nerve to stand up and talk in front of an audience. I can do it now, but I can tell you that it took many years before I felt comfortable with doing so. Nowadays I can knock up a one hour long PowerPoint presentation on the day before a talk, and deliver it to the audience without any rehearsal at all. In the early days though, I'd prepare months in advance, practice every day for a fortnight and still be scared rigid on the night! If you can do this sort of thing naturally and confidently, you've got a head start over those that can't. If not, I'd recommend that you practice with small groups of friends to start with to build your confidence, and then progress to small local events. It will probably come as a relief to those struggling with the prospect of doing a talk, that I have always felt the audience has been on my side and all, without exception, have been very welcoming and appreciative that I've taken the trouble to try and entertain them. Remember also that the more you do, the better you get at it. It's so much easier nowadays with digital presentations, which are far simpler to put together than a slide show.

Preparation is the key to doing a good presentation, and that includes being prepared for every eventuality. Amongst the many unforeseen disasters I have endured I include slide projectors being knocked over and my carefully prepared slides strewn everywhere, equipment suddenly not working (take your own if possible), mobile phone nuisances, hecklers, drunken hecklers, snorers and even farters, yes farters! You need to be ready for how you will deal with these things, and if possible try to turn it around to get a positive response from the audience. It is, however, vital to make these appearances in order to get closer to the anglers who are actually the people that keep your business alive.

By far my most financially rewarding business activity has been my involvement in making films for satellite television. That chance meeting with Matt Hayes at Ringstead Grange Fishery was to lead to

I HAVE BEEN FORTUNATE TO TEAM UP WITH MATT HAYES – A GREAT ANGLER AND LOYAL FRIEND.

us getting together later to produce several popular TV series like Wet Nets in 2000, The Great Rod Race in 2003, Record Breaking Fish in 2004 and Total Fishing in 2006. In total we appeared in over 80 films together. This was general angling entertainment though, and very few of those films covered pike fishing. It is probably not widely known that Matt also has a passion for pike fishing. The pike is up there with his favourite species, and we would have really loved to have made more pike fishing films together. We had plenty of opportunity to do so, but chose not to and took on other subjects instead. The reason is quite simple – publicising pike fishing venues was proving to be a short cut to ruining them, causing pike damage and even deaths. Venues that we did film at were soon invaded by over zealous pike anglers in their numbers, and these venues suffered as a consequence. This does not happen with most other species (perhaps with the exception of zander) as they can take a much higher degree of fishing pressure before this occurs. For this reason, the viewer has had to accept alternatives from us such as pole fishing, feeder fishing and trout fishing. We do enjoy these other styles of fishing ourselves, and we get paid the same regardless of the species we catch for the camera, but unfortunately the poor pike fishing viewer has been robbed of his viewing preference. Sadly, it's another case of a few spoiling it for the majority.

For the very same reason, I have not over indulged in producing further video's and DVD's about pike fishing, even though I know it would have been highly possible to produce some really stunning work. DVD's are frequently pirated, and that has been another reason why I have not bothered. It's a great pity, but human nature is what it is! Even my magazine features have been compromised by the need to protect venues from being descended upon with the likelihood of them being ruined. I have had to go to great lengths not to draw attention to the venues I fish, and that really makes my job very difficult and a lot has had to be held back.

There have been several other ways of supplementing my income, such as working with angling holiday companies like Anglers World Holidays and various tourist boards, including the Irish, Swedish and Danish, in order to promote angling destinations overseas. In doing so I have been lucky enough to have fished for pike in many countries including Canada, Sweden, Norway, Finland, Ireland, Denmark, France and Holland. This has certainly been an eye opening experience which, apart from making me realise that we do not have a monopoly on pike fishing methods in the UK, reinforces my feeling that pike fishing in the UK is not actually that bad at all!

In the UK there is another type of professional pike angler - the fishing guide, of which we have an increasing number. Some are part timers but several work at it full time through the pike season in their area. It has crossed my mind a few times to go down this route, and indeed I have made several starts, but before too long boredom has set in. I'm not saying that the job is boring, but it doesn't suit me as it lacks the variety that I prefer in my work. Keeping guiding to a minimum has kept it enjoyable for me and a welcome break from my routine. Of those who I have taken fishing, some on bank and some on boat trips, many have caught personal bests and there have been lots of twenty pounders landed by my clients. I would, of course, have liked to added them to my own personal tally of big pike, but business is business, and at the end of the day, lists and tallies of big pike are of no value unless presented in a meaningful context. We can all get carried away though, as have several of my clients who have published their catches and forgot to mention how they were caught! Some of my clients have been out with me several times, and many I look upon nowadays as good friends and we keep in contact on a regular basis. It's quite satisfying to see other anglers grow in confidence and feel I have played a part in putting them on the right track.

A very useful consultancy in more recent times has been that with Dynamite Baits, and at the time of writing I am still with them. The opportunity to develop and promote their range of pike products has been an interesting chapter during which I perfected my controversial 'kebab' rig, a system for presenting multiple chunks of deadbait. Sadly, it has not been well enough accepted by the pike fishing public and many have yet to see it used with devastating effectiveness as I have (ahead of its time maybe!).

Unfortunately, pike bait products are not as lucrative to manufacturers as are general coarse fishing baits, and my duties at Dynamite have eventually reflected this and I now spend more time working on promoting pellets, boilies and groundbaits than I do pike baits. At least it keeps my bait bill to a minimum and the extra income is always useful!

I even spent a recent year working with a fly fishing tackle company, Guideline from Sweden, working with Matt Hayes to widen their UK profile by making features for Trout Fisherman magazine. It was very useful to fill a financial gap created by the recession of 2009/10 which forced me to reconsider my business plans. I really enjoyed it too, and also used the time to improve my technique!

THERE HAVE BEEN LOTS OF 20 POUNDERS CAUGHT BY MY FRIENDS AND CLIENTS.

For a self employed person like me, free tackle and bait are a hidden but welcome part of one's income. Sponsors generally have been very good in supplying me with tackle and bait and I have always treated this 'perk of the job' with respect, only asking for what I will use. Mind you, with the amount of fishing I have done it has been quite a lot, although a mere drop in the ocean when offset against the advertising benefits to those companies.

Now for a few word of warning if you should think that this sounds like the sort of lifestyle that could suit you too. When you become well known through your work, you are given the label 'high profile'. The problem associated with this is that you are expected to have an opinion on everything related to your specialist subject. Worse still is that everything you do or say is closely scrutinised, and it seems that there is a self appointed policing minority that are continually on the lookout for people like you to do something in any way controversial. This might be political or have some bearing on your technical ability. It's easy to loose your temper and retaliate, but that's often the reaction they take delight in. It's better to be as professional as possible, behave like a politician and endeavour to turn it round to your advantage. Always be on your guard and be very careful what you say or do. If in doubt, do or say nowt!

Talking of politics, and believe me pike fishing is full of it, I have done my best to steer away from any great involvement. It takes a certain type of person to deal with political issues, but I know my limits and also know that it is something I would not be very good at. I certainly admire those who do fight the corner of the pike and pike angler in this manner, especially the committee of the Pike Anglers Club of Great Britain. This sort of political involvement is not for me though. I feel I best serve the interest of the species I love, by encouraging and helping anglers to fish for them in a considerate and responsible manner. Fortunately, I have not been caught up in many major controversies, although the infamous 'Blithfield affair' in 2000 needed careful consideration with regard to how I dealt with it, having been drawn into it by an unexpected attack from the PAC committee of that time.

Now, I have already stated my respect for angling politicians, but sometimes, as in this instance, I think they can go too far and overreact and interfere. In this situation such overreaction, in my opinion, only served to make matters worse and eventually created division and bad feeling between pike anglers, one which still exists in part to this very day. To find myself, and others, under a sudden and unexpected attack from the PAC committee for fishing an event where pike under 15lb had to be killed was, I believe, a turning point in my attitude towards the PAC and its increasing interference with the activities of pike anglers. The furore which followed rocked the pike fishing world for many years afterwards, and several PAC members who took part in the event were expelled from the club, including me!

Knowing all the pike anglers involved, no pike would have been killed by our hands, and we were well on the way to forging a better relationship with a trout fishing club renowned for killing pike. We felt that the dogmatic stance taken by the PAC committee was unnecessary, but I can now see the chain of events that led them to react as they did. I have no ill feeling to anyone involved, but wish we could all have handled it in a better way. Extremist views were aired from both sides and if we have learnt

Blithfield pike flourish nowadays like this 23 pounder taken on a spoon on a members pike day.

anything, I think it is that extreme views can be dangerous, and we should look at future situations in a more considered manner. I am much happier with the attitude of recent PAC committee's, and would still advise and encourage all pike anglers to join up.

The Blithfield pike flourished in the years that followed when pike anglers became more involved with the fishing on the reservoir. I enjoyed fishing there so much that I even joined the trout club! During my years as a member of the Blithfield Trout Club, I witnessed a modern attitude towards pike rapidly take over from the mindless slaughter of the recent past. This is, of course, my personal view after ten years of hindsight, but if you want some interesting reading and you have plenty of time on your hands, I suggest you research the archives of the internet forums and try to make some sense of this issue yourself. It certainly created a very heated debate at the time, mainly fuelled by those who had nothing at all to do with it!

Most of my 'professional' years have been very happy ones, but all good things eventually come to an end. After spending many satisfying and interesting years developing and promoting equipment for Fox International, the recession brought things to a sudden halt in December 2009, when consultants became no longer financially viable. This happened throughout the trade, and at this point in time the prospect of carrying on as a professional angler has been greatly lessened. Fortunately, the knowledge I have gained over the years, and my connections in the trade, should allow me to start a new chapter in my life and career, but in these uncertain times there's no knowing where it will lead me.

The lifestyle I have led over the last twenty years or so has been very satisfying, but it would be wrong for me to allow you to believe that every day was filled with sunshine and big pike. It was possible though, to earn enough money to get by on and to lead a lifestyle which, to a fanatical pike angler, is second to none. The way of doing this, as I think I have shown, was to become involved in a wide range of related activities, none of which pay particularly well, but together combined to make a reasonable total. From remarks I have heard, I am sure that anglers in my position often tend to be looked upon as wealthy playboys, flitting around the globe and using the very best tackle. You can be quite certain that no one gives you anything unless you give them something in return. The reality is that the travel and tackle are rarely paid for and are part of deals brokered with sponsors. You may also have realised at this point that 'the dream' might be slightly tarnished because of the commercial implications, but the lifestyle benefits have helped me to live with it!

So, that's how my business developed and what's been involved in running it. You can see that it's not all about simply going fishing, but it's been essential to do as much fishing as I can to be able to do my job properly. More importantly it's been about getting involved in every aspect of pike fishing, using every method on all types of venues. It's the experience that this kind of activity generates that gives you the knowledge you need to be able to meet the demands of sponsors and the media. In reality, my work has probably been filled with all the challenges that anyone faces in any job or business, but the big difference is that my work is based upon something that I simply love to do, i.e. going fishing! I still have to run a home and family, and that involves earning enough money to do so. Choosing to do this through my fishing activities means that I have to run a very efficient business, no different to any other self employed person. It must be quite an unusual situation where the product is me and the fish I catch! In fact, at an interview with the Inland Revenue, a most perceptive inspector challenged me by suggesting that I have found a loophole whereby other people are funding my hobby. Damn right they are! It's all legal and above board though, and I have always paid my tax and national insurance as I should!

Having set the scene, the rest of the book will tell you more about the places I've been to, some of the fish I've caught and what I've learnt or concluded along the way and most chapters start with a story that illustrates a point. I hope you will find it entertaining and that it inspires you to do as I have done and go your own way, not following fashion but fishing where and how you want to, being determined and never giving up too easily. I advise using practice as your yardstick and not to follow dogmatic theories from others. There are no training courses, you have to teach yourself! You won't always be right, but you will eventually learn what is. Follow your own dreams and take a few chances for, without doubt, chance comes into everything. Above all else, take time to enjoy the wonderful journey!

'...I FOUND MYSELF FISHING THROUGH GAPS IN THE ICE TO WINKLE OUT A PIKE OR TWO...'

CHAPTER 2

Cold Water Killers

As my business is based upon catching pike, I can't afford to make excuses for not going fishing. Even when it may seem crazy to venture out in extremely cold winter conditions I have no choice but to keep going if I want to pay my bills! Sessions now become filled with hope rather than expectation, but I've always relished the challenge of pitting myself against the worst that nature can throw at me. If nothing else, I can take photographs of the conditions that are making the fishing so difficult, and they can be very useful for illustrating articles and talks. Above all, I still want to catch pike! I am well aware that my tactics will now need to be 'spot on' when the water is icy cold, and it's important to understand what I'm up against. I am now trying to catch a fish that has almost closed down its system, and in this temporary torpid condition is almost oblivious to anything around it. Quite a challenge!

Fully prepared for difficult fishing, I wasn't going to let the very cold winter of 2009/10 prevent me from trying for a very big pike I'd stumbled across a few months earlier in a large weed choked lake. I'd waited for cold weather to arrive before starting my assault on this lake which I'd been trying to come to terms with for the previous two seasons, but I didn't expect it to be so cold though! My permission to fish there didn't allow me to start fishing until December 1st anyway, but at least that had allowed the dense weed to die back a little. After just one days fishing, which was a complete blank, the country was suddenly hit by one of the coldest winters for years. Day after day, week after week, we endured bitter cold weather with snow at times, and the lakes surface was frozen for quite a while. Even the rivers were freezing over and I found myself fishing through gaps in the ice to winkle out a pike or two and it was hard going. Fishing everywhere was rock hard and this was not a time to be tackling waters like this, but I couldn't let an opportunity to try and catch a huge pike pass me by.

As we entered February, I hadn't had another chance to fish there due to the ice, and I realised I'd soon be running out of time as my permission to fish the lake expired at the end of the month. When the ice finally started to clear, I took the water temperature and it was just over two degrees centigrade on the surface near the boat jetty. The shallows were still frozen solid and it was bordering on the possibility of the deeper water freezing over again. It didn't look very inviting! That evening, in the sub zero temperature of my tackle shed, I prepared for another attempt the following morning as the forecast was for a light breeze which should clear any remaining ice, making conditions perfect for float trolling livebaits.

I was soon fumbling with the metal gate at the estate entrance in the grim morning light, trying not to let my fingers weld to its icy feel. My thoughts wandered back to a day in July when I first spotted a big pike there, the memory of which would not leave me. At first glance I hadn't seen her camouflaged body lying in the marginal weed as my eyes were drawn to the outline of a large tench lying on its side. Then I realised why it lay on its side - it was firmly clamped in the jaws of a very big pike! Through the breeze swept surface and amongst the thick dark weed in which they lay, I tried to estimate her size. Seconds later, she melted away with her meal. She was ENORMOUS and I had to catch her!

I was rather surprised to see her lying in shallow water in July with the water temperature being so high. Although pike are far more at ease in the colder months, they do have to feed all year round, and in warm shallow water I have noticed such feeding tends to be quite unpredictable. I had to temper my enthusiasm to try and catch her there and then, but I really had no other choice than to obey the syndicate rules and wait until December when pike fishing is allowed. I was happy to do so though as summer pike fishing appeals to me less and less as the years go by. With a six pound tench to digest, who knows how long it would be before she fed again anyway!

I would mainly be concerned that she, or any other pike I caught when fishing in the summer, might become exhausted or stressed from the fight, or may even die when the water temperature is elevated and oxygen levels are low. The lake is typical of many I fish for pike, plagued with really dense weed in summer, making the potential of snagging a real possibility and a further good reason why I should wait until winter. Furthermore, there is life outside of pike fishing as I have finally learnt, and summer is a time to catch up with family life and….. Oh well….. I'll be honest, its time for catfish, tench and barbel too! I love pike fishing of course, but wouldn't want to miss out on my other activities either.

These thoughts are put to the back of my mind as I load the boat with the gear. I'm in no hurry and take my time. Very cold weather slows me down too and I make sure everything is well organised should I hook into a big pike. My plan is quite simple, to troll a livebait round the lake and cover as many likely places as possible where that big pike might be lying in the icy cold water. I'm going to troll on the oars and use just one rod, as I've found it better to get one bait fishing perfectly rather than try to control two and continually have to adjust one or the other. I'm not expecting the pike to be in a chasing mood, and know I must fish the livebait within inches of the bottom where any pike will be lying in a silent, timeless world, oblivious to anything more than a few feet away from them, and sometimes not even then.

The breeze is gentle and allows me to troll extremely slowly. In fact, I can almost bring the bait to a standstill when the echo sounder indicates that I'm in a potentially good area. I'm working the medium depth contours for the day, staying in about eight to nine feet and paying special attention when I'm

'TIME PASSES QUICKLY, AND THE BREEZE DROPS TO A FLAT CALM...'

adjacent to shallower water, especially near steep drop offs with weed on the edges. There's deeper water to fish at a later stage, but the bottom there is flat, uninteresting and uninspiring. The shallower water can be ruled out at the moment as it's still covered with ice, but it can never be dismissed as it has plenty of weed cover and a few slightly deeper holes. Although the shallows are frozen, it nags at me that the big pike might find warmer water beneath the ice, and I could be wasting my time by fishing deeper water.

Hours pass, I can't remember how many, maybe four or five. My back is starting to ache and my hands are raw from gripping the damp oars after getting them wet while removing weed from the rig every now and again. I think about other places I've fished and big pike I've caught. I daydream about catching catfish in the summer and what it would feel like to have the sun warming my aching body right now. I also think about the log fire burning at home and what it will be like when I get back there and lie in front of it. Time passes quickly and the breeze drops to a flat calm as the grey sky starts to blacken, and although I don't want to go home, I can feel my body weakening from the cold and damp. I decide to turn the boat around and run along a drop off again just once more, a hundred yards from where I'd seen her in the summer.

The average size of the pike in the lake is quite good, but the one I'd seen in the summer was exceptional. If something should grab my livebait, it could be any pike in the lake, I had considered that and was not hoping for anything more than a chance to try and catch her. Even when the red float suddenly buried out of sight I didn't get too excited, it was just a relief that it had!

I wound down and tightened the braid line to set the pair of size four trebles, and the very fact that nothing budged told me straight away that this was a biggish pike which probably didn't even know it was hooked. When it did realise its plight it came steaming towards me, but without the anchor down it was a formality to walk her round the boat to follow her without the need to apply excessive pressure and risk the hooks pulling out.

The cold and pain forgotten for a while, I eased her higher in the water until I could see the stop knot clear the surface and the float show itself. Five or six feet below me in the iron grey water she appeared, slowly and menacing, her mighty snout gripped firmly closed with both hooks inside and just the tail of the unfortunate roach showing. Just one flare of the gills though, and she could throw out the bait and the hooks, so I had to net her calmly.

With extreme care, I slowly sunk the round landing net into the water and wondered whether it would be big enough. As she lay almost motionless just beneath the surface, I slipped the net under her. It was only just adequate in diameter, but had a very deep mesh into which she sunk safely. It just had to be the big one, she was colossal and I started shaking with excitement, totally forgetting how cold I was or how damp it was getting.

By now I had drifted to within fifty yards of the north shore and paddled the rest of the way while she lay quietly in the net, not moving or struggling due to the coldness of the water. Numbed by the cold, I don't think she was too aware of exactly what had just happened. Neither was I for a while until I had unhooked and weighed her. She was not far from my estimate, and at six ounces over 34 lb, it made her my fourth biggest pike. After countless thousands of captures, taken over several decades, this was a very special day indeed!

As I waited for Jan to drive up to photograph her, I contentedly guarded the sack in which the pike lay quietly while I tidied the boat. The roach bait lay mangled on the deck, still attached to the trace, and the line on the reel had spilled from the spool and needed untangling. I was soon tidied up and could not hold back my excitement any longer and phoned my mate Dave Kelbrick to tell him the news. We had only been talking about the possibilities of catching pike in the current cold spell just a few evenings beforehand. If fishing alone has one big drawback, it's that you don't share these special moments with anyone at first hand, but it's something you have to live with if you go your own way.

Captures like this are vitally important to my work. What I am selling is my experience, and it is necessary to build up a degree of credibility when teaching other anglers about catching pike and advising tackle companies about the equipment they should be producing. This has meant pushing myself

'... AT SIX OUNCES OVER 34 LB, IT MADE HER MY FOURTH BIGGEST PIKE EVER.'

to fish every type of venue, with every method I can think of and in all weather conditions. The vast knowledge gained from doing so is not scientifically sound, but is more than sufficient to build up a working understanding of pike behaviour. Much of this is no more than 'gut feeling', as a lot of what I have concluded cannot be seen or easily proven.

I really do like fishing in the coldest part of the year. Pike are in the best of condition and can be caught with less chance of stressing them while their system is slowed down by low water temperatures. Many pike anglers don't like to fish in this colder period, preferring the spring and autumn months when sport can be quite brisk, but mid winter has a special magic for me. It often has a forbidding atmosphere that is urging you to go home and not to bother, but once you start to crack the cold water code, the rewards can be immense in terms of catches and satisfaction. When the banks are barren, and there are no other anglers in sight, that's when I like to go pike fishing!

I have learnt that pike do not follow strict rules and you cannot predict their feeding behaviour with any great certainty. There are so many natural variables to take into account which we have no control over like temperature and the wind. Then there are other influences which anglers don't fully understand like feeding triggers. It is never all that clear how your pike fishing results might be affected by different combinations of these factors. It seems to me that there is a balance at work, with positives working against negatives, and the outcome is rarely clear. For this reason, I will go pike fishing whenever I feel like it rather than trying to gauge when it is a good time to fish, and some of my greatest catches have come when I have least expected them to. Like the big pike mentioned in the opening story. How many would have stayed at home by the fire on that day? Most of my fishing mates did! You have to be a little philosophical to carry on like this and enjoy every fishing session, seeing it as a learning experience whether you catch or not.

Pike are certainly much more comfortable about feeding in very cold water than I first realised, but you can never be sure what the actual water temperature is where a pike is hooked. We tend to take surface water temperatures with our thermometers and fish finder gauges, but this is only a guide to what the temperature might be further down the water column. Water is moving up and down the water column all the time as its density is affected by temperature. It is also circulating in a complex way due to currents set up by the wind and thermal variations between different parts of the lake. With so many forces at work, it would be very unlikely that a simple angler could understand the temperature distribution model for a given water in a given period. All I need to know personally is that this dynamic phenomenon is taking place and that, even on the calmest of days, there will be currents and variations in water temperature. With this constantly in mind, I keep on the move if I am not catching, with the knowledge that pike (and other species) will be positioning themselves in the most favourable places. I just have to find them! This might help the reader to understand why you can search a water and catch nothing for a long time, and then suddenly drop onto a lot of pike in a tight area. There may be other reasons too of course, making our conclusions less sound, but as I have already intimated, there are many factors to be considered.

This is an interesting topic to study further if you have time to do so. I find it quite fascinating and think about it a lot when pike fishing, especially in very cold weather when catching pike can be more difficult. The only clues I have are the air temperature, the water temperature at the surface, the depth

Pike are certainly much more comfortable about feeding in very cold water than I first realised.

of the water and the wind strength and direction. How they work together on the day provides clues to where pike might be and how they might be reacting, and it's up to me to try and interpret this. Searching the water is therefore vital. You might find them by an educated approach or simply by luck, but either way involves keeping moving and usually keeping your bait very close to the bottom at this time.

Even before I considered things in this way, I was never put off by low water temperatures as long as I fished my bait tight to the bottom, because I instinctively knew this was the right thing to do. When echo sounders with temperature sensors started to become widely available, it was possible for boat anglers to gain a better understanding of the effects of water temperature and quantify them. When trolling in Finland many years ago, we found the water temp in one bay to be just one degree Centigrade at the surface, but took pike after pike by trolling our lures so that they followed the bottom contours very precisely. Feeling the lure bump bottom and picking up occasional debris, confirmed that we were trolling deep enough. Those who I fished with on that trip who followed the rule caught pike; those that fished a little higher in the water didn't! That's something I've found time and time again on so many venues, and a valid reason why the method of jig fishing, with its bottom contour hugging capability, can be so effective in winter.

The waters I fish at home tend to be mostly less than twenty feet deep and fishing on the bottom in such depths is quite practical, but fishing on the bottom in water deeper than this at very low temperatures is beyond my experience. I have been successful at catching pike in very deep water overseas of up to 300 feet or so in the summer months, when they can be found suspended in the upper layers, but English anglers do not get much chance to find out much about pike in such deep waters as we just do not have many of them.

Shallow water is the first to warm up, and winter pike might move to shallower water when a sudden temperature rise takes place. Then again they might not! It depends upon how long the warmer weather lasts and how quickly the main body of water cools the shallower water down again by conduction and circulation. Water temperature can certainly vary quite dramatically around a lake in winter, and surface thermometer readings can vary enormously from place to place. Shallow bays catching the sun can be several degrees higher than the temperature over deep water, but this is only very close to the surface and may not reflect the temperature lower down the water column. Many other things can also be happening which will gradually lead to further changes. Wind can move water around and push it to unsuspected areas. Shallow areas might freeze first, but the temperature below the ice might be quite acceptable to pike. Such factors serve to reinforce the lessons I keep repeating to myself any time I go pike fishing. I keep on the move, use a searching approach and have an open mind.

It is confusing and that is why we don't always understand why we catch where we do and when we do, but we do know that there are frequently areas which are more favourable than others. Water temperature often plays a big part in this and finding water of a favourable temperature can be the key to catching pike. In all but the most prolonged and settled of conditions, water temperatures will be all over the place so I am always looking for other clues to where pike will be. Fortunately, the pikes prey is affected by water temperature too, and if you can locate prey, you are probably getting very close to catching pike. In severely cold weather, prey fish don't tend to give themselves away, so trial and error is all you are left with. Boat anglers have a great advantage as they can find prey with their sonar. This doesn't always mean you will easily catch pike amongst them though, especially on waters with huge numbers of prey fish as the pike will be well fed, often making them less responsive to your baits.

I find that fishing in very cold water is most successful when using livebaits, and when everyone else is struggling to catch pike, I often prefer to use them as my first line of attack. When livebaits are not allowed or available, I sometimes use deadbaits, usually small ones. Twitching or inching them along the bottom occasionally can often help, and I usually pop them up to give a better presentation without snagging when I put movement into them. Lures which fish tight to the bottom, and which can be worked very slowly, can also succeed and my next line of attack would often be to use jigs in venues where they can be presented well, particularly in areas where I know that pike are definitely present. There's more about this exciting method in the relative chapter. Winter lure fishing requires patience

YOU WILL NEED TO PERSEVERE TO CATCH PIKE WITH LURES IN COLD WATER.
THIS FEBRUARY PIKE OF 23 LBS TOOK A FOX MICRO DEMON.

and some degree of skill to perform well, but in my experience lures can be worth persevering with even in the lowest water temperatures.

When livebaiting in cold water I have two distinctive approaches. Sometimes I will tether a livebait in a fixed position if I feel that there are pike in the swim, or that they could pass through at some time. To tether the bait I use a 'sunk float' paternoster rig which is very amenable to using multi rod tactics from the bank when rigged with 'drop back' bite alarms. Such alarms are essential as 'slack line' bites have to be detected quickly when a pike moves towards the rod with the bait. I have also devised a 'double float' paternoster rig for boat fishing which has a sunk float to keep the rig in tension and a smaller, secondary, surface float which acts as a bite indicator. This rig can be very useful for bank fishing too without the need for alarms.

Paternoster rigs are fine if I want to fish a known area for long periods of time, but can also be very effective when used in a 'leap frogging' approach when bank fishing, moving the rods along the bank and covering much more water if I'm not so sure that I'm 'on pike'. Dropping the rigs in gaps between bushes on a river is a typical example where this tactic can be productive and a great number of swims can be checked out in a day if you have enough livebaits.

Other waters demand searching tactics to put the bait in view of lethargic pike, especially those fish which are at greater range. The 'leap frogging' approach along the bank can cover a fair few swims in a day, but nowhere near as much water as is covered by float trolling a livebait from a boat, a particularly favourite method of mine. The trolling approach obviously permits fishing in areas beyond bank casting range, and in conjunction with an echo sounder as I've described, you can locate both prey fish and favourable bottom structure, giving a huge advantage.

Whether fishing from boat or bank, another excellent searching technique is covering the water with a livebait mounted under a drifter float. You need a favourable wind, of course, of adequate strength and from a suitable direction, which often limits when it can be used. On waters with uneven contours, you might not get a drifted bait deep enough in places as the depth setting tends to be a compromise to minimise snagging at the shallowest point of the drift. The deeper areas you miss as a result of this could be where the pike are holed up!

On rivers, I make use of the current to search swims by trotting my livebaits under a float, but snagging can be a big problem as in cold weather you do need to get the livebait as close to the bottom as possible. Once again, a compromise depth setting might cost you fish if it's too cold for the pike to come up very far from the bottom for a meal.

As you can see, there are plenty of very effective options for presenting livebaits for cold water pike, whether in a static or searching manner. The biggest problem will most likely be in obtaining them! To comply with regulations you are not allowed to transfer them from one water to another which is a big handicap, and they will usually be very hard to catch on the day. You will have to be very resourceful to stay within the law!

A WINTER PIKE CAUGHT ON MY 'DOUBLE FLOAT' PATERNOSTER RIG.

There's bound to be a lot of theory in my conclusions about cold water piking, and it would be much more plausible if I really did know how pike reacted in the coldest weather. Well I would never wish to presume that I did so, but I've seen enough examples at first hand to reinforce my judgement that they do everything extremely slowly, and none more noteworthy than an incident that happened a few years back when I was running my annual Pike Master Class at Horseshoe Lake in Gloucestershire, ironically organised by the Carp Anglers Society! This was a weekend event attended by about twenty anglers wanting to learn more about pike fishing methods and have a fun weekend at the same time.

The great advantage of a fly is it's delicacy of presentation.
Pic: Matt Hayes

The event of 2007 was greeted with very low air and water temperatures and we arrived to find the lake frozen over! We had two choices. We could have just drunk the barrel of beer that was laid on for us in the clubhouse and had a good laugh, or we could fish if we broke the ice! In actual fact we did both, and the fishing turned out to be unexpectedly interesting. David Mannell, the Commercial Director of the organisation, bravely took out a boat in the early hours of the icy cold February morning and proceeded to break the thinnest ice which had formed over the Summer Bay, which is only about four feet deep. The ice was blown away by mid day and my anglers caught a few pike. Restricted to lures and deadbaits I think they did well, but I know that livebaits would have fared much better. However, we obviously could not import them and it would have been almost impossible to catch any. It was not a 'catch at all costs' weekend and they all soldiered on, with plenty of food and entertainment to make up for the slow fishing.

On my travels between swims to try and help the anglers, I noticed a pike lying in gin clear water, some ten yards from the bank. I was carrying my pike fly rod, having just demonstrated casting, and couldn't resist the chance to run a favourite home tied buck tail fly past it to see if I could get a reaction. Several casts proved that it was unlikely to take it, but it was a challenge I felt like going for!

In similar situations I've cast deadbaits and livebaits close to pike, and with perseverance have tempted a few to take them. Some I've landed but most have just clamped onto the bait and held it, sometimes for over twenty minutes, before I've pulled it away from them. I've even balanced a sardine on a 'known' thirty pounders nose for several minutes after spotting it lying in the margin on a very cold day. It eventually swam away, totally uninterested in it, and despite being what I would consider a prime bait.

Here in front of me now was another challenge. I wasn't really bothered about actually catching the pike, just hoping to see how, if at all, it would respond. After three or four attempts I managed to land the fly on the bottom, about six feet to the left of the pike which was facing towards me. I watched and waited patiently for four or five minutes, in which time I'd assembled a small audience behind me. We

'IT'S VERY CLEAR TO ME THAT PIKE CAN BE CAUGHT IN EVEN THE VERY COLDEST WEATHER CONDITIONS.'

all kept very still, staring at the pike and the fly. Then I noticed something quite significant. The pike was gradually turning its body through 90 degrees to face the direction of the static fly on the bottom. It was only by staring at the pike very intently that I could tell it was turning at all, just a few degrees at a time. It was several minutes more before it was finally looking straight at the fly, which was still several feet away!

It appeared to be motionless, but I could see in the clear calm water that it was approaching the fly at a snails pace. I could barely detect its micro movement as it passed over the small gravel chippings, and the distance between pike and fly became less and less. This took another five minutes or so and we were spellbound and fascinated, and no one could draw their eyes away.

More than ten minutes after the fly had first landed, the pike was within an inch of it, and its tail and rear fins were rippling gently to show it was primed for an attack – but when? More time passed but I could wait no longer and twitched the fly, no more than a few centimetres but enough to make the pike react and inhale it in a flash!

She was hooked and behaved as all cold water pike do by shaking its head from side to side without moving away. Amazingly, two more pike appeared from nowhere to come and see what was happening, but darted away as I slowly winched her to the bank where my good friend Mike 'Hoss' Neate chinned her for me. It was an incredible incident which became the talking point of the day, especially for the two anglers nearby who had had deadbaits out for twenty four hours without a run!

It's very clear to me that pike can be caught in even the very coldest weather conditions. Whether you want to go to a lot of trouble to catch them, or wait until a better time, is another thing! Although they may not wish to feed at this time they can often be tempted by good bait presentation, and frequently enough, in my experience, to make it worth going pike fishing regardless of how grim the situation might look. What we are feeling is not what the pike are feeling. The pike is cold blooded and does not need to keep itself warm; it simply adjusts to ambient temperature. It may shut down its system to some extent, but may be aware of what is going on around it and could be tempted.

We are equipped today with cold weather clothing that is warm, light and comfortable, and there is no reason why we should not fish for pike in the coldest of weather, provided that the water is not frozen and we can cast a bait. If it is frozen, pike can be caught by drilling through the ice, but this is a practice that is fraught with danger and I would not recommend it unless you know what you are doing. Anglers in colder climates do so very successfully, but the ice formed on our waters is generally nowhere near the thickness experienced in other countries to the north, so I would not even suggest anyone should try it!

I never let cold weather put me off. It all depends upon how anxious I am to catch pike and in my line of work I need to be catching regularly. I would prefer to temper my enthusiasm and wait until temperatures start to rise if possible, but would never go pike fishing in the coldest weather and feel it is completely hopeless. The ultimate winter pike fishing experience for me is to catch them in the snow. We don't get much snow nowadays in the UK, but when it comes, you can be sure that I'll be out there – and fishing with confidence!

The ultimate winter pike fishing experience for me is to catch them in the snow.

I've managed to get some good shots of pike in action.

CHAPTER 3

Dog Eat Dog

Photography is an important, in fact essential, part of my business. Apart from illustrating my articles, I also have to supply material to my tackle trade sponsors for their catalogues and advertising campaigns. I also make useful extra income by supplying such material to anyone who will pay for it, such as for web sites and calendars. Trophy shots are obviously of some value, but more sought after are well composed pictures of anglers doing something, like playing fish or netting them. 'Big fish' mug shots are 'ten a penny' and it's something different that's wanted, something which stands out from the ordinary. I need to have my wits about me and to be on the look out all the time for something which is really special. The best opportunities always seem to come totally out of the blue so it's vital to be very aware of everything happening around me. Above all, I have attempted to get shots of the most awesome sight of pike in action. When you witness pike attacking prey, or even each other, it is very rare to capture it on film as it happens so quickly. It does come right every now and again, and I've managed to get some good results.

I'd been drifting the East shore of a large gravel pit all morning, alternating between fly and wobbled deadbait methods. It was well into May and the trees were green again after a long harsh winter, and with the water rapidly warming it would soon be time to put the rods away again for a while and give the pike a rest. Time for just one more session though! The breeze was gentle and pushed the boat along so slowly that there was no need for a drogue.

Then a commotion started, close to the bank upon which new reed growth was breaking through. All hell broke loose, and from a splashing and crashing of water, a small pike frantically emerged and flipped itself onto the bank. A fish of about four pounds had jumped onto the bank and wedged itself in the vegetation in an attempt to escape from being eaten alive!

In the gin clear water, some eight to ten feet deep, my Polaroid's clearly revealed its persecutor. It was a very big pike and clearly over 30 lb, probably the 32 pounder I had caught in the winter, and she was rapidly quartering the area looking for the escapee. Just beneath her massive frame swam another big pike, looking to be all of 25 lb. They were all fired up, ready to attack, and apart from being privileged to witness such an amazing spectacle, I sensed I had a chance of catching one of them, either on rod and line….. or on film! If it was the 32 pounder I had caught before, there would be no real reason to catch her again - except maybe on a home tied fly! I just had to do it as the chance of a 30 lb pike on a fly rod rarely comes anyone's way!

Suddenly, the pair of them swam under the boat, just three feet beneath the surface, and I fumbled with my fly rod and camera, not being sure which one to get ready first. They passed by again, searching for the small pike, but they were too deep for me to photograph them so I started to strip line from the fly reel and got ready to cast.

I had been experimenting with a Di7 sinking line out in the deeper part of the pit and was already clipped up with a buoyant fly which I cast as close as I could to the land bound victim. The fast sinking line pulled at the fly which begrudgingly followed its downward arc. The big girl was alert, very alert to anything and everything, and was soon aware of its presence. She turned in an instant, and as I stripped the fly back she came round from behind and opened her massive jaws, completely inhaling my little home tied offering. Like a bloody fool I yanked the line with my stripping hand, intending to set the hook but only succeeding in pulling the fly from her mouth! Why oh why didn't I just let her turn and hook herself?

Then she was gone. I'd had one chance and mucked it up. Ten minutes later when we were getting concerned about the jack on the bank, it just flipped back into the water and went to find somewhere better to hide. No pike or photo's this time. It doesn't always come together!

It will come as no surprise to seasoned pike anglers that bigger pike eat smaller ones. There is no love lost between them, and if they are hungry they will eat smaller pike without a second thought. If another pike should threaten them by coming too close to feed in their territory they will do likewise, sometimes eating it and at other times giving it a vicious warning bite! At spawning time the females will eat their male suitors for a snack, before, during or after the ritual, and at such times I have caught big pike with as many as three tails of smaller pike showing in their throats! Wherever there are too many pike competing in any situation, they will naturally thin themselves out. I have kept tiny pike of just a few weeks old in aquariums and always ended up with just one very fat one, and have seen similar instances in nature where cannibalism starts almost from birth. It may seem cruel, but it's nature's way of selecting the fittest and the strongest for future breeding and ensuring that there is enough food to go round.

A pike is the master of its own territory you would think, but there does seem to be some sort of pecking order, naturally decided by size. Pike seem to instinctively know this and pike of different sizes tend to keep apart unless it suits them to get together, notably at spawning time. Even then there is a strained relationship, the males knowing when it's safe to come into close proximity with the larger females– and when it's not!

This separation is something I've noted many times. A separation of males and females is a possibility, but as it is difficult to tell one from the other, this would be no more than a guess. Males rarely reach double figures in weight, so size is one way of distinguishing males from females, but single figure fish can, of course, be of either sex. In waters where pike do not achieve large sizes, it's reasonable to assume that the bigger ones are females. At the point of spawning we can make a positive identification through any evidence at the vent of eggs (female) or milt (male) which is useful to back up any guess work. There are enough pointers to indicate that females are the main aggressors in this unforgiving world of cannibalism.

Close study of a river system for many years revealed to me just how much bigger and smaller pike stay out of each others way. In the early autumn when food is widespread and plentiful, pike tend to be well spread out and it's common to find pike of all sizes all over the river. It's a time when bigger pike are, apparently, less aggressive to their smaller friends who tend to use this time to feed while they can. Things change when falling water temperatures and migratory instincts see prey fish packing together in huge shoals, partly for the safety of numbers and also to assemble to move to their spawning grounds in side streams, backwaters and tributaries. This is the time when the separation starts to take place. Now the concentrated shoals of bigger prey are shadowed by big pike, and jacks are noticeably absent, as evident from my catches.

In river backwaters and sheltered areas where prey fish fry gather in big numbers, an order of pike size has been noted too, but it is often accompanied with a sort of sharing system whereby some day's big pike are feeding on the shoals, and on other days smaller pike take over. In the main river through the colder months, the shoals of bigger prey are normally accompanied by bigger pike only, with smaller pike being spread around parts of the river where the feeding is sparser. This continues until early spring when the bigger pike follow the mature prey fish to their spawning grounds.

It does seem logical that pike will attach themselves to prey of a suitable size for their needs. Small pike will be better served amongst small prey items, but bigger pike can, of course, eat anything which will fit into their mouths, be it large or small. For this reason, bigger pike can also be expected to be caught amongst fry concentrations too, but smaller pike have little to gain by attaching themselves to shoals of large prey.

When pike spawn, males and females obviously have to get together, and for a while in early spring, pike of different sizes might be caught in the same area indicating that spawning is imminent. After spawning, bigger pike will stay in the spawning area if it also makes good habitat for prey fish to spawn in and they will wait for them to arrive. At this time, the main river now seems full of small pike only, with them obviously keeping away from bigger pike or becoming food!

If you really want to see a pike attack another pike, the months of April and May offer the best

'JACKS ARE NOTICABLY ABSENT WHEN FEMALES LIKE THIS 23-POUNDER ARE ACTIVE.

chance. Carnage takes place at this time when voraciously hungry females put smaller pike onto their menu and thin them out without mercy. Try catching a small pike at this time of year and watch for a big girl coming in to stalk and attack it. Cruel it might seem, but that's how it is. Pike really are cannibals of the highest order, but they kill for food without malice or evil intention. And it really is a sight to behold as this next observation left me in no doubt!

I was busying myself with my deadbaiting rods and re-setting a drop off bite alarm after recasting. Jan, fishing a swim behind a bush to my left, suddenly called out in terror. I'd seen her striking a run a minute or so earlier and I wondered what the devil had happened. On the way in to the net her catch, a six pounder, had been snatched in front of her very eyes. In calm clear water she was witnessing a rare sight. A monster pike had grabbed it across the back and was swimming slowly away with it. It was only days beforehand in the same swim that I had seen a similar big pike in the most unusual of

'...SHE GRIPPED AND SQUEEZED THE LIFE FROM THE POOR JACK PIKE...'

circumstances. Standing at the waters edge watching my floats, I noticed a grebe come by at high speed, not on the surface but swimming about a foot beneath it. Seconds later a huge pike followed, its bulky body powered by a massive tail and huge rear fins, working overtime to catch up with its feathered prey. They both disappeared out of sight but the grebe did not surface and was not seen again! It had to be the same pike, I thought, with the memory so fresh in my mind.

I was round to Jan's swim like a shot as she shouted out what was happening, and just in time to take the rod from her as she wanted nothing to do with it! The shock of the sudden appearance of the big pike had really shaken her up! Whilst I tried to guide the pike back into view, Jan made herself useful by setting up the camera, but not before lighting up a cigarette to calm her nerves!

The huge pike came closer to the bank, so close that I could have reached her with my net pole. She lay perfectly still, her victim writhing and wriggling in a futile attempt to escape from the painful bite from her large teeth. I managed to fire off a few shots, rod in one hand and camera in the other, and having a few pics in the bag I got down on my belly to get as close as I could to lie face to face with a spectacle that is so rare to witness. As I looked straight into her eye she gripped and squeezed the life from the poor jack pike which bucked and squirmed in an attempt to become free of her deadly grip. She wasn't letting go though, and was so focused on her intentions that she seemed oblivious to my presence. Eventually she let go after she became aware of me and it was all over. We'd caught a special moment on film and such captures are, to me, better than reeling them into the net.

If only I could have captured every such magical moment I have witnessed. They are etched into my memory of course, but I can only try to relate them to you in words which seem less than adequate to describe them. Take, for example, a December morning when I was a much younger man and lying on the bank of a stillwater watching my floats, but as always looking at everything around me. I've noticed in nature that you get days when everything seems to be happening and other days when all is very quiet. This was one of those days when the wildlife was very active, water birds busying themselves and rabbits popping up here and there in this rarely trodden location.

Suddenly the straw coloured grasses around me were alive with the rushing and crashing of rabbits and pheasants and goodness knows what else. I couldn't see most of them, just sensing them scurrying through the unkempt landscape. I knew this meant that the 'shooters' were approaching and the dogs were driving everything in front of them. Suddenly the water in front of me burst into life, and a shoal of about a dozen tiny rudd sprayed up onto the wet gravel which was being gently lapped by the swell from the windswept lake. They were obviously being chased, and the culprit, a tiny jack pike of around eight inches long, slithered amongst them, nipped onto one and flipped itself back into the water with it. His moment of glory was short lived though when a bigger pike of no more than a pound and a half in weight grabbed hold of him, turned sharply and started to disappear down the slope and into deep water. Dog eat dog! Seconds later, a bigger shadow came streaking past in their general direction and followed with obvious intent. Dog eat dog eat dog! There's no love lost amongst hungry pike!

Shortly afterwards, I had a run on a herring that I was fishing in the margin which produced a five pound pike. It was bitten so badly at the back end that as it tried to swim away its tail hung down limply, only being held together by the remaining integrity of its backbone. An hour later a dead perch fished in the margin was taken and I landed a 46 incher which weighed 30 lb 10 oz. She proved to be the biggest pike in the lake and must have been the only one which didn't have to watch its back!

From the above episode, it's clear that any pike will be wary of another pike which is bigger than itself. At feeding time, it does seem pretty obvious that the bigger the pike the more dominance it will assert. This does not necessarily mean that the biggest pike always get the first shot at the prey as I have often heard suggested. I think they will do so if they want to, but will also allow smaller pike to feed as well, and smaller pike feeding can sometimes be a trigger for bigger pike to investigate. Two examples of this come to mind.

On Blithfield in 2003, Matt Hayes and I found good numbers of pike feeding in the 'stone cages' area of the North reservoir, and using jigs we promptly caught a couple of jacks followed by two 'high doubles' and a 23 pounder. Then Matt hit the jackpot with a 32 pounder, and at this point we decided to rest the swim and go trolling for an hour. Our fish had got progressively bigger and a '30' would take some beating! This was probably the biggest bad decision we have ever made because experienced pike angler Eric Edwards dropped into the swim and made history by taking a brace of monster pike weighing 37lb and 41 lb! At least they were caught by one of pike fishing's most skilful anglers and were well deserved. Well done Eric! The biggest ones had waited till last it seems, and although it appeared to indicate a reverse pecking order, it could have been smaller pike triggering bigger pike into feeding – or maybe just co-incidence. We don't know these things for sure, but anglers do like to speculate!

Jan and I had a similar experience on a local stillwater. We launched the boat for the last few hours of the day to tackle a deep trench situated behind an island where we had prebaited over several days as it looked the sort of feature that we could draw pike into. Having rarely fished the swim for pike before we were not too sure what to expect, but Jan's float fished deadbait was away immediately and she netted a 13 pounder. While unhooking it, my float was away and I landed a 14 pounder. I then made the mistake of ribbing Jan by telling her I was now in front, when her float came

'THERE'S NO LOVE LOST AMONGST HUNGRY PIKE!'

to life and I was soon weighing an 18 pounder for her! The banter became as lively as ever when my next run produced a 19 pounder! We certainly had pulled a lot of pike into the swim, and by keeping as quiet as possible were extracting them one by one. With darkness approaching, I made my next error of judgement by declaring that the loser should cook the dinner when we got home, not expecting my 19 pounder to be beaten in the final throes of the session.

Minutes later, Jan reminded me of my words as I weighed a 23 pounder for her which she had tempted by craftily twitching her bait very slowly back to the boat. I often wish I'd never showed her that little trick! By now the tackle was in a right mess, with the unhooking and weighing gear spread everywhere and the boat littered with bits of squashed herring and mackerel. Basking in her glory, Jan tidied up while I fished like fury to try and get another 'take', inching my bait along as Jan had done so successfully. Suddenly my pencil float disappeared from sight and I felt the line pull through my fingers. Having momentarily lost my concentration by turning to Jan to ask her to make up the landing net again, I struck without disengaging the bait runner, and the spool of my reel quickly resembled a cheap nylon wig as it spun out of control! I had no alternative but to hand line the pike to the boat which was a lot easier to do than one would expect, and Jan slipped the net under it without any problems. Jan could tell she would be doing the cooking when we got home as it was clearly the best pike of the session. It wasn't quite as big as we thought, but at 24 lb 8 oz it was big enough! This lake is full of small pike which are easily caught in the spring and early autumn months, but they rarely show up in the midst of winter, clearly another example of pike separating into size order. It is quite rare on this water to catch jacks in areas with large prey fish or pre-baited swims at any time of the year. They know their place!

Big pike will fight amongst themselves at times and we can only guess that this is over food or territorial issues, but how their minds work is beyond me. Even in swims where there is more than enough food to go round, I have many times had a big pike grab another big pike across its back. Sometimes it might be a ten pounder grabbing another ten pounder, but my most noteworthy instance came when I found myself playing a 26 pounder which was held onto and badly mauled by another pike for over ten minutes. I didn't see the aggressor, but it is reasonable to assume that the pike which grabbed it was bigger, and there were bigger pike in the lake!

THE SPOOL OF MY REEL QUICKLY RESEMBLED A CHEAP NYLON WIG

Elsewhere in nature, we certainly see conflicts due to bad blood between all the warm blooded species, so I see no reason why this should not appertain to cold blooded creatures either. Maybe, in the case of hooked pike being grabbed, it's the 'dog on a lead' syndrome where an aggressor sees its victim tethered or restrained, thus making it an easy target and a chance to settle old scores. Let's face it, we don't really know, but if enough observations are accurately recorded and not romantically exaggerated, time will eventually lead us to draw more sensible conclusions. These events must be fairly rare and only feature at certain times of the year, otherwise we would find lots of pike covered with battle scars or their numbers would dwindle away. This is not the case and I don't think that pike are under constant threat from their own kind and know how to live in harmony for most of the time. They are probably more concerned with threats from other creatures, something they learn from an early age.

'...at 24 lb 8 oz, it was big enough!'

Pike may appear to be the masters of their domains, roaming fearlessly in search of their prey, but they do need to be wary and have their wits about them because they are always in potential danger. Small pike in their first year are frequently snapped up by grebes and herons, and as they start to grow to a couple of pounds or so they become of more interest to cormorants and mink. Even the very largest of pike can come under attack from the biggest pike killers of all – otters. Not so many years ago, otters were not a problem in the UK, and until recently I saw little evidence of otter predation on pike. Since the recent reintroduction of otters around the UK things have changed dramatically and all of our fish stocks, not just pike, are suffering as a result.

Then there is the threat from humans who would kill them out of ignorance or take them for food. Very few UK anglers take pike for eating nowadays, but pike populations in some areas are under serious threat in this way again from Eastern European anglers who have come here in recent years for work. As it is in their culture to take pike for eating, they are doing so whilst in the UK, often unaware of the problem they are causing to anglers and sometimes with total disregard. It's very sad to see the great pike fishing we have worked so hard to achieve wiped out in some areas in a very short time, and a decline in other areas to a point where local anglers don't bother to fish any more. Hopefully, new legislation will limit any future damage and we can turn things around again.

Pike are no longer the biggest predators in many of our waters since the widespread stocking of catfish into hundreds of venues in the Midlands and southern parts of the country. Earlier catfish introductions into a very small number of waters in the middle of the last century resulted in catfish topping out at a little over 30 lb in weight, but more recent introductions, however, seem to be of faster growing strains which are reaching unbelievable sizes. Sixty pounders are not at all uncommon and are present in dozens of waters and these fish are still growing, with individual fish approaching 100 lb in weight. There is no evidence to suggest that catfish eat a lot of pike, but nevertheless there is the potential to do them harm. Fortunately, these species tend to feed at different times of the year, the catfish preferring the warmer months and the pike the colder months. There is an overlap, of course, and there will be times when pike and catfish are competing for the same food supply. There is positive evidence that catfish attack large carp when they both compete for the same food, so it is likely that there is a skirmish or two between catfish and pike. At the moment, I don't detect any serious problems directed towards pike on the waters that I fish which contain both species, but it's an ongoing situation that has not yet reached a final conclusion.

'...MODERATING THEIR OWN NUMBERS...'

When tackling up for pike on waters which have both pike and catfish, I'm nowadays posed with a dilemma. I usually start to fish for pike in early October, but as catfish can still be very active at this time I worry that I will hook one on my pike

Catfish are becoming increasingly likely to be caught by pike anglers.
This 63 lb 8 oz fish came from a UK water which also has pike.

gear. The cats in these waters are big and getting bigger and I've had them take over 200 yards of 20 lb mono on five pound test curve rods so I'm pretty sure they would spool me out on normal pike gear and they'd swim off with two trebles in their mouths, or worse still in their throats. On the other hand, if I left the pike alone till later and carried on cat fishing into October, I might hook pike and get bitten off without a wire trace as they will be more active when the water starts to cool down. As it happens, neither disaster has yet befallen me, but it has to others who fish there.

If this happens too frequently, I can see the need to make rules which protect both the pike and the cats. Instead of starting pike fishing on October 1st, as we do at present, it might be safer, given the circumstances, to start on November 1st or even later when the cats have become more dormant. Alternatively, catfish anglers might have to stop fishing for them at the end of September as they become more likely to hook pike on their rigs which have no wire traces. Then again, we might have to insist that catfish rigs must incorporate wire traces when using fish baits. Prebaiting could become a problem, and might have to be banned as it would attract both cats and pike into a swim. We will have to face up to this problem eventually on waters where pike exist alongside catfish if both species are to be protected adequately.

The carnage that takes place under the water is largely unseen, but we are privileged to get a glimpse from time to time and it makes fascinating viewing. Pike are only doing as nature intended, controlling the numbers of lesser fish and water creatures and moderating their own numbers to enable a healthy balance to be achieved. It might seem cruel at times but it's necessary, and for anglers like me who make a living from their knowledge and observations, it also gives us something interesting to write and talk about!

CHAPTER 4

No Mercy!

'THEY ARE CLEARLY DESIGNED BY NATURE TO KILL WITHOUT MERCY'

I was driving along a road which runs parallel with the River Nene, just a mile from the sluice where it empties into the tidal river. With my window wound down I was enjoying the late summer sunshine, scanning the water as usual for anything interesting. From the middle of the river came a mighty swirl amongst a group of coots sending them screaming and scurrying in all directions. I was left in no doubt that one of their numbers had been dragged under to a certain death!

It's often said that pike taking waterfowl is just exaggerated speculation, but in the many years I have spent by water, day and night, I can tell you from first hand experience that pike do tackle water birds, not to mention other creatures like voles, rats and frogs. They are clearly designed by nature to kill without mercy. I could relate many sightings such as the mother moorhen on the Hampshire Avon frantically doing her damndest to get her brood back into the nest, but nature had told them it was time to make their own way in the world. It was quite sad to watch a pike pick them off one by one as they drifted with the current and then got swept away, too innocent to know the impending danger beneath them. Nature can be cruel in this way, but the wicked way of the predator does hold a certain fascination for us.

I'm always listening out for any snippets of information which could lead me to good pike fishing or to expand my knowledge of pike behaviour. Finding things which are interesting to write and talk about is obviously very useful to a writer. There are so many stories about pike, most of which are a load of nonsense or exaggeration, but every now and again I'll discover something worthwhile. Like the 'swan eaters' for example! In 1994 I followed up a phone call which sent me in search of 'swan eating pike' and started a project which kept me busy, on and off, for four winters! Rather than dismiss the phone call as a waste of time, I was very eager to find out more. A previous observation of swans in potential danger from pike had already stirred my interest in this topic.

Pike don't eat swans do they? Of course they do, but not the big ones! A swan is just as much on the pike's menu as any other living creature, but this is clearly limited to eating them at cygnet stage when they will fit nicely into their mouths and stomachs! How long after birth they are in danger for is debatable. Certainly, on a pit at Bainton in North Cambridgeshire where I fished in the late eighties/ early nineties, the adult swans were taking no chances with their precious offspring. Right through until late summer they would carry them around on their backs when venturing away from the island on which they lived. It was quite funny to watch when the cygnets got bigger. It was a bit of a balancing act, but their parents knew a thing or two!

There were very few pike in that pit and only four of them exceeded double figure weights during the time I fished there, but all of them were destined to grow into massive fish. I caught them all, and even recaptured two of them whilst getting to know the pit. They were very distinctive individuals and I gave them names, simply for my own ease of recollection. They topped out at the following weights:

The Donkey at 31lb 9oz. When my mate witnessed it, he was convinced you could fit a saddle on its broad back! My first capture of this fish was at 24lb 6oz and it reached its maximum weight two seasons later.

The Animal at 31lb 5oz. A brute of a fish with a wicked jaw which, at the first capture, had the tail of a recently swallowed tench showing in its throat. I caught it again just four days later weighing 30lb 15oz, the tench having now disappeared into its stomach.

The Silver Fish at 31lb 1oz. An amazingly clean and unblemished pike, sleek and silvery in colour and looking like it had never been caught before. I caught this fish again at 30lb 13oz, just five days after its first capture.

The bruiser at 30lb 5oz. I had caught this pike previously at 20lb 1oz when it had quite a delicate appearance. When it appeared three years later showing a massive increase in weight, it had developed the most awesome head and impressive body profile. A real bruiser!

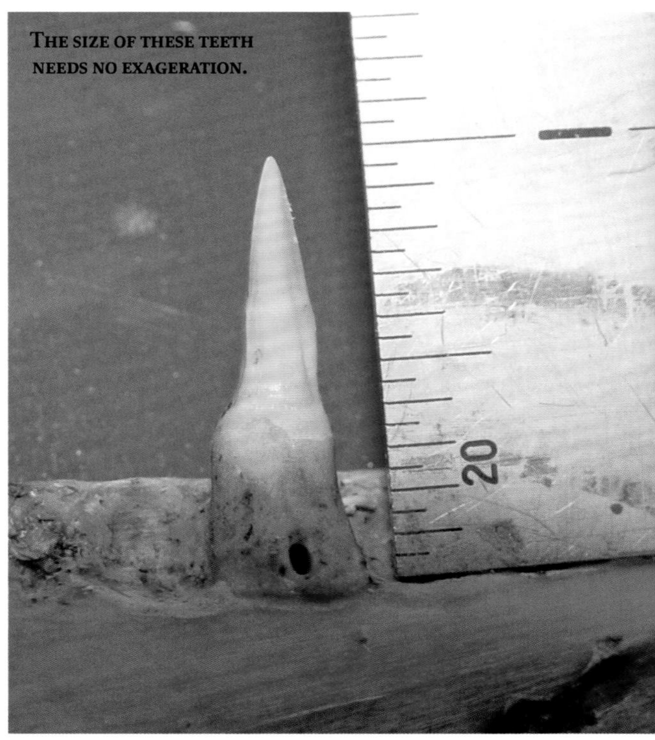

THE SIZE OF THESE TEETH NEEDS NO EXAGERATION.

Pic: Mick Rouse

The swans were taking no chances with bruisers like this around.
She weighed 30 lb 5 oz and took a popped up trout deadbait.

I don't think it takes a lot of imagination to see why the swans that lived on the lake were wary, just as water birds must be anywhere there is danger from big pike. Pike eat water birds and other swimming creatures much more than is realised. That's my conclusion, although there are limits of course or there would be nothing left! Like us they take advantage of seasonal harvesting, and spring and summer are times when nature supplies them with food aplenty, not only in terms of young water birds but small mammals like voles as well. This is the time of year when I have witnessed most activity of this kind, and its nature's cruel way of sorting the weak from the strong. Mind you, I think even the strongest can be caught out at times as the pike is capable of striking in a lightening attack that can outpace almost anything it fancies eating. Luckily for its prey, what the pike gains from its speed it often loses through its poor accuracy! Even where such prey is not abundant the pike, being an opportunist, just can't help itself at times as it's in its nature to seize anything that moves within its territory. Birds and mammals clearly come into this category.

Hunger can also drive pike into taking birds and mammals when prey fish stocks are either insufficient or difficult to obtain, such as in very weedy water where small fish can hide away. When pike are forced to take birds as an easier option they can become labelled as gratuitous killers, leading to their persecution.

All of these thoughts were running through my head as I drove north to meet the warden of a North Lincolnshire nature reserve. Initially he had phoned Angling Times to voice his concern about pike eating his swans on the reserve, and had asked whether they could offer any advice. Angling Times then phoned me, and from the tone of the messenger I could tell that they hadn't taken him very seriously, but they did promised to pass the details on to pike anglers in the area that might be able to help, and this is where I came in.

Arrangements were made, and a few days later I was to meet pike fishing legend Neville Fickling at the water with the prospect of us both taking a look. Neville had also been notified by Angling Times, and like me he had taken notice as a chance to fish an otherwise unfished nature reserve was well worth looking into, even if the warden was a 'nutter' as my informant had described him!

After meeting the warden, he turned out to be quite the opposite. He was an intelligent man, and after he had told us about the recent history of the reserve, it all started to become clear. As the reserve became developed it attracted increasing numbers of birds, many of them being fish eaters like grebes, cormorants and herons. The food supply for the pike subsequently became greatly diminished, and in desperation the pike started to pay more attention to water birds than would be normal. In particular he was concerned that they were responsible for the disappearance of most of the cygnets each spring. This seemed a reasonable assumption, but we needed to find out more about the pike population in the lakes before we could offer our opinion regarding appropriate action. There are several lakes in the complex and the swans could move from one to another, so the whole water system required examination.

We started by tackling the biggest expanse of water on the reserve, but became quickly disillusioned by its shallowness. It just didn't seem to be somewhere that we could enjoy pike fishing, and casting into open water of no more than two feet deep just didn't inspire confidence. We also tackled a couple of smaller lakes in a wooded area but found them too overgrown, and the limited swims available were fished out in no time at all. We gave it the best part of the day and then went our separate ways, but not before I'd asked about another lake on the reserve which looked a better prospect, one which we'd written off as it was totally surrounded with dense bushes which made it almost unfishable. With permission granted I stopped off there for the last hours of daylight, hoping to find a way of casting a bait in.

It wasn't easy as the bank was steep and the bushes were sharp and shrouded with prickly brambles, but I managed to forge a gap between them so I could cast into the open water beyond. It turned out to be worth the struggle though as six pike up to 17 lb 4 oz were caught very easily with deadbaits, nice looking fish as well. Perhaps not the 'monsters' we had anticipated, but interesting pike fishing and the sort that I enjoy, with plenty of runs, good fights and very pretty fish.

During the day I met Bob Pask from Scunthorpe, a good friend of the warden, and although only a very casual pleasure angler, he fancied having a go at catching a few pike and we became very friendly. It was through Bob that I eventually had the chance to discuss with the warden the possibility of fishing there again, and I was quite delighted to be offered the chance to do so occasionally by arranging it through Bob.

Another day was organised for the end of March, a day which was to open my

'...An otherwise unfished nature reserve...'

'... WHEN A 15 POUNDER, WITH A DISPROPORTIONALLY HUGE MOUTH, HAD A DUCK SHOWING IN ITS THROAT...'

eyes as to just how many pike were in the overgrown lake. Bob had located another swim we could squeeze into, giving us two options on opposite sides of the lake. The fishing was simply amazing with runs galore and 15 pike came to my rods that day including a 23 pounder, caught twice from opposite sides of the lake! Several others were caught by Bob and a few more by my brother Ralph who came with us. It was very sociable fun fishing for Bob and Ralph, but as a keen pike angler I could see we were onto something rather special. The warden's suspicions about the pike eating the birds were clearly confirmed when a 15 pounder with a disproportionally huge mouth, had a duck showing in its throat, the green tinge to its wing indicating it to be a teal.

I now had a dilemma. Do I suggest that the pike needed thinning out, or do I just enjoy a bit of good fishing and leave the pike to their fate from other hands? It was pretty obvious that the warden wanted some action to be taken so, rightly or wrongly, I said I would remove some pike the following winter, preferring to do so at the coldest time of the year when moving them would pose minimal risk to their welfare.

As spring arrived the new broods of cygnets were born, but to the dismay of the warden they quickly disappeared, and he was now getting very anxious for some action to be taken!

I was onto the case as soon as October arrived, and the first trip produced two 20 pounders weighing 20lb 4 oz and 21 lb 9 oz. They were very long fish, looking rather empty and being 42 ¾" and 42" long respectively. We caught several other pike that looked in need of a meal too. I decided that the water was still too warm to move any pike and said I would return in November when the temperature had dropped down to a safer level.

November came around and the first three pike were removed, all single figure fish. One nine pounder had a very pronounced bulge in its stomach, which was undoubtedly a small water bird. Fortunately I'd found a water not too far away which was being stocked for pike fishing and was more than happy to take them. Three more visits that winter saw another ten pike removed, mostly middle size fish but one 'big double' was taken away as it had an enormous mouth and was potentially a 'bird killer'.

After the next spring bird count it was notable that not all the cygnets had been taken this time, some sort of success we all thought, but it was agreed to remove a few more pike the following winter. In fact for each of the next three winters, I made three or four visits to the reserve and took another 20 or so pike away, all middle size fish. More big pike were encountered but were returned. Five different big pike, which all hovered in weight from just under 20 lb to more than 25 lb depending upon how hard they had been feeding, were left in the lake along with smaller pike which we hoped would be proportionately males to maintain some sort of balance.

We removed about 150 lb of mid sized pike in total with the purpose of reducing the competition for food and assisting the roach and bream to increase their numbers. With a balance of prey and predators being restored, it was our expectation that the pike would pay less attention to the birds. The plan seemed to be working as increasingly more cygnets survived each year and the warden was delighted.

Once this had been achieved, I saw little point in catching the same pike again and I have never been back. Keeping in touch with Bob for the following three years, he informed me that of the 16 to 17 cygnets produced each spring, just the occasional one was now disappearing.

It had been an interesting project which had produced some great pike fishing and saved a lot of swans from a gruesome death. Looking back though, I have to wonder whether it is wise to interfere with nature. We now have too many swans on our local waters and I am the first to curse them when they pick up my tench baits in shallow water! This is for others to judge, but at the time I did what I thought to be the right thing.

The fishing had been very enjoyable and the pike in the reserve were very aggressive at times. My most vivid memory of that lake would have to be wading out into shallow water to chin a seven pounder, when one of the bigger pike snatched it from my grip. Next cast, I hooked and landed a 22 pounder. Great memories, I must go back one day!

Rats and Voles

Do pike really eat rats and voles? They certainly eat voles and I have seen quite a few instances of them disappearing in the midst of an almighty swirl, and the Old River Nene, near March in Cambridgeshire, always offered a good chance to witness this phenomena. It happens suddenly and like lightning, and you need to be the sort of person who is observant and has their wits about them or you will never see it. For several years I had a boat on this narrow fenland drain type of river, and it was always a great pleasure to drift with the wind along it's heavily reed lined course, casting spinnerbaits in front of the boat. We never caught any big pike there but we caught a lot of pike. Big pike were there though and this was proven beyond all doubt when a local resident caught pike of 29 lb and 32 lb from next to my boat mooring where I regularly baited with chopped fish at the end of each session. You can't win them all!

When drifting along the river, although not an everyday occurrence, I would occasionally see a pike attack a vole or a terrific swirl as one scurried away to the safety of the reeds. Voles disappear in silence when pulled under, unlike birds which let out an almighty scream when attacked, starting every other water bird in the area to do the same whilst scattering far and wide.

One special day stays in my memory. We had seen a vole taken and this encouraged us to start fishing the area with surface lures. In the course of the hour that followed, we took several pike on a wooden American surface lure known as a Smitty Slap Tail, a rather large lure with a blade at the back end that flapped all over the place on the retrieve. Sure enough, whilst unhooking one of these pike I detected what looked like a shoelace protruding from its throat. With a little teasing from my forceps, I easily extracted the pike's last meal – a large vole upon which the digestion process had not yet started. It was probably the one I had seen taken!

What about rats? These shy creatures tend to keep themselves well hidden in the daytime and feed mainly at night, and probably for this reason we rarely see them connected with pike attacks. There are huge numbers of rats, and they must be another great potential food source for pike. Unlike voles, which tend to swim across drains and rivers and smaller waters, rats tend to stay close to the bank when they venture into the water. I have never seen a rat taken by a pike, but my good friend Paul Fitzgerald from Birmingham had a hair raising experience one night when bivvied out on a stillwater near my home during one of this visits.

The regular barking from his little Jack Russell drew his attention to a rat which kept scurrying backwards and forwards under his rod rests, which were positioned in shallow water with reed beds to either side of the swim. Naturally, his dog's reaction was to jump up and bark every time this occurred. Then suddenly, out of the blue and frightening the living daylights out of him, and probably his dog as well, a large pike came hurtling between his rods, jaws wide open and its body half out of the water as it tried to grab hold of the rat. It never did so as far as is known, but neither the rat nor the pike were seen again for the rest of the night. It must have been an awesome sight and one I would have loved to have witnessed myself.

Stories of pike taking birds and mammals add colour to the pikes character and ruthless reputation. To see it at first hand is a rare and special moment, but it is possible if you are observant. If you spend your time reading a book while waiting for a run, or like to get comfortable in a chair on the river bank and shut your eyes, you will miss these things. If you are alert and in tune with your surroundings you will witness, from time to time, some amazing spectacles of pike in action which you will eventually cherish as much as catching them.

Where voles are plentiful they are on the pikes menu!

Choosing a suitable lure requires careful consideration.

Pic: Matt Rand

CHAPTER 5

Food Glorious Food

To be able to catch pike on request on a regular basis, as I have to do in my work, it's useful for me to know as much as possible about their eating habits and patterns. This will ensure that I arrive at the water with suitable bait for the session and I can't afford to get it wrong too often, especially if I have to catch for the camera. A pleasure angler can go home moaning about a poor result, whereas I would go home without having earned anything, not to mention the prospect of not working again!

Bait is very important and I must have the most effective bait with me for the day. Livebaits and deadbaits must be the ideal type and size, and lures need to be of the ideal style, size, action and colour. I must also ensure that I have sufficient bait but not overburden myself with too much, especially if I've a long way to walk. With so many variables to consider it's not always possible to make a quick decision, but a hasty one might see me wasting bait or, worst of all, not getting the result required to get the job done. This means that I need a good working knowledge and understanding of what pike might eat in different circumstances, what they are capable of eating, and how natural food availability and weather conditions affect their desire to feed.

First of all, just how much can they eat? Forget all the old wives tales you might have heard such as 'they can eat their own weight in a day'! Whilst this could be true of a small pike eating one of its own kind of a similar size, it would be unusual for bigger pike to attempt to do so. In rare instances where pike tackle a massive 'outsize' meal, maybe another pike or a very large prey fish, it cannot swallow it straight away. Such pike are occasionally seen with their prey protruding from their jaws, with part of it digesting in their stomach as it gradually feeds it through its system. Typically they will do this with large eels or after seizing other pike. Sometimes they cannot help themselves and get very greedy, and will tackle further food even though their throat is already blocked with a large food item which may even be protruding outside of their mouths. The angler concerned with the weight of his catch is now faced with a problem. Should you catch a large pike that has another fish wedged in its throat, do you include the weight of the prey fish? Fortunately, I have never faced this dilemma with a very large pike, although I have had one or two where there has been just a tail showing in the throat. Should I catch a thirty pounder with best part of a three pound eel sticking out of its throat, to be quite honest I don't really know what I would do. I would probably consult my peers for their opinion. It really doesn't matter provided you are honest about it. When feeding on smaller prey, things are very different because each food item is taken straight to the pike's stomach and is therefore immediately added to the pike's body weight. Clearly though, their stomachs will only hold so much - but how much?

In reality they can swallow quite a lot when it suits them to do so, but there are limits as to how much their stomachs can hold which may be more than most pike anglers would think! The most extreme example of gluttony I have witnessed at first hand is of a pike gorging on a meal of almost half its body weight!

It all came about on a day when I was out piking with my brother Ralph, who had driven nearly a hundred miles for a day's fishing with me. The trip was arranged at short notice with Ralph ringing up the day before and telling me how desperate he was to get away from business and to have a quiet day by the water (not that my days by the water tend to be very quiet!). He especially wanted to fish my latest pre baited swim which I'd been telling him about.

He'd fished some of my pre baited swims before and taken some good fish, including several twenty pounders. That's one of the benefits of preparing swims in this way, so that you can be confident of catching when time is limited. A problem I had this time was that I wasn't intending to fish the swim for a while as I'd had a freezer clear out, depositing over 20 lb of chopped herrings and mackerel into the swim the night before. I had no worries about it being eaten eventually as the lake held, to my knowledge, at least five 20 pounders and a dozen others over 15 lb. There were many smaller pike in the pit too, but they were rarely caught in the pre baited swim, the bigger pike typically controlling a prime food source. The smaller pike obviously knew that it was wise to keep away. It would be rather like walking into a pub frequented by twenty big blokes and where the beer was free! You wouldn't risk it!

I explained the situation to Ralph and we spent the day flitting around several other waters, but struggled to catch much of any note. As we entered mid afternoon he twisted my arm, and we were soon chugging along in my truck to the pre baited swim. I prepared him for the worst, telling him it was too early to fish there and I would have given it a few days' rest myself. With nothing to lose, however, he was prepared to spend the last hour or so of daylight there.

Having the rods already made up in the back of the truck enabled us to cast out our deadbaits within minutes of arriving, and our two pencil floats were soon glinting on the flat calm water, highlighted against a beautiful red fenland sunset. It would have been enough to sit there and have yet another cup of tea and just chin wag for an hour, but we didn't even have time to get the kettle on. One of the floats, which were previously laid flat, suddenly stood upright and slowly disappeared as it wandered away. It's a sight I will never get tired of and yet I must have seen it thousands of times. It was on my rod too, and although I offered it to Ralph, he declined.

The swim had been good to me through the winter, and it was very familiar to feel a heavy lump lumbering around the swim before quietly giving up and being guided into the waiting landing net. I'd been fishing that water for a few years and was pretty sure I knew all the bigger pike and I liked to try to identify each one as it approached the net. I was just telling Ralph how lucky we had been to get a run, but by Sod's Law it was one of the smaller pike that occasionally visited the swim and it usually weighed between 14 and 15 lb. I had no doubt it was that fish, in fact I'd caught it the previous week, but as it rolled into the net I immediately noticed how fat it was! I could see that it needed very careful handling.

I lift any fish with care in the landing net, making sure that the fins aren't getting bent and that the fish's own body weight is not contributing to any unnecessary damage, and proceeded to turn it onto its side so I could gather the excess mesh to cradle it better. As Ralph helped me carry it across to the unhooking mat, a few choice words clearly described my amazement of how heavy the fish felt. I was staggered when the scales read 21 lb 12 oz, over seven pounds heavier than at its last capture a week previously!

She was quickly photographed, and as we slid her from the weighing sling back into the icy cold water you could not only feel the chunks of pre bait inside her gut, but actually see some of them deforming her bulging belly. The greedy sod had bolted down over seven pounds of my pre bait!

'...And slowly disappeared...'

This interesting capture immediately altered my views on how to go about pre baiting, and furthermore, started me thinking about just how much pike can eat - if they choose to! I have added this last phrase because I am beginning to think that what they can eat and what is available can be very different things. Just because food is there doesn't automatically mean that they will eat it. For whatever reason pike seem to only consume as much as they want to, judging by the fact that most pike in my pre baited swims do not put on anything like this sharp increase in weight. I have caught plenty of pike in more natural situations where prey fish are plentiful, but they have not gorged on them to excess either. This is probably one of the reasons why pike fishing can be so unpredictable and interesting as you never really know what's going to happen next.

'...See some of them deforming her bulging belly...'

It is clear to me that rapid weight gains are more possible when pike are consuming prey which is easy to swallow. That 15 lb pike could, in theory, eat a seven pound prey fish, but by the time it had all finally entered its digestive system, its increase in weight would not have been anywhere near as dramatic as it would have excreted most of it through its vent in the process. Pre bait or any discarded anglers baits, can soon fill a pike's belly and I can think of quite a few 'known' pike from other waters which have added three or four pounds to their weight between captures. A seven pound increase in weight is exceptional in my experience, happening partly because the food was easily available in a suitable size and quantity and then through its desire to eat it. It's a pity the resident 25 pounder didn't feel peckish!

In natural situations, pike do not normally find such quantities of dead fish except after 'fish kills' of various kinds. Of the 'fish kills' I have witnessed, other than from pollution, the most notable have been when pumps from side drains have suddenly started up, drawing thousands of roach through them and maiming and killing them in the process. When the pump at Pode Hole Basin in Lincolnshire was started up one year, thousands of dead roach littered the bottom in the outflow into the Vernatts River. I tried to catch pike just below where the carnage had taken place but found them very difficult, and only a livebait would tempt them as the bottom nearby was still awash with corpses, easily seen in the gin clear, shallow water. The few pike I did catch were small, but obese in the extreme because they had eaten large quantities of the dead roach. In retrospect, I regret not spending more time fishing in that area in the days which followed, and I wonder what the weights of the Vernatts 20 pounders we had caught there previously had been temporarily elevated to. Life is never as straightforward as this though, and I am sure at the time there was a very good reason why I never continued.

A similar sighting was made on the Great Ouse River, but I was only passing through in my boat and not in the area long enough to see how much the pike took advantage. In this instance, a pump from a side drain was started up to discharge water which was building up on the land after heavy rainfall, and the numbers of dead roach pumped into the main river had to be seen to be believed. The pump could only have been running for a few hours when I witnessed the event as it had not been working when I had passed it earlier on in the day. Even so, a few pike had already started to feed in the area, a couple of which I caught on livebaits, but it seemed that other pike had not yet homed in on the rich feeding. As the current took the floating carcases downstream (goodness knows how many other dead fish were under the water), seagulls and cormorants came from all around to feed on them. I can just imagine the feast that later took place in the dark hours that followed after I had gone home. Pike, zander and eels must have all been piling in together, not to mention signal crayfish and mitten crabs which are present in this part of the river nowadays in increasing numbers. It must have been an amazing sight, but kept from our eyes by the deep water and darkness! Once again, I was unable to go back to fish the area, this time for a couple of weeks, so I probably missed out on catching some really fat pike as the weights of the local fish must surely have been boosted well above their normal winter weights.

Many pike anglers are obsessed by weights, and I would not deny them the right to get excited when pike exceed the bench mark targets of 20 lb, 25 lb or even 30 lb. How that weight is achieved is purely academic and I don't think we should be concerned as long as the angler has not purposely attempted to feed pike in order to artificially raise their body weights. This would not be too difficult to do I should imagine. I have never done so myself, purely using pre baiting to get pike into a localised area and make catching them a lot easier. I dare say, based upon the story of the greedy 15 pounder, that it would be quite possible to elevate the weight of a 'mid twenty' to over 30 lb. A hollow victory comes to mind, especially if the pike is made to look obese, but what of the angler who catches a very big pike which has gorged on someone else's pre bait? Dilemmas, dilemma's! It's not life threatening though and of no importance in the great scheme of things, so I personally would just enjoy the capture and accept it for what it is!

Pike weights can also be boosted naturally when they gorge on easily available live prey, typical of situations where huge shoals congregate in winter. Here it is quite normal to find pike with distended guts and a couple of pounds heavier than they ought to be. They will naturally hold quite a lot of spawn at this time, accounting for a lot of the increased bulk, but some pike are clearly crammed with small fish which can be felt through the skin of their undersides. The unexpected capture of a 30 lb river pike was made in such a situation, where prey fish were abundant in huge numbers and pike were feeding heavily on them.

I regularly fish all my local fen rivers in both Lincolnshire and Cambridgeshire, often from a boat, and although they have been very productive in terms of numbers of pike, have never produced anything really special. Twenty pounders were caught but were rare visitors to my net, and I fish these venues purely for sport rather than expecting to catch a huge pike. I am always happy to catch a 'big double', and in winter some of them are really fabulous looking fish. For my work, this sort of fishing is ideal.

I always start looking for prey concentrations on rivers in the autumn, and once I have found them, regular visits to the river are necessary to keep me in touch with them as they can move around quite a lot. In the mid winter of 2008/9 I found a very big concentration of roach, and there were lots of pike in attendance. Each visit produced reliable sport and lots of doubles up to 18 lb were caught, which is a good fish for the river. They were stocky fish, well padded out with spawn and topped up with roach and skimmers.

'I AM ALWAYS HAPPY TO CATCH A 'BIG DOUBLE', AND IN WINTER SOME OF THEM ARE REALLY FABULOUS LOOKING FISH.'

For some time I'd been expecting the river to produce an 'upper twenty' after already catching some stunning looking pike, one of them being over 25 lb to a client. That pike was exceptional for the river though and I didn't expect to beat it easily, but I always felt there should be something bigger when taking into account the vast numbers of prey fish I had seen on my echo sounder. Not only did the pike have massive shoals of roach and rudd to feed on, but also a huge shoal of bream that roamed up and down the river. I am sure my mates became bored with me telling them of the river's potential based on my instinct, but they would soon be made to sit up and listen!

When the big event happened, it just came like a bolt from the blue! The bait, a small live roach, was cast

PIC: IAN SLOAN

'...I KNEW THE SIGNIFICANCE OF A 30 LB FEN RIVER PIKE.'

down the river and alongside a moored boat. There was no agenda, I was simply relishing every second of fishing in the mild, damp air that was following on from a long cold spell. The float 'plopped' under, just as it had already done a couple of times earlier that day when I had boated an 11 pounder and a 16. This fight was in a different class though, the pike just plodding around and feeling heavy. As it rolled I said to my good friend Ian Sloan, my boat partner for the day, that we were about to have a 'twenty' coming into the boat! It rolled again and I said that it might even make 25 lb. While slipping the net under it I suggested it might even be a bit bigger, but when I unfolded the landing net mesh I could see that it could be no less than 28 lb! Then it just seemed to grow and grow as I rolled it into the weigh sling. In disbelief, I lowered the sling back to the bottom of the boat to get my breath. Ian, being a fairly casual pike angler, could not quite understand why I was getting rather emotional, and I must say struggling for words!

I lifted again, this time turning the face of the digital scales in his direction, and he confirmed that it read 30 lb 3 oz. Then I totally lost it, and without another word spoken I put the pike back in the landing net and held it over the side of the boat. I really was stunned as I knew the significance of a 30 lb fen river pike. Even in normal condition it would have been a very big pike, but being close to spawning time combined with rich feeding, it had elevated its weight to surpass that which fanatical pike anglers like me dream about. It had taken a tiny four inch livebait, the size of prey that the pike clearly preferred at the time as they fed amongst a huge shoal of them, picking out my tiny roach livebait from the tens of thousands of others around it! I've caught many thirty pounders, but to this very day I'm still feeling shell shocked from this one!

It's never a good idea to try and hypothesise about what size of prey pike eat. I am convinced that they just eat what's most easily available, and much of the time it can be prey fish of mixed sizes. I have seen this at first hand when working for a netsman for a while back in the eighties. Big pike kept in tanks overnight often regurgitated their stomach contents, and there was usually quite a variety on display. I have also held pike in tanks myself when helping with fishery management projects and I'm never surprised what they spew up. It's interesting that even the biggest pike often contain large numbers of quite tiny fish, only one or two inches in length and of a size you would not think they would bother with. Certainly not of a size you would consider using for bait! Probably a hundred of them would weigh no more than a few ounces, but it's obviously in the pikes nature to grab anything that is easy for it to do so. Facts like this are always on my mind and the reason why I am always trying something different when I'm pike fishing, not sticking rigidly to the same tactics all the time.

A lot of the waters I have fished in my area contain good numbers of larger prey fish, mainly tench, bream and sometimes chub, and waters with an abundance of these species occasionally throw up very big pike. Those that are also stocked with rainbow trout, as some are, have even more potential for rapid pike growth. The potential for big pike in these waters is fairly predictable, but even less well stocked waters can produce the occasional outsize pike from time to time, and I am always looking out for any water with such potential even if it doesn't have a reputation. At the time of writing, I am fishing a still water where the pike are what I would describe as 'average', typically from 5 – 15 lb in weight and with an occasional low 20 pounder. Listening to reports from those who fish it, I haven't bothered to fish there much. It seems like a very ordinary pike water and it has never really appealed to me - that was until I saw a pike which made me think again!

A July bream session on the lake two seasons ago was progressing very nicely, and towards the end I had taken about 25 fish for a total weight of about 100 lb. That wasn't unusual as the lake is crammed full with them, mostly weighing from three to four pounds with the occasional bigger one. Towards the end of the session I hooked a smaller one of about two pounds or so, and as it came to the landing net in the clear water, I could see a very big pike following it and snatching at it.

I held the bream in the landing net without unhooking it so I could get a bait to the pike without delay. Several casts with a totally unsuitable lure, snagging in the weed whilst doing so, told me I probably wasn't going to catch it. In my haste I'd also forgotten that summer pike fishing is not allowed there and thought it best not to blot my copy book and lose my season ticket! I put my rod down, unhooked the bream and released it, already planning ahead to how I would fish for that pike later in the year. As the bream swam over the shallow margin the big pike appeared from nowhere, opened its mighty

THE LAKE THAT WAS FULL OF THESE CHUB PRODUCED TWO 30-POUNDERS.

jaw and sucked it in. With just the tail of the bream showing she lumbered away, down the slope and into deeper water.

She was undoubtedly 28 lb plus, potentially a 30 pounder in winter condition and well worth catching. Unfortunately, through the following winter I was very busy. The lake was also frozen for a long period and I just never found the time to fish there. The club members that did fish reported pike to about 17 lb and I would have known if she had been caught. I now had to decide whether to try and catch it in the following winter.

I worry about fishing for 'known' big pike as they are approaching the end of their relatively short lived lives, and often die when they have reached such specimen sizes. You could easily be fishing for a pike which has died of natural causes or, as so often happens with older fish, from being spawn bound, so I was in two minds whether to try and catch it during the following winter, as time is precious and cannot be wasted on wild goose chases. I'd started to talk myself out of a winter campaign when, last summer, exactly the same thing happened again in the same swim. This time a four pound bream was grabbed and I was instantly nipped off, but I saw the pike very clearly. It was a monster and very likely the same pike I'd seen the previous year.

From these and other observations, I'm quite sure that any venue that has large bream shoals, whether river or still water, will most likely have bigger pike 'attached' to them; pike which follow them around and feed on them when they need to. It makes sense to keep close to a food source of a size which gives optimum return for effort. I'm paying a lot more attention to this nowadays, and in a recent season I followed a river bream shoal over several weeks and caught pike to over 27 lb from amongst them, not to mention zander over 12 lb as well!.

Up to now I've only talked about successes of the past, but this pike I've seen is now a challenge for the winter following the publication of this book. I feel confident that if I apply myself I will catch it, and hopefully, by describing my planned tactics, will inspire readers into seeking out their own bigger pike and consider how best to catch them. It can happen by luck, but is more likely through a carefully considered approach.

In October, when pike fishing is once again allowed on the lake, I will begin my campaign with a two or three day session. Unless I am lucky (who me?), it will take more than a few short sessions to get it right. I will start by bream fishing and focus on getting them into my swim, and once they are there I know there's a good chance that the big pike could be within casting range. Whilst bream fishing I will have two large deadbaits out, one cast either side of the bream shoal. To get the deadbaits noticed I will pop them up, and using a float rig I'll twitch them occasionally to give them a bit of movement. I use small baits for pike quite a lot but I am not dogmatic about it. In early winter, bigger baits can be a better option at times, and as in this situation I will use them when I feel it gives me an edge.

I'M AFTER THE PIKE THAT'S EATING THESE!

When the bream are finally in the swim my plan will be stepped up a gear and I will change one rod over to a livebait rig. First I will have to catch livebaits as it's not allowed to take any to the water. To catch roach I'll need to change my feeder tactics from a method feeder with a maize or pellet hook bait, to a maggot feeder and double maggot

Caption: '...I followed a river bream shoal over several weeks and caught pike to over 27 lb from amongst them...'

hook bait. There are very good numbers of bait size roach in the lake, so this should not take too long that early in the winter.

You can learn a lot about pike by fishing for their prey. When fishing the method feeder with hard hook baits, I almost exclusively catch bream from three pounds upwards. You could not use soft hook baits when after bream as small fish demolish them within minutes. When fishing the maggot feeder you do catch the odd big bream, but mainly small roach which can be very annoying, recasting every few minutes after unhooking yet another one. When you want bait though, you don't mind! I should easily catch roach of 6-8 inches which are ideal, and as big as I can rig safely and efficiently with the leger rig I use.

Something important I learnt from maggot feeder fishing on this lake was that there are a lot more smaller bream in there than I had realised, and 'one pounders' are very common but they are rarely caught on hard hookbaits. This means to me that the lake has the food source to grow pike quickly and to good sizes and further big pike can be expected to be coming through. It

CATCHING INACTIVE PIKE, AS THIS 29 POUNDER WAS, TAKES A LOT MORE SKILL.

would be unwise to ignore the potential for a big pike there!

Getting the livebaits out in good condition so that I can expect them to stay alive for long periods of time is my next consideration. Casting them more than a rod length or two will easily damage them, and in the early part of the season when the water temperature is still quite high, they will not last for long. I would ideally like to use my bait boat to gently drop my livebaits, but they are banned due to the carp angler's antics of previous seasons. Margin placed baits might work, but I would be too frustrated not to have the capability of positioning them well out into the lake and close to the bream shoal. I have a way of doing it though!

As I often repeat, but with good reason, you can import a lot of what you learn from fishing for other species into your pike fishing tactics. Catfishing has taught me a lot about livebait rigs, and for getting my catfish livebaits out a long way I use what is known as a 'winch rig'. It's too complicated and unnecessary to go into great detail, but basically you cast a heavy leger weight to where you want to put your livebait, and when doing so the main line is connected to the line of another rod. In effect you have cast out two lines. The second rod, or 'winch rod' as it is known, is then used to pull your pike line back to the bank while the leger weight remains where it is, making sure that your pike reel has an open bale arm to allow line to be taken during the retrieve. You now clip on your livebait rig, which is a special buoyant rig that will initially float on the surface. The rig is then wound back to the weight using the pike rod, winding very carefully so as not to dislodge the weight. When the rig is above the weight, you keep winding to pull it down tight in its popped up position, setting your bite alarm as you would for any leger method. You now have a fresh and lively popped up livebait in position and it should stay lively all day if you have done it correctly. As I've already said, this is not intended to be a technical book. The rig is not quick and easy to describe, but you can find more detail on any catfishing website if it interests you.

Whether I catch that pike will largely depend upon how much effort and perseverance I put in. It would be easy to become disillusioned if weeks and months pass by without a result, but you need to be prepared for that. I'm sure I will catch other pike to keep things lively, but I will also be fishing other venues as well rather than putting all my hopes into catching that one particular fish. As long as I'm enjoying it I will persevere. When I'm not, I'll move on!

It's clear that wherever you fish for pike, you need to be aware of the facts about the water and not expect pike fishing to be similar on each one. Within each water it's possible to deduce what pike eat, and sometimes when they eat it. Knowing these basic facts, it is then a matter of weighing up what your chances are of catching pike and how to go about it.

I look at it like this. I divide the pike's time between feeding and digesting periods. During the feeding time I have my best chance of catching them while they are actively hunting, but I also have another chance, albeit a lesser one, of catching them while they are digesting their meal, and I accept that catching pike at this time of inactivity will require a lot more skill. It's worth looking into this philosophy in more detail as I think it will explain, to some extent, why pike fishing results can vary from day to day and why waters vary in levels of difficulty. The feeding time and the digesting time, and how they are related, are points worth considering in more depth.

The length of the feeding period is dependant upon the ease in which the pike can satisfy its needs and will vary from water to water. On 'average' waters, where prey is plentiful and of a modest size, I'm sure that pike are nipping in and out of feeding and digesting periods quite regularly during normal winter conditions. Feeding periods will be frequent, although not neccessarily a daily occurance and a sensible approach should find that catching them is not too difficult at most times, although they may need a little coaxing every now and again.

Then we have what I refer to as 'hungry' waters. Typically, pike in such waters tend to be long and thin as they are frequently on the move looking for food. In this instance, the balance between the numbers of prey and predators has probably been disturbed. This could happen, for example, where cormorants or other water birds have depleted the prey fish stocks to such an extent that the resident pike have insufficient food and spend a lot more time hunting than digesting. The feeding window on this type of water will be much wider, its pike will be constantly on the look out for food, and digesting time is a luxury. The fishing on these waters tends to be easy and most baits and methods will work. If fished for regularly, they are often poor looking specimens through excessive handling. On the contrary, pike in rarely fished waters where food fish are in short supply, or where they have to work hard to catch them, can look very sleek and beautiful, typical of many large Irish and Scandinavian waters I've fished.

At the other extreme are waters where the feeding time is minimal and the digesting time excessive, usually as a result of an abundance of large prey fish. These waters can be very hard to come to terms with but often contain very large pike. Catching them can be very difficult and almost impossible at times because opportunities come briefly and rarely. This would be typical of a well stocked rainbow trout water or a water that holds vast shoals of bream, tench or other large prey fish. This could be the case on the water I have described where I am planning to fish this winter, where large bream are present in vast numbers. If a big pike grabs such a food item, typically weighing from two to five pounds, and if it can do so with ease, it will have no reason to feed again for a very long time. Its feeding time will be brief and it's digesting time lengthy. Water temperature can help, and the warmer it is the better in this respect as the food will pass through the pikes system more quickly. In very cold water it will take much longer to digest prey and the chance of being in the right place in the very brief moment when the pike take's its next food item is very slim indeed. You have a better chance in a water where there are several large pike, but when their numbers are low you are likely to struggle and these waters can easily break the will of all but the most determined or dedicated.

I've hinted previously that inactive pike can be tempted, although this requires more skill from the angler. The chances of tempting inactive pike are, in my view, somewhat dependant upon how well they have fed previously and how far into the digestive phase they have progressed. A pike that has recently eaten a very large meal for example, may be difficult to catch for a while, but will eventually enter a period when it is considering its next meal, making it more possible to tempt. On the other hand, pike that are digesting 'lean pickings' will undoubtedly present the angler with a better chance of catching them as they are still hungry. Fortunately, there are those pike that are just plain greedy and don't know when to stop feeding, no matter how much they have consumed! Such pike are encountered from time to time, often big ones, and they are the ones I like to catch!

These are my feelings based upon fishing for pike for four decades, and I may not necessarily have reached accurate scientific conclusions, but when faced with so many different pike fishing situations where pike have varied immensely in difficulty of capture, I have had to console myself with at least a basic feeling about what is going on under the water. Applying this theory to new waters I am tackling, gives me the confidence to come to terms with my results, and from a practical point of view, choose my tactics. On hungry waters for example, I will not waste good bait and I will not get up too early in the morning because I know that whenever I fish, I will have a good result. On the other hand, if I am fishing a very hard water, a short session is unlikely to put me in the right place at the right time, and the longer the session, the better chance I will have to put myself in that short feeding window. I also know that on such a water, it will pay me to reposition my baits regularly to try to drop onto static pike which are less likely to come to me. This is why slowly trolling livebaits on such waters can be a winning method if it's allowed, and one I prefer to use whenever possible.

Knowing what my chances are likely to be, on any water, keeps me going when I appear to be getting nowhere! I have reached the conclusions I've detailed after many years of sitting on banks and in boats trying to fathom it all out. It's staring to make a little sense to me now and a lot less frustrating than it used to be!

Sometimes they cannot help themselves! With another pike wedged in its throat it took my lure!

Captures from hard waters, like this 20 lb 1 oz fish, are particularly satisfying. This one took a lamprey in a very weedy swim.

'...THE RED TOPPED 'SLIM SLIDER' FLOAT SLAMMED UNDER TIME AFTER TIME...'

CHAPTER 6

Little and Often!

There's nothing quite like the thrill of catching a specimen pike, but I don't have the luxury of being able to fish for them as often as people might think. Most of the time I am looking for action packed sessions where I catch lots of pike. Pike of any size will do – although I don't complain if they are big! My work as a tackle development consultant is much better served by catching a lot of pike rather than just a few big ones. The tackle needs to be properly tested and decisions cannot be based on just one or two fish captures. Big pike are never far from my thoughts though, and I'm always looking for opportunities to fish for them when I do have the time!

A couple of seasons ago I was out for a mid winter 'bagging up' session to test some of a new range of Fox pike gear. My chosen venue was a river in East Anglia which has never had a great reputation for bigger pike, but it usually produced very good sport. A dozen pike in a day was always on the cards, usually with a 'double' or two thrown in. The winter rains had put paid to consistent sport after Christmas and I had been struggling elsewhere, but this is an interesting place to fish and somewhere I can get away from the crowds and get on with my work undisturbed. I just love to launch my boat there every now and again as there's still a lot of river I haven't fully explored yet, and I learn more about it with each visit.

On a cold January morning I drove across for a session, intending to try a few areas where I had previously found big shoals of roach and expecting to get a rod bender or two to put some of the new tackle items I had with me through their paces. The first two swims produced nothing, but my third drop of the anchor was to remind me that you never know what's coming next when you go pike fishing!

As usual I was fishing alone, something I prefer to do when I'm working on new tackle development as there is more to do than just fishing. Anyone who came with me would soon get fed up when, for example, I chopped and changed between a couple of dozen different lure patterns to check their actions, usually in swims they would rather not be fishing and when they would rather be deadbaiting elsewhere. My work eats into the fishing time and would frustrate anyone with me who is expecting a day's sport. It's a great job of course, and on this particular day I was testing the final samples of a new boat rod and a new 'quick change' trace system. I needed to catch as many pike as possible. Nice job eh?

As I approached a new swim, roach dimpled on the surface and a pike swirled amongst them as I dropped the anchor. I'd been deadbaiting up until that point, but I could see it was now time to get out the livebait catching kit! I slung out a couple of deadbaits while doing so – just in case! To be honest, bait catching was too easy, and I started catching one small roach after another. They were quite small, averaging about five inches long, but I don't have a problem with using such small livebaits in many situations, especially when it is really cold. It didn't take long to fill my bait bucket and I was soon reeling in the deadbaits which had gone undisturbed, and replaced them with a couple of livebaits suspended beneath floats. They were mounted on just one size four treble and a red 'bait flag' was used to retain them and make them more noticeable in the coloured water.

'IT DIDN'T TAKE LONG TO FILL MY BAIT BUCKET...'

I actually slung the baits out without too much thought while I started to organise the boat, but one was taken straight away. A real tussle followed and a good sized pike was soon guided into the large diameter net which I nowadays favour, finding it much more practical than the popular triangular type. It features a rubber coated, large diameter mesh, which is very easy to remove hooks from compared to the 'carp friendly' soft micromesh material.

The pike was very fat, its stomach bulging after gorging on small roach, and I thought it was a contender for pulling the scales past the magical 20 lb mark. It was not to be though, weighing in at just over 18 lb. Out went another bait, but before I could make any progress with tidying the boat, the float was gone again! This time a 12 pounder was chinned and easily unhooked whilst still in the water.

'Time to get organised' I thought, as another pike struck near the boat. With two rods now back in action I tried to put the kettle on to boil on my stove in the cuddy, but it was obvious that I wouldn't be having tea for a while as both floats slammed under at the same time! An 11 pounder was quickly chinned and returned whilst a 17 pounder was put into the sling for weighing. It was clear that this area of the river was crammed with roach and pike, probably the reason why I couldn't catch anything in other nearby swims. Catching those pike and playing them in the swim seemed to start a feeding frenzy as roach were now being scattered everywhere.

For the next half an hour, I waited no longer than ten minutes for a 'take' and put another four double figure pike in the boat, the biggest going 17 lb 2 oz. With eight 'doubles' boated in such a short time, and the prospect of more, I decided it was time to start writing down their weights in my notebook rather than trying to remember them, as this had the makings of a very memorable catch!

Pike activity was not confined to the immediate area where I was anchored as, in other nearby swims, pike could regularly be seen scattering the roach, and there would often be several strikes at the same time. It was an awesome sight and I now had the enviable job of working my way through them! It was the sort of pike fishing I live for and which doesn't come along too often, so I was going to make the most of it. I had plenty of livebaits, and if I ran out, it would be easy to catch more. What's more, I was really giving the new rods and traces a thorough testing too! I almost forgot what I was there for!

Using my lightweight anchor, it was possible to fish an area, lift it for a while, drift a few yards further down the swim and drop it again without making too much disturbance. Following this procedure, I methodically worked through the swim getting take after take. In fact, I reached the stage where I could see there was no point in using more than one rod. This was frantic fishing, and with darkness fast approaching I decided not to waste time weighing any more of the larger pike unless they looked like they would make 20 lb.

After catching so many pike over the years, I am happy that I can estimate pike weights pretty accurately. The weights of such pike are not that important anyway, but when I totted up the fish recorded in my notebook and realising that all fifteen pike I had caught were in double figures, I set myself the challenge of taking the score up to 20 'doubles'. I was quietly confident I could do so because they were still striking everywhere!

Two things occurred to me during this session. First of all, there were no 'jacks' about. Where were they, and why didn't the females want them joining in the feeding spree? Secondly, every pike was very lightly hooked, yet I would have expected some of them to have swallowed the small livebaits. Was it the fact that they were all extremely fat and were just topping up their already full stomachs? Was there so much food around that it was unnecessary to bolt it down? A few things to ponder, but probably never fully understand.

More pike came to the net as the red topped 'slim slider' float slammed under time after time – every one a 'double' and several of them in the 17 – 18 lb bracket. Only darkness and running short of livebaits made me decide that enough was enough. I'd got a long haul ahead of me, sorting the boat out and then driving home. The final tally for the day, recorded in my slime and mud soiled notebook, was 22 pike with every one weighing in at over ten pounds with a conservative estimate of a total weight of over 300 lb!

Over dinner that evening, Jan heard the tale over and over again. She knew what I was leading up to – would she come down with me for another session and take some photos? It was a great opportunity to get some pictures for articles - and an excuse to catch some more!

Two days later we headed straight for 'the' swim. The rods were already set up and I spent the first

'At 23 lb 12 oz it was 'well in' and I breathed a sigh of relief.'

hour catching livebaits which came on board aplenty. As often happens, if you tell someone about a great swim, it never lives up to its expectation. I really had to work for the first run and it took an hour before the float finally plopped under. When it came, a 17 pounder was hooked and then a 15 pounder took a livebait just a few minutes later!

As happened in the previous session, catching one sent the others into feeding mode. Swirling started everywhere and then a bigger vortex rocked the area. Jan said she'd seen the back of the pike and it looked big. She's rarely wrong, so I tossed a tiny four inch roach livebait right into the boil it had made. The float disappeared so quickly, I never even saw it go under! All the pike had been fighting well, so I never expected anything special with this one until it appeared in front of me. As it slipped over the solid rim of the net I knew I'd got a 'twenty'!

At 23 lb 12 oz it was 'well in' and I breathed a sigh of relief. It's not all about big fish, but I really wanted this haul to be topped with a 20 pounder to make it especially memorable, and this one meant more to me than bigger pike I have caught from other venues where pike of this size are not that unusual. The day continued with plenty of sport, but nothing to match the previous session. 11 pike were landed, all on tiny livebaits, with eight in double figures, the others being just shy of that weight, and 'jacks' were not in evidence once again.

It had been a memorable two days fishing with 30 double figure pike including a 20 pounder. In my earlier years of piking I would have been delighted to catch thirty doubles in a whole season, a fact which brought into perspective just how far my pike fishing had progressed.

To make this mega haul of quality pike, it was essential to offer them the right bait, and I instinctively knew that small livebaits would work in this situation. I have tried taking the easy option and using deadbaits in the past, but usually found them to be a poor second best to livebaits in swims crammed with prey fish. The size of livebait was important too. I have frequently experienced the use of smaller livebaits to result in more fish landed than if using larger livebaits, when pike are in amongst huge shoals of fry and small prey fish. They will take the bigger livebaits, but dropped runs and missed runs have been an annoyingly regular feature.

I've tried to analyse why this happens, and I think it may be to do with how pike deal with baits in cold water circumstances. When water temperatures are higher, pike swallow baits of any size very quickly as their fast metabolism at this time demands a high throughput of food. When it's very cold though, the demand is greatly reduced and there is no need to bolt baits down quickly; in fact quite the opposite. Where there is plenty of food, they seem content to nip onto them quite gently and take their time because there are plenty more. Because we tend to strike immediately nowadays, we will have a better chance of a 'hook up' in cold conditions by using a small bait than we would if using a big one. Even small baits tend to lead to lightly hooked pike when it's very cold, further evidence that they are in no hurry to swallow them. My success rate is much higher with small baits in cold water, and I catch plenty of bigger pike in the process too. I don't think for one minute that this is a hard and fast rule to be applied everywhere though. You have to work out what's best for each water at different times. It's something I believe in though, and experience to pass on which might help the reader to think more about his own approach if he feels set in his ways!

When pike are pre occupied with smaller prey fish, it is often referred to as 'fry feeding'. This term is a little misleading so I will first of all clarify what it means to me. I tend to think of 'fry' as young fish in their first winter, not even a year old yet and typically from one to two inches long. On many venues they can be found gathered together in winter time in vast numbers, and you will find them packed into culverts, under boats, around landing stages and in quieter backwaters. They pack tightly together to give them a feeling of safety from predators, not only from fish but from birds such as grebes and cormorants. Each one hides behind many others thinking it is safe, but it doesn't work like that though and predators just pick them off one by one. It is remarkable how quickly a livebait can be taken when cast amongst thousands of similar sized prey fish. When pike are all fired up they don't miss a thing, and the keenness of the pike's senses easily enables it to detect anything which might be vulnerable from the visual and audible signals it is sending out. This makes them the odd ones out, and as the other fish move away, the livebait on the hook becomes an easy target!

Individually they may not be much of a meal, but collectively they can provide quite a feast, and even the very largest pike will join in with this seasonal harvest. These tiny fish might seem to be of little interest to larger pike, but the fact is that they are, and especially where they are prolific and easily available. Wherever I fish I always consider trying small baits, whether they are livebaits, deadbaits or lures, and rarely feel that they are an inferior offering.

When in their second and third winters, prey fish will obviously be much bigger having gone beyond the 'fry' stage and now becoming even more attractive to pike. They are now typically three to five inches long dependant upon their species and thus a far better prospect for pike to eat. In reality, winter concentrations of prey fish often consist of both sizes and some even bigger ones in amongst them as well. The larger mature prey fish often gather separately, probably with spawning in mind which will not be too far away. Winter pike fishing for me is frequently dependant upon finding any big shoals of prey fish if I can do so.

Finding concentrations of prey fish is not easy if they don't give themselves away, so I am always looking for other clues that will lead me to pike. Seeing pleasure anglers catching them for sport is a useful pointer, and I also take an interest in 'accidental' captures of pike by those fishing for other species or their encounters with 'nuisance' pike which may be related to the presence of prey fish shoals.

On trout reservoirs for example, many large pike fall to trout anglers flies, and trout anglers frequently relate tales of being bitten off by pike. They are often caught by those using flashy lure patterns aimed at fry feeding trout, but it's not unusual for pike to be taken on small nymphs and even occasionally on buzzers which resemble not much more than bare hooks! The logic defies my understanding but does not dispel the fact that it does happen and quite frequently at that. I think that some of the time such captures are connected with fry feeding pike – but not always! It would be very neat and tidy for me to say that these anglers have caught fry feeding pike, but I don't think this is always the case. I'm sure it's simply that pike are conditioned to snap at anything which moves from an early age. Finding them regularly in the stomachs of large pike, as mentioned elsewhere, supports this theory. Further evidence comes from the fact that large pike are frequently caught on small flies from my club trout fishery, which has no small fish species at all!

I have already detailed how this fact gives me great confidence in using small baits, and this particularly applies when fly fishing for pike where casting a smaller fly is so much easier than casting a big one. Having tried both, the use of smaller flies does not seem to be a handicap and they catch plenty of bigger pike too.

An interesting phenomenon of fishing for pike with a fly is that I have hooked quite a few in the tail. I have also experienced many 'knocks' on the fly which I believe are also from pike hitting a potential food item with its tail in order to disable it. It makes more sense if you visualise a pike wading into a group of small fish. Some will probably enter its mouth, but if it swirls round and lashes into them with its massive rear end fins, it will almost certainly disable or disorientate several more, which it can then pick off at its leisure. More food for thought!

One of the great visual moments in pike fishing is when a pike (or several pike) strike into a shoal of prey fish and send them scattering all over the swim, often with an audible accompaniment sounding like someone throwing in a spade full of gravel as the prey erupt on the surface and scatter everywhere. It can be particularly spectacular where prey fish are gathered in big numbers and is something I'm constantly looking out for at any time and which has led to many an unexpected capture after an opportunist cast to an attacking pike. Whether I catch or not, such inspiration has often spurred me on when the going has been tough.

The most amazing display I have ever seen occurred in a small bay of about two acres, which is joined to a much larger expanse of water of more than 40 acres. They are joined by two narrow channels, and as soon as the weather turns cold, all the roach from the larger expanse of water enter the small bay and pack tightly into it. If you wanted to catch roach on all but the very coldest days, this would be the place to catch them. That is, if the pike would let you!

When this water changed ownership, the new owner built a platform in the bay so

'These tiny fish might seem to be of little interest to larger pike, but the fact is that they are...'

that he could fish for the roach. His first session, on a mild October morning, saw him hook several dozen roach, none of which he got into his keep net because every single one was snatched by a pike within seconds of being hooked! Not being a lover of pike, he lost his temper and said 'they have got to go'. One way or another, he was intent on removing them, 'dead or alive'!

When I heard of this, I had to poke my nose in because there was talk of culling the pike, and by the time I got to speak with the owner I know a few had already been killed. There was no time to waste and I had to take action to save these pike from a certain death. I agreed to catch a few and remove them to two much larger lakes nearby where they would be welcomed.

On the first session, I arrived for an afternoon's fishing complete with a tank of water that would hold four or five average sized pike and was greeted by the owner. The sight before us in the flat calm lake was awesome. As many as six, eight, maybe ten pike would all strike at once, scattering thousands and thousands of small roach all over the place. Even if you turned your back on the lake, you could hear the carnage taking place behind you. It was a sight that any pike angler would travel a long way to witness, and even better I was about to cast a bait in amongst them! I don't think it mattered what I cast into the swim, a livebait, a deadbait or a lure as there were so many pike - and they were in 'killing mode'!

To make my life easy, I tossed out a float with a small piece of herring with just a size four treble in the tail. The float didn't even settle and I was bent into an eight pounder which fought like stink, sending roach scattering everywhere as it battled to the net. With just one treble the unhooking was quick, and a similar bait was soon flying out to a different part of the swim, only to be taken within seconds again! I hadn't even had chance to set the stop knot properly, but it was obvious that this was not critical. After landing the second fish I adjusted the stop knot so that the deadbait would be suspended in mid water, not that it mattered that much! Within less than half an hour I landed another six pike ranging from 5 – 12 lb. With five in the tank and three more in sacks, I had to stop fishing and take them over to the other lakes.

To cut a long story short, the action went on all afternoon and I never waited more than a few minutes for a run, and removed a total of 18 pike from the swim! I could have caught a lot more, but my time was being taken up by carefully transporting them. The smallest was about four pounds and the biggest around 14 lb but I returned a 17 pounder which I hoped would grow a lot bigger with less competition from the others. As we drove away from the lake for the last time, there were swirls galore highlighted against the red sky of the setting sun, confirming that we were nowhere near to resolving the situation. I was asked if I would come back the next day, otherwise they would get someone else onto the job. I didn't take much persuading!

The next afternoon was almost a repeat of the previous one and this time I caught and removed another 20 pike of similar sizes. I won't give a blow by blow account, but needless to say it was non stop, arm breaking action again. It didn't stop there though and I returned for two more sessions as we didn't seem to be making any inroads into the pike numbers at all. In those four afternoons I removed 76 pike from this single swim, but I had to call things to a halt as I was now getting worried that the other lakes would not be able to support any more. As it turned out it was just what the lakes needed,

'...MY TIME WAS BEING TAKEN UP BY CAREFULLY TRANSPORTING THEM!'

'...IT WAS NON STOP, ARM BREAKING ACTION.' PIC: STEVE MARTIN

and they have settled down into a good pike waters, providing many anglers with excellent sport.

If you just like catching pike for the sheer fun of it, as I do, this had to be the ultimate pike catcher's dream. Even after we had finished the exercise you still didn't have to wait long to see a pike strike, but at least it was possible to fish for the roach without being bothered too much by them. Returning to the lake the following year, the pike fishing sport was still very brisk and the average size and condition of the pike was slightly better. It's always a dilemma knowing whether to interfere with nature in this way, but confronted with seeing dozens of pike bashed on the head or taking such action, rightly or wrongly, I would do it again.

Catching pike amongst big shoals of prey fish can often be very easy as illustrated in this story, and even though your bait might seem quite insignificant amongst the vast numbers in the swim, pike soon pick it out when in a frenzied feeding mode. In this instance, bait choice was not important as the pike were hell bent on eating everything in sight as their demand for food was high in the early autumn water temperature. It was a very different scenario to the earlier story about catching pike in very cold water conditions when a small livebait was the superior method.

When a pike has been seen scattering prey under more 'normal' circumstances, I've many times tossed a livebait in its direction and experienced a quick response. Quite frequently though this doesn't happen, and it's easy to think that the pike has moved on and start casting all over the swim and damaging the livebait in the process. I think that this is because the pike sometimes waits a while before making another attack if its chances of success are low. Otherwise it would be chasing all over the place and wear itself out. The pike is an ambusher, not a chaser!

I find I have better results in this situation if I sit it out with a paternoster rigged livebait rather than a roaming bait which keeps swimming out of position. Alternatively, I will wait ten minutes or so before trying again if it looks like the pike isn't likely to make an imminent attack. It might, of course, be digesting a prey fish after the attack you have seen, giving it less reason to strike again immediately. We will never know such things for certain, but when faced with several 'unknowns' we mustn't beat ourselves up if we don't always get it right. Part of the fun of pike fishing comes from trying to outwit them!

In amongst congregations of fry or small fish, there may also be other predators at work as well. You can sometimes find perch nearby, and in waters where they are present there might be zander too. The use of smaller baits is useful as they could tempt perch and zander whereas if you only use bigger baits, you could miss these 'bonus' fish. I refer to them as 'bonus' fish when I am fishing for pike, but when it is obvious that there are plenty of perch or zander present, I will often make them my target fish and scale down the hook sizes on my baits or use smaller lures if necessary. Sometimes I will decide to target perch with worms if I have any with me, and it's surprising how often pike will pick up a big wriggling worm!

Lure fishing for perch and zander amongst fry can be very productive, especially when the water is quite coloured as it often is in river backwaters in winter for example. Pike also fall for smaller lures quite regularly in these situations and my most memorable catch of recent years was a pike of 20 lb 12 oz from a River Severn backwater which fell to a tiny Vibrax spinner, but it was a bit of a lucky catch really. My fishing buddy, Matt Hayes, had to leave the boat for five minutes to answer a call of nature, and rather than waste time I decided to see if I could catch a perch as there were tiny fry scattering within casting range of where we were anchored up. Expecting a perch or possibly a zander, I was caught off guard when the tiny spinning rod rammed round and I was into a great battle from a fish that would not give up, despite the cold water. It was obviously a pike, but I wasn't at all surprised that it had snapped at such a tiny offering.

We hadn't yet made up the landing net, and chinning the pike over the deep side of the Warrior boat was not easy, so I had to wait for Matt to get back and help me land it by making the net up. It was a real bruiser of a fish with a very big head, and it had taken the spinner just a few feet from the bank in about three feet of water where fry were gathered. As I always say, have faith in your own judgement, keep trying different things, and you will make your own luck. I have faith in small baits in the appropriate circumstances, and regularly reap the benefits!

The pike is an ambusher, not a chaser. Pic: Matt Hayes

'...A PIKE OF 20 LB 12 OZ FROM A RIVER SEVERN BACKWATER, WHICH FELL TO A TINY VIBRAX SPINNER.'

'...DEADBAITING IS THE MOST POPULAR PIKE FISHING METHOD IN THE UK.'

CHAPTER 7

I'm Not Eating That!

Surveys constantly remind us that deadbaiting is the most popular pike fishing method in the UK, as it has been for many decades. It is often perceived as a very simple method, not too difficult to rig up for and perform, and frequently described as 'easy' or 'boring'. I don't agree with this at all! It's true that any fool can sometimes cast out a couple of deadbaits, sit back and relax, and catch a few pike when they are on the feed, but this is a world apart from being able to consistently produce good catches from a variety of different types of water and under a wide range of weather conditions. To do so needs a good working knowledge of rigs, methods and tactic, and most importantly an acceptance that pike can sometimes have a preference for one bait over another.

Success with pike when using deadbaits requires a lot of thought, and when carried out with a pro active approach there is little time to get bored! Before proceeding any further, I would ask the reader not to expect to read this chapter and then quickly become a successful deadbait angler. The topic is more complex than one would think and cannot be learnt entirely from a book. It will require a vast amount of time on the bank before the points I mention can be appreciated to a stage where they may become of any practical value. I will start by emphasising this point and also encourage the reader to carry out his own experimentation with deadbaits from water to water. It is vital to keep trying different deadbaits and variations in their presentation and enhancement, all of which can lead to much improved results at a local and general level.

I would also like to point out a fact that many pike anglers don't seem to realise. Deadbaiting, as effective as it can be, is not the best way of catching pike in very cold water. When the water temperature is below four degrees centigrade at the surface, pike rarely respond well to deadbaits in my experience. They become very lethargic, and years of experience tell me that livebaiting becomes a far superior method. I will be brief on this point, but ignore it at your peril. Fortunately, in the UK, we only experience such low water temperatures for very brief periods during most winters.

It's also important to realise that as effective as deadbaiting might be, it is only one of several weapons in the pike angler's armoury, and I rarely fish a session with deadbaits only. There are many times when it is not a handicap to do so, but I usually also have lures with me, and if possible livebaits too. A multi method approach will often catch more pike, but is not always necessary as I have had some blinding sessions when using only deadbaits in situations where I have identified this to be the best method. Whether fishing deadbaits exclusively or using them as part of a multi method approach, it will still be necessary to determine the best deadbait species for each session as taking 'any old bait' is rarely a good approach. It needs more than a little thought if you want to get the best from deadbaiting.

It's likely that any deadbait that is cast out will be taken by a pike eventually, but the thinking pike angler will be working to cut this waiting time down to a minimum, and in doing so will catch considerably more pike than the angler who chucks out any deadbait without much thought. I am firmly convinced that pike can show a preference for one deadbait over another, although the degree to which they do so varies from water to water. If this was not the case we could use the same type of deadbait all the time. Most experienced pike anglers do not do so, as experience shows that using a variety of baits is necessary to keep the 'runs' coming. I am also convinced that pike do not always simply accept or reject our baits when they find them, and a degree of inspection often takes place. Max Cottis and I made some interesting observations when making the *Fox Guide to Gravel Pit Pike Fishing* DVD in 2006.

The fishing wasn't easy due to the low water temperature, but we had to demonstrate a variety of methods. We were getting a few runs however by chopping and changing our baits and tactics to try to find something that worked. A useful observation was made that day which is worth relating. In the very clear water, I noticed a pike would regularly follow our deadbaits in as we retrieved them ready for recasting, or sometimes it would just appear in the margin as if out of curiosity. It wasn't a particularly big pike, but making films is not all about catching big fish. We are attempting to make them interesting and discussed how we could use this observation to our advantage, deciding that it would make good viewing if we could film that pike actually taking a bait. The obvious choice, to me, was to paternoster a livebait in the margin, positioning it near the top of the steep marginal slope. We did so, focused the camera on it, and waited in readiness for the pike to approach. What could be a better offering on a cold winter's day than a tethered livebait?

Whilst we waited I reeled in another rod, only to find the lamprey bait looked a bit tatty so I decided to change it for a fresher piece. We had plenty of bait so I tossed the free offering into the margin, no doubt to be sniffed out by a pike over the next day or two. I guess you are probably two steps ahead of me now and can predict what happened next!!

The pike approached after about twenty minutes or so and our cameraman flicked the switch. We all kept very still and concealed, with our eyes firmly focused on the livebait going round and round on the paternoster rig. Yes that's right – the pike swam past the livebait, totally ignoring it and proceeded to start rooting around for the lamprey section in the thick bottom weed, five or six feet away from the livebait. It spent several minutes doing so and it was unclear whether it actually swallowed the lamprey, but it then emerged from the weed and turned on the livebait, taking it in a flash as though it had remembered it was there.

Drawing conclusions is always a dangerous thing to do with regard to pike behaviour. I wouldn't like to speculate about bait preferences based upon this one observation, but this little episode, if nothing else, certainly tells you something about the pulling power of a lamprey bait and the effectiveness of livebaits. It also makes you wonder just what thought or instinctive process goes into a pikes feeding procedure. First of all it had clearly detected the scent from the lamprey section from some distance away, even though it was buried in the weed. Did it know that the livebait was as good

PIC: MICK ROUSE

I NEVER UNDERESTIMATE THE PULLING POWER OF LAMPREY!

as 'in the bag' so concentrated its efforts on getting the lamprey as well? Was it greedy or clever or just following the instinct given to it by nature? With two choices, did it show a preference?

We later filmed another pike in the margin, this time taking a popped up mackerel tail. Here we witnessed a quite intense inspection of the bait take place with the pike responsible making an examination of it with its nose rather than just eating it straight away. Was it curious, cautious or simply checking it to see whether it was edible? Who knows?

Such events lead me to wonder what has happened before each run I get or when I experience a dropped bait. I don't think that we can automatically assume that a pike simply comes along, finds the bait and takes it. How many pike have rejected it? How many rejections have taken place on a day when you have blanked? How many times have you made a poor choice of bait and limited your chances?

Other sightings I've made have left me wondering whether such behaviour is purely instinctive and nothing to do with them being crafty, clever, thinking or even learning through experience. It does seem that they can easily tell one type of dead fish from another and decide whether it is safe or desirable to eat. I think it's not unreasonable to take this further and suggest that such identification could lead to a preference? I would also suggest that such fussy behaviour is more likely from well fed pike rather than those in 'hungry' waters where hunger will most likely override caution. Many pike anglers independently conclude that a preference is shown at times, as I do myself. When fishing at Horseshoe Lake in Gloucestershire one winter's day, another sighting left me feeling very much this way.

I had noticed a couple of pike patrolling along the shallow bush lined margins at the top end of the Summer Bay, and it was a great chance to put deadbaits in their paths and wait to see their reactions. A couple of smelts and half herrings were used, as that's what we had with us. They ignored the herrings completely, but homed in on the smelts. It was interesting to note how cautiously they approached them and I was quite fascinated to see how they examined them with their noses and then swam away. They came back several times over a period of an hour or so to make similar inspections. Eventually, one came into the swim and took a smelt quite freely, seemingly having weighed up the situation from a distance. They may be dumb creatures, but this tells me that some thought process, however primitive, is taking place.

It would be easy to apply a dozen or more different interpretations on the examples I've used in this chapter, or indeed about any personal theories on other matters I've passed on throughout this book. We are trying to understand a wild creature and our conclusions could be way off the mark. It could well be that, in the last example, the pike could detect our presence and were simply acting with caution and impulse because they were afraid and wary. I will never pretend that I know the answers; I'm still searching for them!

When we can't see what's happening under the water, which is most of the time, we have to draw conclusions about how pike react to our deadbaits from whatever information we can glean from our fishing results, and you can draw some evidence through experimenting with them rather than just sitting and waiting for floats to go under. Trying to work out what deadbait and method to use is what makes this style of pike fishing so fascinating to me, and even when I'm catching I'm always aware that I might not have found the best bait or method for the day. Most sessions see me chopping and changing deadbaits and their presentations to try and see if I can find something that works better, and how I proceed mainly draws upon gut feelings from previous experiences. Experimentation has to be conducted within practical limitations though, as you can only take so much bait with you. You are also limited by the constraint of time, and it's easy to see why it is difficult to arrive at meaningful conclusions in the short term.

I'll now look more closely at the different types of deadbaits we might consider using. Why not just take what you can get, you might ask? Why not use whatever is cheapest and most easily available? On many venues you can do this and in my neck of the woods that would mean using herring and mackerel, and it's a fact that these two baits have accounted for more pike captures for me than any other deadbaits. It's equally true that if I took them to some waters they would fare second best, or sometimes be a total waste of time. These are typical of waters where commonly used baits are treated with suspicion by the pike as they have been hammered on them so many times in the past. Waters in this category require something different or a little more unusual, and my next consideration would be to try smelt or lamprey. When first introduced to UK pike anglers, both baits were difficult to source and were often in short supply, but using them could really turn things around. If you could get them they literally took waters apart and are the two most devastatingly effective deadbaits I have ever used! Nowadays they are readily available from most good tackle shops, resulting in them losing their edge where they have been used too much. Where they haven't though, they can still be very productive! Some seasons they can be in short supply, and if you have them and others don't, it can give you a serious edge. In other words, stock up with them when you can get them and keep well in front of other pike anglers who don't have them!

My next line of attack would be to consider even less popular deadbaits (in my area), like trout, eels and sardines, although some or all of them might be widely used in other areas. The modern day pike angler really does have a great range of baits to choose from, and it should also be remembered that they can all be presented in a variety of ways to make their presentation different, such as half baits, chunks, kebabs and even spiced up with the addition of the multitude of fishy smelling flavourings and oils available.

I will also use coarse fish deadbaits, which often provide an edge on hard fished waters. Most pike anglers either cannot or do not wish to catch them, although they are becoming more available from bait suppliers nowadays. All the silver species such as roach, bream, chub and dace, make great deadbaits. Dead perch are extremely good baits too, but hardly anyone seems to use them locally. Having caught two 30 pounders on perch baits, one on livebait and one on deadbait, I am more than happy to use them! I have already mentioned about a dozen different deadbaits and you can't take them all on every session, so that alone is good reason, by a process of elimination, to find out what works best on each of the waters you fish.

Waters you have little knowledge of can present a dilemma when choosing bait. It can take a while to determine which deadbaits work best on any new water and I think it's unwise to start with predetermined assumptions. I don't base my conclusions on just one or two sessions either. I also consider that bait alone is not always the solution and I am simultaneously considering feeding times and location too. A point that is never a waste of time repeating!

How then, do you use all this hard earned knowledge to decide what deadbaits to take with you on a pike fishing session? If you covered all the bases you would have about two dozen different types which is just not practical or affordable, but this is a question I ask myself every time I prepare for a session. On waters that I know well, I have a pretty good idea what to take based upon what I have learned from trial and error, and the following examples of preparing deadbaits to fish two very different waters should help the reader to understand this better. As catching pike indirectly pays my bills, I have to get it right as often as I can!

My first example is a mature gravel pit which has a very good head of pike and is absolutely crammed with roach and bream of all sizes. Even though it screams out to me to use livebaits, it is also a fantastic deadbait water. It is a very reliable 'runs' water and I can expect to get through a lot of bait, and its not worth struggling to catch livebaits as the pike take deadbaits just as readily. I could also use lures there but the pike wise up to them more quickly than they do with deadbaits and my catch would be limited. In actual fact, I usually try to catch a couple on lures just for the hell of it if I can, but for most of the session its deadbaits all the way. These pike are fished for quite regularly and yet they never seem to wise up, provided that you keep varying the bait presentation.

For this reason I need to take plenty of bait with me, and there is no point spending a lot of money on it or going to any trouble in preparing it. For this venue I have a good clear out of my bait freezer and take with me all the 'rubbish' baits accumulated from previous sessions. There will be heads and tails cut from whole fish and also squashed or damaged baits of all sizes and species, all of which I have been specially saving for such venues or for pre baiting. If I don't have such bait in the freezer, I

A 21 POUNDER FROM A WATER WHERE THE BIGGER PIKE HAD A PARTICULAR LIKING FOR MACKEREL.

will use the cheapest and poorest quality baits I do have because there is absolutely no point in wasting my good baits. Every scrap of bait can be used and this venue is ideal for fishing with chunks, kebabs and half baits, all prepared from old and damaged baits, making it very economical to do so.

Compare this idyllic scenario to another water where the pike are very fussy. Weed makes lure presentation difficult and livebaiting is not allowed and the pike have seen all the common deadbaits like herring and mackerel, and in more recent times even smelt and lamprey. I will put one or two of these baits in my cool bag, but I will mainly rely on roach and perch. I never see anyone else using them and I do well on them, but they do need to be of a very high quality to work well. Knowing that I will be fishing this venue several times throughout the winter, I stock up with roach, perch and any other silver fish at every opportunity. If I have plenty of livebaits at my disposal, I will kill a few to use as deadbaits to get the freshest bait possible. If you intend to use coarse fish baits, catching and preparing them yourself is usually much better than buying them as they do need to be really fresh and shop bought ones rarely are. Advance planning, as always, will pay dividends!

Packing deadbaits for a session on this water is a lot different than for the first venue mentioned, and hopefully illustrates the importance of being prepared with the right deadbaits and not taking similar ones with you every time. Every water I tackle with deadbaits needs thought and consideration in a similar way and I have worked out what to take to my regular venues. What of new waters though, which I'm fishing for the first time or trying to get to grips with?

When tackling new waters with deadbaits I'll make full use of the opportunity to use four rods where allowed so that I can try a range of baits to help me to arrive at conclusions more quickly. On my first day on such a water, I would probably have the four rods rigged with herring, mackerel, smelt and lamprey, and fish them in several different areas. If these do not work, I would not panic straight away as it may not be a good deadbait water and might produce better by using livebaits or lures. Then again, it might have been a day when the pike were not feeding so I would need to have another few sessions there before I ruled any of those deadbaits out. I might also have made a bad swim choice or not have been there through a feeding period. It can often take many sessions to start to really understand the pike's preferences, and it's not a good idea to walk away from a water or write it off on the basis of a few poor sessions. It may well be that you have simply not cracked it yet!

Ideally I am looking for a water where the pike will take any deadbait offered. This happens quite frequently and pike are not at all fussy in many of the waters I fish except those which receive excessive angling pressure. These I try to avoid but not everyone has several waters at their disposal and has to make the best of the waters they have.

Fishing pressure can, to some extent, dictate which bait to use, but even on unpressured waters there can be days when the pike show a preference for one type of bait over another. It's something that I can't understand but it's a fact that it does happen. I have had days when all of the runs have come to one type of bait, while other top quality bait offerings have been totally ignored. With this always being a possibility, I like to also have a small selection of alternative baits to try, just in case the pike are not responding to those I expect to work. I don't always get it right, and I'm frequently left with no doubt that pike fishing is not an exact science and I am not infallible!

When the pike have seen it all, I start thinking beyond the type of bait and look more closely at bait presentation. The size of deadbait can make a difference and I tend to use smaller deadbaits where the pike seem wary, or even chunks or kebab style presentations. Sometimes you have to concede that it's not a good deadbait water and consider livebaiting if it's allowed.

Observations I've made of pike approaching baits and taking them have really affected how I think about bait choice. I suspect that there is a

A BIG PIKE TAKEN ON A WINDY DAY. DID IT FOLLOW A SCENT TRAIL?

'When tackling new waters with deadbaits, I'll make full use of the opportunity to use four rods...'

lot more going on under the water than we would care to imagine and pike that have been fished for are more wary than we suspect. In the search for a more effective deadbait, some anglers have gone down the route of flavouring their deadbaits or injecting them with fishy smelling oils. I have done so myself and have spoken to and fished with many other pike anglers who, at some stage, have done likewise. Our comparative conclusions, like this topic, are full of contradictions, but I believe there is mileage in using additives to increase or improve scent trails from our baits, whether they are applied directly to the deadbait or in groundbaits to attract them. A deadbait has a very adequate natural scent for pike to follow, but when pike are not in the immediate vicinity it may take a long time for them to detect it, and the addition of dispersible additives can, I'm convinced, lead them to our baits more quickly. Sometimes our baits can be a little on the stale side and would benefit from an extra boost of scent, and additives can provide this. Then we have to accept that the flavour itself modifies the smell of the bait, making it for all intents and purposes a different bait. If asked a few years ago as to whether these additives offered any advantage I would have been very sceptical, but nowadays I am more aware of the effect of the scent trail from a bait and its ability to attract pike from a distance. It may not make the bait a better proposition for the pike, but I think it can make it aware of the bait more quickly. I have certainly had many occasions when the flavoured baits have been the first to go and this has happened enough times to give me confidence in using them. The question I always ask myself though is whether the additive itself led to the pike taking the bait, or simply that it offered a better scent trail than the undoctored baits!

There is a lot more work to be done on flavours, and I do enjoy experimenting with something different on one rod to try to make a meaningful comparison. There are dozens of deadbait additives available though, not to mention endless fishy smelling carp products which can also be used, and it would be a mammoth task to experiment with them all. Opinions and experiences differ vastly and I do wonder whether there really could be one additive which is better than all the others. If there

Pic: Steve Martin

I always expect some action when there's a good flow on a river to send the scent trail downstream.

is, I have not found it or heard about it! If there was a definitive bait additive that would make a big difference on a widespread scale, anglers would have found it by now and the manufacturer would have made a fortune from selling it! However, at a local level, it's worth trying a few of these additives on the waters you fish regularly, to see if there are benefits. Once in a while I find something that works for a while, but I have yet to find a particular additive which has changed my results in a sustained way. For now my conclusion is that it's the strong scent trail which is the key and not so much the specific flavour.

I firmly believe that, whatever the smell or flavour might be, natural or artificial, 'scent trails' do lead pike to your bait. A day spent on a new water resulted in an incident which really confirmed my views about this. The evening before fishing, I had dropped three test lines in the margin in three different places. Deadbait offerings of herring, mackerel and roach were tied to thin cotton lines with small polystyrene markers, and if I found that they had moved by the following morning, it would give me a head start with bait and swim choice.

On my arrival at daybreak, I found that all three markers had moved. Two of them were close to the marginal reed beds and I managed to cast over one of them and retrieve it and found the bait had gone. The other didn't appear to have a pike attached either as it drifted with the breeze along the reed bed. I got it back a few days later from further down the lake without a bait attached. The third marker was well out into the lake, just beyond float casting range and appeared to be stationary, and I suspected a pike was still temporarily attached. I tried to cast one of my baits as close to it as I could, but was a good fifteen yards short.

The morning passed but the marker didn't budge, and neither did the float fished herring I'd cast near to it, although I had three small pike on the other two rods. My eyes were continually drawn to the marker and I was willing it to move, if only to see in which direction it would travel. It was a fairly calm day with just a slight ripple appearing every now and again, not the sort of day I like for deadbaiting because I want the wind to set up an undertow which will spread the scent of my deadbaits over a much greater range. Maybe the lack of underwater movement was the reason why I waited for four hours to witness what was to happen next.

Without any warning the marker float, obviously attached to a pike, quickly headed in the direction of my float fished herring, and as they came together my float shot under and the float and marker were dragged along together. The pike had detected the presence of my herring from quite a distance despite the lack of undertow, and headed towards it and found it quite easily.

Draw what conclusions you will from this incident, but my mind is made up that regardless of how good your deadbait may be it will not necessarily guarantee that a pike will find it quickly. Weather conditions can make a difference and wind is particularly important in stillwaters for setting up an effective undertow to draw the scent trail from the bait. The slightest of breezes can set up small currents on which a scent trail travels, but a big wind can have a much more dramatic effect. On the flat calm day in my illustration, the scent dispersal must have been minimal, but enough to eventually reach the nearby pike which reacted by following it to its source.

Scent trails can be masked if a bait is cast into dense weed or lands on a muddy or silty bottom, and although the pike's finely tuned senses will eventually detect it, it could mean an unnecessarily long waiting time. This is one good reason to consider enhancing deadbaits with flavours in order to increase their scent trail on such waters, and also good reason to pop them up to permit better scent release. We should also remember that the simple act of puncturing a deadbait to release body fluids will clearly offer a similar benefit at no additional cost. We must recognise too, the extra pulling power of chunks, kebabs and bait sections with their high scent release.

I became very aware of how scent trails can be limited by mud and weed when filming some underwater sequences for a DVD in the hope of getting footage of a pike picking up a deadbait from the bottom. When casting the bait in front of the underwater camera which was set up in a known 'hot' pike area, Stu Morgan the cameraman emerged in his diving gear and told me something which shocked me. When he told me that the deadbait disappeared completely in the silt when it hit the bottom I was amazed. I'd caught plenty of pike in that swim in the past, but now it made sense why moving the bait often provoked a strike and why popped up baits work so well. Some times the pike must have been digging the deadbaits from the mud, and this probably happens more than we think. Does pre baiting condition pike to digging in the mud in these situations? More questions!

There's nothing cut and dried about the practice of deadbaiting and how it relates to the pikes behaviour. I hope I have illustrated that it's not 'easy' or 'boring', and in fact is very interesting and thought provoking. To be a good deadbait angler requires much more knowledge than just knowing how to tie a rig and cast out a bait. I'm still learning myself as I try to improve my catch rate and that's what I'm continually working at!

'...I had hooked most of the bigger residents of the pit...'

CHAPTER 8

Time for Lunch

It can be very annoying when you have driven seventy miles in the early hours of the morning to find someone already in the swim you have dreamt about all night! It's bad enough when it's the 'hot' swim, and probably the only one where you have a good chance of catching, but even worse when you've dragged your wife out of bed to come with you to do some photography! On a chilly February morning quite a few years ago this happened to me, and with the knowledge I had built up about the venue my heart wasn't in fishing another swim. To add insult to injury, the angler in 'my' swim was someone I had come across before, a casual pike angler who rarely caught much, but what he did catch was not handled particularly well because of his lack of experience. The pike in this water are stunning in appearance, and I baulked at the thought that he might soon have one bouncing about on the bank which was strewn with all sorts of sharp debris that could easily damage it.

It's not my water, of course, and I had no right to dictate any terms so I was polite, suggesting that if he had a big fish he could shout to me as I would be fishing on the adjacent lake. I settled in a swim on the other lake and caught a 'jack' on a deadbait and a perch on a spinner, but my mind wasn't really on the fishing. At mid morning I went across to check his progress and wasn't surprised to hear he hadn't had a run. I reported that the same had happened to me, and using a bit of 'kiddology' I suggested it was 'just one of those days'. I was sweating though and the reason will soon become apparent!

I returned to the other lake and took three pike up to 11 lb on wobbled deadbaits, but this didn't take my mind off the fact that I wanted to be in that other swim. Just after mid day I nipped across for another chat, and the angler, still fishless, said he was getting bored and was thinking about fishing the other lake too. I told him what I'd caught and he decided that enough was enough and that he would move to the other lake as he was now getting anxious to catch something to save the day. I casually remarked that I'd try his swim for an hour or so while I ate my lunch, and probably have an early finish myself if nothing was happening, having already had a good morning's sport on the other lake. He reeled his rods in and I went back to collect my gear. Oh yes, what a result!

Like a man possessed I quickly scrambled down the steep bank and positioned three sets of rod rests in the shallow margin. Sweating profusely I climbed back up the bank, clipped the weight back onto the leger rig and reset the depth on the two float rods. I re baited with fresh baits and propelled the one on the middle rod to the horizon on the leger rig and spread the float fished baits well out to either side. The swim was fairly flat bottomed, shallow and uninteresting, and had no features that I knew of. I did know though that around one o'clock, the bigger pike had a very short, sharp, feeding spell and I'd got my baits out just in time!

Almost on cue, a float went gliding away and I was into battle with a good fish that fought really hard in the shallow water and I had to wade out to net it, away from the marginal brambles and overhanging bushes. Jan had barely pressed the shutter of the camera to record the 23 pounder I was holding aloft when the other float was off, and I was soon landing another of the pit's bigger pike which normally goes over 20 lb, but on this occasion weighed in at 19 lb exactly. For the next 20 minutes, mayhem ensued. I was just about to net yet another obvious 'twenty' when the bobbin on the leger rod dropped down and the alarm sung out. The hook pulled out of the 'twenty' but there was a 16 pounder on the ledger rod, this one having taken a sardine. Annoyed with myself for dropping off a 'twenty', I was cheered up just ten minutes later when a mackerel tail was taken and I landed a fish of 20 lb 8 oz. Half an hour later a legered sardine was taken by a really good looking pike weighing just short of 17 lb which marked the end of a really hectic feeding spell. We stayed on until dark, but without any more runs. When the other angler passed by, after deciding on an early finish, we naturally kept this to ourselves and made sure the slimy weigh sling and landing net were kept well out of sight!

The early afternoon feeding spell that I had predicted had exceeded all expectations, and I had hooked most of the bigger residents of the pit which, it seemed, had all come on the feed at once. In a small water this is quite possible and I am sure this also happens on bigger waters as well. You would need to be very lucky though to find them all in front of you and have enough time in the feeding spell to catch more than just a few of them. I have seen this happen on bigger waters many times when, after a long quiet spell, I look around and see anglers in other boats catching pike. When this happens, I know its time to put in extra special effort as it will all be over before too long. It's very important to recognise this and not spend that time taking a nap in the bottom of the boat!

It would be very useful to know the precise pike feeding times for all of the waters you fish. Can you imagine turning up at just the right time, bagging up for a few hours and then going home? This might seem fantasy, but something close to this is possible when you get to know waters really well and you are up to speed with the pike's feeding habits. It takes quite a while to work it out though and is subject to change as the season progresses. To have a working knowledge of more than a couple of waters at any one time is as much as you could hope for but it is possible, especially on local waters which you can visit more frequently.

Feeding times are far from straightforward, but are something worth recognising and looking for. Many pike anglers have scratched their heads and wondered why they are not catching, even though conditions seem ideal. One of the reasons, and there are others, is that there has not yet been a feeding spell in their swim during the time they have been fishing. They might have missed one by arriving too late or a feeding spell may come later in the day. They must also consider that they might not be in the swim where feeding is taking place or is going to take place. There are several things which have to come together and location is just as important as timing.

When pike are not feeding, for whatever reason, it is possible to be in a swim that is full of pike and still not catch any or even be aware of them, as I have indicated in other chapters. When I'm blanking, especially in a normally productive pike area, I always think about this and work extra hard at 'inducing' one to take a bait. This might be by twitching back a popped up deadbait for example, or putting a lure such as a jerkbait through the swim to wind one up. It's not always possible to have the option of livebaits, for various reasons, but their use can make an enormous difference. I used to think in terms of catching the occasional 'bonus' pike at these times, but there have been many occasions when extra effort in the ways described has led to some big catches. For example, I have had many days when every run on deadbait has come within minutes of moving it by a short distance, or it has been grabbed while being moved; static baits being totally ignored. The ability to catch inactive pike is, I believe, a major difference between an average pike angler and a good one.

This lesson was brought home to me in a really big way when fishing on the Baltic Sea with Anders Forsberg, the fishing guide from the Vastervik Fishing camp. His knowledge of this vast water is second to none as he has spent so much time fishing there. He told me of a swim which was full of pike, but which you could fish for hours without even suspecting they were there when they were not in a feeding mood. He assured me though that as soon as one was caught, it would usually trigger the others into feeding. Recalling similar experiences of my own, which I had not really thought deeply enough about up to that point, I suspected that he could be right.

We anchored in water of about 20 feet deep and about 100 yards out from a reed lined rocky island. Three of us thrashed the swim for more than an hour with everything from jigs to jerk baits, but nothing happened. On any other water I would have up anchored and moved long ago, but while we sat and had a break, drinking Anders 'rocket fuel' coffee, he persevered with a lure. I really thought that this was leading nowhere when a pike slammed into his spoon and he shouted that we should start fishing again quickly. Anders made sure his pike disturbed the swim, allowing it to dart and dive everywhere rather than winching it straight in to the boat, all part of a cunning plan which he had obviously executed before!

'I can't remember how many we boated, but I had six or seven …'

He was absolutely right and we were staggered when we all suddenly started to catch pike after pike. I can't remember how many we boated, but I had six or seven and the others had as many too.

What we had done by catching one pike, it seemed, was to modify their normal feeding time by creating a trigger which alerted the other pike to the possibility of prey arriving in the swim, putting them into premature feeding mode. This was a man made trigger, but other triggers have been observed to occur though natural causes such as weather changes or the sudden appearance of large shoals of prey fish entering an area. These effects could easily be misconstrued as feeding times, but are not the feeding times I'm thinking of where pike get into a routine of feeding at a particular time of day. This does not worry me of course, because I am catching pike, but the two should not be confused.

Many believe that feeding triggers can be influenced by moon phases. Those having more time than I to make such studies believe this to be so, and although once sceptical, I wouldn't dismiss it so quickly now after retrospectively checking some of the catches detailed in my fishing diaries against moon phase charts from previous years. There are too many 'coincidences' for my liking and the evidence seems to be stacking up in favour of the theory being sound, although nowhere near to any guarantee of success as other forces are at work.

My simple interpretation of this theory is that by fishing around the hours when sunrise/sunset and moonrise/moonset coincide with new or full moon phases, you'll have your best chances of making a good catch, assuming there are fish in the area of course. It's a matter of knowing, ahead of time, exactly when the sun and moon will rise and set, in the belief that fish are most active in windows surrounding each of these four daily events. The moon effect is said to be more reliable than the effect of the sun as it has the stronger influence. Students of the theory have looked at the cycle in much greater detail and taken the debate to an even higher level.

Approaching weather fronts often trigger pike activity

Anglers have always known that fish are often very active at dawn and dusk, i.e. sunrise and sunset, but fish activity surrounding moonrise and moonset is less noticeable because these events are likely to occur without affecting any change in the perceived light. The rise and set of a new moon is invisible anyway, and overcast weather often hides the full moon. Without prior knowledge of the moons setting and rising times, two of the best fishing times will be disregarded every day! I'm becoming a believer, although I don't think for one minute it always leads to bumper catches. It just gives an indication of good times to fish, but bearing in mind that pike activity may then be affected by other influences such as water temperature, which could make the pike reluctant to feed even at the trigger points.

Out of interest, I recently checked my diary dates for random notable catches against old moon phase charts. Most catches were made at very unfavourable times! This has not led me to discount the moon phase theory. As I have already stated, I believe that it cannot be consid-

THIS 28 LB 9 OZ PIKE WAS THE ONLY FISH OF THE SEASON FROM A VERY HARD WATER. IT CAME AT A PRECISE TRIGGER POINT!

ered in isolation. Furthermore, inactive pike can sometimes be tempted with skilled application and a degree of perseverance.

We can also never be sure whether feeding times or feeding triggers apply to every pike in the water at the same time. Furthermore, they probably won't all be in the same swim or, indeed, the swim you are fishing, making the whole business rather hit or miss. I'm rather pleased that I don't fully understand these things. To go fishing with a perfect prediction of my results would spoil it for me. I'm glad that it's complicated and that pike fishing is affected by so many variables, least of all our individual skill!

Fortunately nothing remains constant, so every day produces a new challenge. As the seasons change, feeding times will change too and mid winter feeding times will be very different from autumn feeding times with dawn/dusk feeding becoming less reliable and mid day feeding more in evidence on many waters. Very often there will not be a precise and recognisable feeding time in evidence at all, and you might find that pike are catchable throughout the day. The more time you spend on any water, the more likely you are to determine the best times to fish.

Provided nothing alters dramatically with a water, such knowledge can be imported from one season to another. For example, a 60 acre Lincolnshire pit I sometimes fish is always reliable, season after season, for a dusk feed which often results in catching some of the bigger residents of the pit which go up to 25 lb. Knowing this, I can get some work done in the daytime and look forward to a couple of exciting hours as the light fades.

If you start looking for feeding times, you will notice that they will vary in length and intensity. The

DUSK IS ALWAYS WORTH FISHING THROUGH AT ANY TIME OF YEAR.

short, sharp type is the easiest to recognise, when a blank period is suddenly punctuated with several runs and then followed by a quiet spell again. At other times you might find multiple feeding periods throughout the day. A dawn feed might be followed by a couple of quiet hours, for example, and then there could follow several short bursts of activity throughout the middle hours of the day, interspersed with further quiet spells. Then again you might not get any activity at all through the day, and then an intense feed occurs at dusk. Exactly what is happening to induce these patterns we will probably never know, but it does tell any pike angler never to write off a situation as hopeless, no matter how dire things might seem at the time. This is not an excuse for simply putting in rod hours though, it's still important to fish correctly!

Whilst you are never going to know the precise feeding times on all the waters you fish, you will at least fish with more confidence if you accept that there are such things and be ready to identify them rather than putting a run of good fishing down to no more than good fortune. Knowing they exist will also help you to come to terms with venues where you are not getting the result you desire. You might conclude, for example, that it may be due to the fact that you have not been there at a feeding time.

I'm not very keen on fishing for pike around the clock, but that is the only way you will be able to work out feeding times with any degree of accuracy, as pike are likely to feed at any time of the day or night. I get tired like anyone else and also have to earn a living, so many of my pike sessions nowadays are for just a few hours on local waters which I try to target at optimum times. I will attempt to fish from dawn till dusk on waters involving some travelling, but have to accept that I could miss out on any pre dawn or after dark feeding spells.

If I am honest, I prefer pike fishing in the daytime because my enjoyment comes from more than just reeling them in. I like to enjoy the scenery, but above all I like to take a good look at the pike I catch. If I am trying to come to terms with a difficult water, I will do the occasional 48 hour stint and fish through two dark periods but that is rare, and when I do I like to reel my rods in and get some proper sleep at some stage. I'm keen, but also know it's only a glorified, self financing hobby and won't push myself beyond the point of enjoying the fishing. Furthermore, my health and sanity come first!

It can take quite a while to determine feeding times on any water, but over a period of time, usually several seasons, patterns can emerge which can give you a good idea of when pike might feed on a similar type of venue elsewhere. I'm constantly looking for feeding times and they can come at any time of day, but not necessarily every day to make things more complicated! Quite often a day with no runs at all is followed by a day when they go on the feed or vice versa. It's obvious they can't feed all of the time and feeding intensity must vary from day to day to suit their needs. Once feeding times are established, I can save myself a lot of wasted time by putting my allotted hours in at the best time. When I caught my 34 lb 7 oz gravel pit monster, I was fishing for the 'eleven o'clock run' which you could almost set your watch by. With very few pike in the pit, once the feeding time was worked out it was just a matter of perseverance - and maybe a bit of luck!

Why pike should have a specific feeding time is a point I often ponder. I've concluded that they have worked out when they have their best chance of fulfilling their dietary needs for the prevailing conditions. When fishing a huge water in Finland many years back, the boatman told us not to worry about getting up early the next morning as the pike in the large bay he would be taking us to would not feed until mid afternoon when the sun had been on the icy cold water for most of the day. Naturally we got up early because we wanted to go fishing, and reluctantly the boatman took us to the area, but he was obviously not very pleased that we didn't listen to him, thinking that we knew better.

Four hours later we hadn't had a 'hit' from either casting or trolling our lures! We went through lures which had performed well on previous days in other areas, also trying different colours and working sinking lures at different depths, but nothing seemed to work. We had no choice but to concede that we should have listened to him. Then, at the time he'd predicted, pike after pike was caught and from the same area we'd been fishing. There were several 'upper doubles' and a 20 pounder - and using the very same lures we'd used earlier! I'd certainly learnt the importance of listening to experience and not assuming I knew better!

I have also learnt to prepare for unexpected feeding spells and try and recognise when they might happen. For example, I've many times seen how a fast moving approaching weather front can provoke activity and send pike on the rampage. As a front approaches and passes over, I often suddenly start getting runs and see pike swirling as they attack prey fish. I am starting to take more notice of this type of feeding trigger and have accumulated enough facts to suggest this to be another important factor which can be thrown into an already complex equation.

At the time he'd predicted, pike after pike hit our lures like this 19 lb 12 oz fish which took my 18 cm Rapala Magnum.

It could make your head spin when trying to make sense of feeding times and triggers, so at the moment I just accept that these things exist as a starting point towards understanding them. I look for patterns and feel very fortunate if I can use what information I have to ensure I'm fishing any venue at the best time and not wasting my time. After many seasons of study, I can tell you roughly what time of day it's best to fish many local venues at a particular time of year. I have venues which fish well at dawn, others which have morning feeding spells, and others which fish well into darkness for a few hours. Where they are in close proximity I can, if I wish, flit from one to another to maximise on results.

In my opinion, the pike's feeding habits are not as random as they might appear. In their own little worlds they know exactly what they are doing! They know where their food is, and when feeding time arrives they go and get it, much like we would do when visiting the supermarket. If

It was a very large pike, possibly this 31 pounder which was the biggest one in there at the time.

something triggers them into a feeding mood beforehand, they will react accordingly. This final story leaves me in no doubt of this!

With the sun on my back, I was anchored at the entrance to a shallow bay, enjoying a waggler fishing session on an exceptionally pleasant summer afternoon. It hadn't been too productive but I'd enjoyed it nevertheless and decided it was time to leave as it was getting a bit too warm and I was feeling quite hungry. Turning to the back of the boat to start the electric motor, I glanced down the mirror calm surface of the lake and noticed, right at the far end some 300 yards away, there was a strange disturbance. I kept watching it to see what it was, and it was getting closer and closer. Moving at high speed, it was soon approaching the boat and I can only describe it as looking like a torpedo on its way to blast a battleship from the water. It passed my boat within 20 yards and I could now see, without any doubt, that it was a very large pike and looking every inch a thirty pounder. It was propelling itself along with its big tail at quite a considerable pace, and on reaching the entrance to the bay, it dived out of sight.

Feeling I had witnessed something quite unusual I started to pull away, but quickly brought the boat to a sudden halt by slamming the motor into reverse. I stood open mouthed at what was now happening in front of the reed bed towards which I had been casting. Prey fish were leaping, jumping and scattering everywhere as a huge swirling and snapping beast tried to grab them. Seconds later, all went very calm and quiet again as if nothing had happened.

What does this observation tell us? It says to me that the pike had made a decision that it was going to feed and it knew exactly where to go, even from a resting place far away at the other end of the lake. It was feeding time! This decision could have been based upon a sudden need for food, its normal routine, a natural trigger or alternatively a trigger in the form of the vibrations from the feeding shoal fish being detected by its lateral line sensors. Any, or a combination of such reasons, could be plausible.

It travelled quite a long way to reach the prey shoal which I would have thought would have used up a lot of its energy, and yet it had plenty in reserve to make an attack. The pike is known to attack in short sharp bursts, but maybe has a lot more stamina than we think. I suspect the pike has a lot more going for it than we realise, being able to remember where its food is and to travel long distances to intercept it, regulated by internal and external forces no more or less than we are. Not bad for a creature with a brain the size of a pea!

Having detailed how nature can dictate pike feeding times, it is interesting how anglers can modify such times by baiting swims, exactly as they do when fishing for other species. A lesson learnt from pre baiting with deadbaits is that, if sufficient quantities are thrown in on a regular basis, pike will often take the easy option and use it to replace their natural food. Furthermore, they will often adjust their feeding times to suit when the pre bait is applied. Throwing the bait in regularly at dusk, as I often do, usually leads to pike getting used to finding it at that time, and possibly forsaking their natural food to ritually consume it in the dark hours. That's a great ploy for the angler who wants to fish at that time, after work maybe, and also for those who don't want anyone to know what they are up to as other anglers have usually gone home by then! If you want reliable daytime sport though, it's proven best to regularly pre bait early in the day. Without doubt, as I have proven to myself, it is possible to control feeding times in this way.

What can we glean from my experiences over many years and the thoughts they have provoked? Until I sat down to write about feeding times and triggers, I never realised just how complex a subject it is. I am sure they exist, and that is a good starting point for further study of any water I am fishing that is proving difficult to crack.

You could forget about feeding spells if you wish to. If you go pike fishing to simply enjoy the day and accept whatever comes along, then there's nothing wrong with that at all. You would probably catch a lot of pike too, but not I suspect at anywhere near the rate of the angler who has a good working knowledge of feeding times. It's not a competition, but when you have to catch pike for a living as I have had to, catching them quickly and efficiently does become important. If I only have a few hours to spare, I ensure that I use them wisely!

CHAPTER 9

Barrie's Pike

(In memory of a great pike angler)

One of my biggest regrets is that I didn't get to know the great pike angler Prof. Barrie Rickards *(left)* better than I did. We bumped into each other from time to time, chatted about anything and everything to do with pike fishing, and always ended by planning a day fishing together which never seemed to materialise. He always had a busy schedule and so did I, so it never happened.

Barrie was the man who, above all others, inspired me to think more about my pike fishing in my formative years. His writings in the press and his famous book *Fishing for Big Pike* (A&C Black 1971) which he co authored with Ray Webb were instrumental in taking my pike fishing to a higher level by showing what was possible if you put enough thought and effort into it.

I also got to meet Ray Webb (now deceased). A couple of friends and I spent a day with him back in 1974 when he was living in a very old single berth caravan on the bank of the Old Bedford River. It was a shambles of a place and everything was filthy, but he was content and happy just to be living in his beloved fens, far away from his house in Sheffield which he rented out to finance his nomadic way of life. As time has moved on, I can understand more and more why he wanted that lifestyle. I can also understand more clearly now how everything can soon get into a right mess when you are obsessed with fishing and don't see what it is doing to your sanity! On the day we fished with him, he suddenly went off at some point and I don't even know where to. He was a man of few words, but what he had to say was both interesting and useful. Later that day I caught a 22 pounder, a long lean fish of 44 inches which took a half mackerel from a swim he had taken us to!

Barrie passed away on *November 5th, 2009* at the age of 71. The day after the sad news was broken I was fishing alone on a pre planned trip, ironically to the River Great Ouse where he had caught a very rare fen river 30 lb pike several decades ago. As I motored my Orkney Fastliner upstream on a very calm and pleasant morning, my thoughts kept wandering to Barrie and what he meant to so many pike anglers, most of whom had never met him and yet he had touched their lives just as he had done mine.

I anchored up and tried a few spots, but didn't catch anything at all. My thoughts kept returning to Barrie, and I wondered whether he had fished the swims I had got to know so well over the last few years. Were the 'hot spots' the same in those distant days as they are today? Barrie had never boat fished on the Great Ouse, as far as I know, so perhaps he'd seen it from a different perspective to me. We'd talked about him joining me for a day in the boat when we could compare notes about the river, and he was particularly interested to know more about the bottom contours and prey fish movements I had been telling him about. I had been longing to share this knowledge with him, and also let him know about my own fenland river 'thirty' which I had kept very quiet about for quite a while. I wanted him to be the first outside of my close circle of friends to know about it. Pike angling had lost one of its greatest contributors, and I had been robbed of sharing my story with him.

By late morning, I was well up river and anchored in an area where I'd had plenty of pike in the past, although nothing above a 'high double'. It was an interesting swim, and as there were prey showing on the echo sounder screen, I thought it could be a good area to try while I stopped for a cup of tea. Three deadbaits were scattered around the boat, positioned favourably in places where I'd located prey fish.

Ten minutes passed, and as the kettle started to boil I was 'away' with a run on a full herring which went steaming off upstream, staying close to the bank. A quick strike was made but the pike was not hooked and I lost the bait! This seemed a good point at which to finish making the tea and have a break. With Barrie still on my mind, I decided that I would reel in my other baits for ten minutes. It was my own way of paying tribute to him, and if it was not for the event which followed, I would probably have never mentioned my personal feelings to anyone.

'I ANCHORED UP AND TRIED A FEW SPOTS...'

I enjoyed the strengthening sunshine, it felt good on my face, but I felt a nagging sadness pulling me down. I thought about how we pay our respects to others by having two minutes silence. Then it occurred to me that anglers fishing alone are always silent. Maybe I should have two minutes of talking! The silly thoughts left my head as my eyes were drawn to a slick of fish oil breaking the surface, right next to the anchor rope. It was not just a trickle but a great splurge which was clearly, to my mind anyway, coming from a pike that was chewing on a deadbait - and it surely must have been the herring I'd lost earlier!

Almost working on auto pilot, I dropped a float fished smelt just upstream of the oil slick. A paternostered livebait was positioned downstream and I then started to work a 40 gram spoon across the river. It was one of those moments when you are inspired and spring into action. I don't know why this happens, but all of a sudden I often find myself buzzing with activity and just know it's time to get down to work. There's something in the air that's telling me that I am going to catch!

On the first cast with the spoon, the retrieve was met well out into the river with a solid 'clonk' and a fighting mad 12 pounder was soon being chinned after a short display of cart wheeling and thrashing next to the boat. I'd not long slipped her back when, from the corner of my eye, ever watchful on my floats, I saw the deadbait float sink away and run downstream, passing under the boat as it did so. With the anchor rope tied to the centre position rod holder bracket there was no danger of her snagging it, so I fed the rod tip under the boat to clear the engine propeller, caught up with her and wound down firmly.

The fight was dogged in the deep water beneath the boat. It was not spectacular in any way, but nevertheless a great pleasure all the same. I had no doubts it was a 'double', probably a decent one, but this river has a habit of rarely giving up its fish of more than 18 or 19 lb or so. Even as she obliged and swam quietly into the net, I thought it to be a fish of about that weight. She was long, but November fen fish tend to be quite skinny, so I didn't hope for more.

The digital scales read exactly 20 lb, and as I checked again and again they wouldn't give me one ounce more or one ounce less. From a section of the river where I'd never had a 20 pounder before, I'd caught one of the exact weight. It felt more than coincidence that my personal and private tribute to Barry had led to the capture of a pike of exactly the bench mark weight he had set for me all those years ago. It became one of those significant moments in my life when I start to question just how much is fated to happen to us. I thought back to the untimely death of my first wife, back in 1988, and how I couldn't fish for nearly six months. When I finally got started, my first week produced four 30 pounders for me. The feeling I had then was exactly that when taking this river 'twenty'. We all need something to believe in!

The pike was photographed by a nearby pleasure angler, but I didn't tell him the story. I carried on fishing and took five more pike, two being doubles, and then finished by anchoring up in the dark in a known zander area. Two hours into dark, I was away on a full mackerel which was fished right next to the boat so I could see the float quite clearly. I had the shock of my life when a potentially personal best zander came into the head torch beam. Two thirds of her body were over the solid rim of the round landing net when the hooks pulled out! She just slipped away, and no amount of jabbing around into the blackness of the deep water was going to get her back. She was gone!

Had I not lost my 'dream fish', it would have been an amazing ending to a day filled with strange happenings and emotions. On the way home, I thought about how we react to losing something. Perhaps you will understand what I'm trying to say!

It felt more than coincidence that my personal and private tribute to Barry had led to the capture of a pike of exactly the bench mark weight he had set for me all those years ago.

CHAPTER 10

Dinner is Served

The diesel of my old four wheel drive truck rumbled down the damp track, slipping and sliding after recent rain, as I headed for the south east corner of a 65 acre gravel pit. It was the deepest part of the pit and not many pike anglers were aware of the 'hot spot', the deep channels which ran parallel to the bank, just a rod length out from the reed fringed margins. Two channels met at the corner I was heading for, each being quite narrow, and unless you knew they were there the temptation would be to cast further out where the water was much shallower and densely weeded. Even if you knew of the presence of the channels your bait positioning had to be perfect, and a poorly performed cast could easily see the bait landing in the dense weed at either side.

Each channel had a clean silt bottom, only about a metre wide at the most, and on a bright calm day you could pick it out if you looked carefully from a boat. I often wondered whether it had been created by the passage of fish as the pit holds some big carp too which I have caught in the same channel in warmer weather on float tactics. It was in this channel I was going to fish on this cold winter morning, but this time for pike!

In no hurry, I dropped the tailgate, put the kettle on and sorted my old tin mug from the tangle of tackle, stinking and wet from the day before. By the time the kettle had boiled I'd set up my camera on its tripod, focusing the lens on two rod rests set up either side of my large padded unhooking mat. Two float rigs were baited with half herrings which were carefully positioned in the trench, care being taken to remain as quiet and concealed as possible.

Before I'd finished my tea, one of my home made orange and white balsa pencil floats came to life. I was in business – but not at all surprised! I played the pike to the landing net with more care and caution than normal as I knew there would be other pike in the swim. The pike was lowered onto the unhooking mat, quickly unhooked and then transferred to the weigh sling. It was a good looking pike with thick shoulders and a solid belly, and well worth a photo. A couple of shots were quickly taken using the air operated remote shutter release, already set up and in position for me to kneel on.

I carried her in the sling and carefully slipped her into the back of the nearby dense stems so that she could rest and make her way back to deeper water at her leisure. I knew the fish by sight, a big 'double' with an unusually small tail for such a big pike. I'd given her the unimaginative, but descriptive, name of 'Little Tail' and I'd caught her already that season and twice the season before. She was a couple of ounces heavier since her last capture a month ago when she had weighed exactly 19 lb, and she still looked as fit as ever.

I unhurriedly finished my tea and cast in again. This time I waited nearly ten minutes for a run and played a repeat of the action from the first pike, this time with a 23 pounder which had turned up for the first time that season, having put on over a pound since the last winter. My gear was quickly stuffed into the back of the truck and I was off to another venue for the rest of the day, a water where the fishing would not be so predictable!

This is not everyday pike fishing, to turn up at a water and very easily catch two cracking specimens and then just drive nonchalantly away and go fishing somewhere else for the rest of the day. This was the pattern for my fishing though on that particular lake for a whole winter back in the early nineties when I had finally realised how effective pre baiting for pike could be. I'd made many earlier attempts at pre baiting but in a less focused fashion, and although it had been obvious that it could draw pike into an area, I had never fully realised until that season, just how devastating it could be until I took it more seriously.

I don't know why it took so long for me to work this out. It had worked for eels in the early days of my predator fishing, baiting with mashed fish and fish chunks, and had also brought pike (and zander) into swims after baiting up the night before a session, but I hadn't yet seen the full potential. To make it

CAUGHT TO ORDER! THIS IS NOT EVERYDAY FISHING.

work really well, it eventually became clear that I needed to be committed to a pre baiting programme, not just for a few days nor even a few weeks, but rather months or even a full season. When I lived in Birmingham and pike fishing meant travelling long distances, it had been impossible to bait in this way, but since moving to the fens where I have dozens of pits, drains and rivers on my doorstep, it had become very viable. Other anglers were experimenting around the same time and I drew inspiration from their results, particularly those of Nev Fickling who was sensible enough to put himself in a similar position by moving to an area with several suitable waters reasonably close to home. At the same time, another pre baiting project I was undertaking on the River Welland was also proving interesting. All I was doing there was regularly baiting around my boat, which was kept moored on the river at that time. At the start of each session I would drop a deadbait next to the boat and catch a pike almost instantly. This also started me thinking about taking things to a bigger scale on a larger water.

The pit I had chosen to start my first major pre baiting project was only a couple of miles from home and I had previously fished it on a casual basis, mainly for eels and carp. Before starting, I had to convince myself that I was not wasting my time. I knew the pit had a reasonable head of pike, but for its size I expected it might hold a lot more than I had caught up until then. It did not have a particularly large head of small prey fish but there were plenty of eels, which led to the pike being fairly nomadic and hard to pin down as they travelled around looking for food. There were no particular 'hot spots' or good areas which I knew off so this seemed like a good opportunity to try and make my own by concentrating any bigger pike that were in the pit into a smaller area, making them easier to catch. My next task was to pinpoint a favourable area to apply the pre bait.

The lake was leased by a water sports business which was not really interested in the fishing, but would give permission to fish if you asked nicely. I managed to get permission to put a boat on the water for a couple of days, ostensibly to do a bit of fishing but keeping the real reason to myself – to determine where to put my pre bait! With the lake being relatively shallow and gin clear, all this would require would be a good pair of Polaroid's and a calm day! In the whole of the 65 acres, I only considered five places to be suitable because the vast majority of the pit was found to be quite shallow and very weedy. I looked for deeper areas where I expected the prey fish and pike to be in the winter, and after some deliberation I settled for the one with the most interesting contours with proximity to dense weed and reed beds and a small area of relatively weed free bottom. Having selected my swim, I scattered about ten pounds of chopped herrings and mackerel into it, and when the wind died down and the surface became calm, I could just about make them out on the bottom in around ten feet of water.

'How much pre bait to put in was a question that I asked myself many times...'

On my return, a day later, there was not one scrap of bait left! In those early days of pre baiting I questioned everything and was not yet convinced that pike had eaten it. As it was only early October, eels could have taken it and there were also plenty of grebes and cormorants in the area which could have taken it too. No matter, I put another ten pounds of bait in and this time left it for a couple of days as I had something else to do. On my return, it was exactly the same – it had all gone!

On my next visit I dropped a further pile of bait in, and after doing so put two 'test' baits into the swim. Half herrings were tied to thin cotton lines with the other ends tied to small pieces of polystyrene to identify their positions. As I rowed away, the chunks of polystyrene bobbed in the ripple and I felt a tinge of excitement. I had used 'marker' baits on other waters where pike densities are very low and found them very useful for giving some indication of whether pike had been in the swim. If the markers remained untouched I never bothered to fish there, but if they were gone it encouraged me to fish and was often an area that produced some pike, although not always guaranteeing success.

All this previous experimentation was going through my mind as I drove up to the swim the following evening. Would the markers be there - or not? My worries were unfounded as there was no sign of them! Buzzing with anticipation, I decided to cast a deadbait into the swim. In less than a minute it was gone and I had an 18 pounder on the bank, in magnificent condition and with a nice plump belly. In the back of its throat it was spewing up bits of my bait! I was onto something!

From that point, I fell into a pattern of regularly baiting and fishing and pike started to come thick and fast, culminating at the point where the capture of a big pike became predictable. I've always carefully guarded my pike fishing, and there was no doubt in my mind that I had to keep this quiet and not draw any attention to the swim. The manager of the lake was too busy with his water sports business to have noticed what I was up to, and the few other anglers who were allowed to fish there were kept totally out of the loop. I had to tell a few fibs, in fact a lot of fibs, to keep this under wraps because it was good pike fishing which was getting better and better!

'As I rowed away, the chunks of polystyrene bobbed in the ripple...'

This is where we came in at the beginning of this chapter. It was now possible,

'...YOU NEEDED CHEST WADERS TO GET THROUGH THE REEDS...'

as long as I kept up the pre baiting campaign, to turn up at the swim and have a good result in no time at all. It was absolutely fascinating fishing and became very predictable. I only ever caught big pike in the swim, most of them being over 14 lb and there were, in that season, at least a dozen different fish weighing over 17 lb including three different 20 pounders. By choice, I only ever caught one or two fish from the swim each session before leaving it alone because I knew that if I over pressured it, it would be very short lived and the pike would wise up. The key to keeping the sport coming was to keep the bait going in and not overfishing the swim.

How much pre bait to put in was a question that I asked myself many times as the project progressed. To come to terms with this I considered two things. First of all, the condition of the fish was taken into account, and secondly the frequency of the runs when fishing the swim. After pre baiting for about a month I noticed that the fish were not only fat in the belly, but also becoming thicker across their backs and shoulders as well. They were certainly not obese looking fish by any means and they started to look real 'bruisers' as they filled out all over. If they had have become obese I would have cut down on the amount of bait, but this did not happen and I continued with a regime of two or three pounds of bait per day for four days a week.

I would also have cut down the amount of bait going in if the 'runs' had slowed down, indicating that I was over feeding them, but at the rate I was feeding the swim it was always possible to get a couple of runs within half an hour. I quickly worked out the perfect feed rate for the water, but subsequent pre baiting projects have led me to make adjustments as I went along. Once you get into it though, it doesn't take long to work out how much to put in.

This project inspired me to carry out many similar projects on all sorts of different waters and I have proven to myself, without a shadow of doubt, that pre baiting with deadbaits for pike is a tactic that can, in the right hands, lead to large scale captures of big pike. The main proviso is that the angler should be totally dedicated to the project and handle it sensitively.

Pre baiting can bring its problems. My biggest fear is that other anglers will accidentally drop onto one of my pre baited swims, realise how good the fishing is and then hammer it relentlessly. If I think this is a possibility, I take evasive action from the start. I would rather bait swims with difficult access than more obvious swims, and only bait up and fish them when there is no one else around. I will often use a large groundbait catapult to fire chunks of bait to obscure positions which are difficult to cast to. I will even use a bait boat to take my pre bait beyond normal casting range, but this also means having to use the bait boat to drop my hook baits as well. You have to decide whether it's worth going to this amount of trouble, and I would only do so if there was the possibility of some exceptionally good pike fishing.

Pre baited swims can be stumbled upon though and it can be most annoying, especially if you have put in months of hard work. At the first inkling that this has happened, I obviously stop putting the bait in. The pike will still visit the swim for quite a while though unless another baited area is quickly created to draw them away. When one of my top swims was 'discovered', I immediately baited another swim over 200 yards away where you needed chest waders to get through the reeds to fish it. Within a week, the old swim dried up and the pike moved 'en masse' as proven when my first cast into the new swim produced a 21 pounder which was quickly followed by one of 18 lb! Naturally, I went to a great deal of trouble not to be seen baiting or fishing the new area, and it wasn't long before the other pike anglers decided that they were having too many blank and they cleared off!

For those who have not tried pre baiting, it must seem incredible that it is possible to enjoy such predictable fishing, where 'big doubles' and 'twenties' are a regular occurrence. For a while I was happy to simply enjoy the idyllic situation created by my first big pre baiting project, but eventually I got tired of fishing a very tight area and for the sessions to be so short. Due to this, my next big project was to be carried out in such a way that I could have a full day's fishing and provide sessions that would be a lot more interesting.

The water I had chosen for this new project was over 25 acres in area and had a good head of pike of all sizes. The owner rarely let anyone fish there but I managed to win his confidence, even though he limited my access to just one area of the lake. With my recently gained knowledge of pre baiting, I became very excited at the prospect of trying to get all of the pike in the lake into this area by baiting. Luckily, it was one of the deeper parts of the lake, typically 12 to 16 feet deep. The swim I was allowed to fish from was a small promontory, but it gave me about 50 yards of water to cast into from a central point. When my pre baiting campaign started there, I decided that I would not concentrate the bait in a tight area but spread it as far and wide as I could. My baiting up visits became less frequent than with my last project, but on each occasion I put in very large quantities, typically 20 lb or more. I used a catapult to fire out small chunks of bait and I would also throw out a few typical hook baits as far as I could. It had occurred to me that spreading the bait in this way would keep the pike grubbing around for much longer and they would be spread around the swim rather than concentrated in a tight area. Being largely weed free, the swim was ideal for this approach.

It worked like a dream and when fishing finally commenced after a few weeks of baiting, runs came easily and were usually spread throughout the day. The action wasn't over too soon and I could

'...My first cast into the new swim produced a 21-pounder...'

This 32 pounder hogged my pre baited swim!

now catch a dozen fish or more and have a really good day's sport. At end of each session I would put in a further large quantity of bait and also try to bait up between visits when I had the chance to do so. I still had to exercise some restraint though, and only fished when I felt the swim had been rested for long enough.

Although the fishing remained good, it became apparent that sport always hotted up as darkness approached. It seemed that my practice of baiting up at the end of the day was eventually conditioning the pike to feed in the early hours of darkness. As soon as I started fishing into darkness, it was as though all hell was let loose and it was 'runs galore' and on one occasion I had three runs and three twenties in a very short time. The lake produced a lot of 20 pounders and two different 30 pounders over a period of several years until the ownership of the lake changed hands and I lost the fishing. A sad day indeed, but I think I was ready to move on.

Pre baiting has been a real eye opener. It is clear to me now that an ambitious pike angler can take control of the pike in a small to medium sized water, determining where they feed and when they feed. He can also move them around the water and affect their condition. This can all be done in a very predictable way and I know that a concerted effort could result in the capture of very large numbers of big pike if one wished to go down this route. Having worked this out, it might come as some surprise when I say that I don't particularly want to do this anymore. It has been very interesting but I do not want to stack up numbers of big pike just for the sake of doing so. I would prefer to fish a wider range of waters, explore new ones as much as possible and look for interesting pike fishing experiences rather than just play the 'numbers game'. Nowadays I'm happy in the knowledge that I can use pre baiting as a potential solution for solving problems on difficult waters if I need to, and I can bring it into play when necessary

Pre baiting has been very useful to my business in many ways, as catching pike 'to order' is necessary for several reasons. Tackle testing requires a quick result and it doesn't matter where, when or how I catch pike, as long as I test items of tackle thoroughly, and that usually means catching pike with them! Making technical magazine and web features requires a quick result too as time is money for the photographers they send out with me. It was common sense to keep a few swims baited on various waters so that I could test an item of tackle and submit my report about it on the same day if necessary, or shoot a technical feature in double quick time. Naturally I had to be cagey about my swims, but that became second nature a long time ago!

Most of my tuition clients want a 'normal' fishing session, but some just want to sample pike fishing and learn about rigs and handling pike. They often have little or no experience, and at that stage the more pike they can catch the better and I arrange it for them. Pre baited swims are ideal for this and in practice I 'double up' by testing tackle at the same time! It's useful to see how others get on with new tackle items, and less experienced anglers have often helped me realise how important it is to make product packaging and catalogue literature more clear. Experienced pike anglers take a lot for granted and forget that beginners need clearer instruction.

I've got dozens of local waters at my disposal as I've made it my business to forge good relations with local clubs and land owners. Keeping swims baited on these waters means that I get through a lot of bait, and some of my trips to Grimsby to fill my two bait freezers have been very costly. Fortunately, my more recent arrangement with Dynamite Baits has resolved this problem to some extent, and they ultimately benefit from the publicity from my catches.

Pre baiting can have its problems as I have already mentioned, but sometimes they are the sort of problems I like to have! Other species can decide to join in the feast and I have had chub to over five pounds and zander to 12 lb make a 'nuisance' of themselves in my baited swims. I also had a 30 lb pike keep bothering me on one water! I was allowed to fish it once a month during one particular winter and the obvious thing to do was to heavily bait it in between sessions. In the five sessions I fished there, a big pike, which always weighed over 31 lb, hogged the swim and seemed to keep all other pike out of the feeding area. It mauled several other pike while I played them, some of them quite large ones, and it was caught itself on no less than four of the five visits I made! It was a long pike with an extremely large head and thick back. Goodness knows what it could have weighed with a full stomach but it never

'The likes of his smile and his old wall eye, Will never be seen again!'

put on much weight around that area of its body. It is not unusual to have recaptures of recognisable bigger pike in pre baited swims, it's inevitable, and I don't loose any sleep over it as it's just a very small part of my pike fishing.

I've frequently found that some pike will not leave the baited swim, no matter how many times they are caught. I'd like to put that down to careful rigging and handling, but I would like to think that this would apply to all the pike I catch. Certain pike, it seems, just never learn! Jan and I caught one pike so regularly that we gave it a name which was very relevant to its physical characteristics. 'Odd Job', as we called our friendly pike, never increased in weight from about 13 lb over several seasons and was easy to identify. Despite its weight, we always felt it was a male fish, but it never carried spawn so we never found out for sure.

His bottom jaw protruded further than the top one and it was twisted so that the bottom teeth showed all along one side. As if that was not bad enough, he was skinny, scruffy and had a 'duff' eye! When we found him dead one spring morning, it was like loosing a family pet and very upsetting. That you can feel that way about a pike is embarrassing to admit, but he provided us with no end of fun and banter. He always fought like stink, never coming in easily, and because of those protruding teeth, unhooking him was always hazardous, causing quite a few cuts and grazes. Happy memories!

Ode to Oddy

He used to love his weed lined hole
And the tit bits he found there
He knew he'd be caught from time to time
But that was only fair

He knew we'd play him gently
And never cause him pain
The likes of his smile and his old wall eye
Will never be seen again!

Mick Brown - January 2004

Deadbaiting is the most popular UK pike fishing method and will be for years to come, and pre baiting is helping to keep it alive by making it more interesting and productive. It is a very British method which hasn't spread to the continent in a big way, but I think there will be a surge of interest at some stage when it is promoted in a better way. I have written in German, Italian, French, Danish, Dutch and Swedish magazines about deadbaiting, and made major presentations in Germany and Sweden, but so far the interest is patchy. My personal feedback is that there is some interest and I am regularly receiving correspondence from all of these countries, and others, for more information about deadbaiting equipment and how to purchase it. I think that in Europe, deadbaiting has a huge potential tackle market which has not yet been exploited as there are thousands of waters where it could be practiced very effectively. If only I was 20 years younger!

'...RIGGED UP FOR FLOAT FISHED DEADBAITS, WHICH I WOULD POP UP WITH BALSA INSERT STICKS CONNECTED TO CAPTIVE WIRE LINKS.'

CHAPTER 11

Taking the Rise

A casual conversation at an angling club dinner where I had just made a pike fishing presentation, unexpectedly led to me being invited to fish a very private water. I had fished it before some 15 years previously, but had lost my contact there and never thought I'd get a chance to fish it again. It was a mature gravel pit with a good head of pike and I'd taken some cracking looking pike from there, including a few 20 pounders, with the biggest going just over 21 lb. Time moved on, and so did I, and the last I heard on the grapevine was that cormorants had devastated the roach shoals in the lake and the pike were now very thin. That wasn't going to stop me from taking up the invitation though as I know that rumours aren't always true, and even if they are, things can change over a few years - sometimes for the better!

In the few times I'd fished there in the past, I'd worked out the best tactics and was pretty confident that I knew where on the lake to fish. I left home just before daybreak with my rods already rigged up for float fished deadbaits which I intended to pop up with balsa insert sticks connected to the trace by captive wire links. Popping up the deadbaits had been instrumental in getting a good result on this lake as it had a lot of bottom weed growth, even in late winter. Popping up also allowed the baits to be 'twitched' every now and again without picking up weed. This movement often induced a 'take' and this is a very effective trick I use a lot. It is easily carried out with a float rig, but when legering a popped up bait, picking up weed when moving it makes it far less effective. Legering pop ups has its time and place though, usually when the bait is required to be held static for longer periods of time.

I was also using a float rig for another important reason. After several decades of fishing deadbaits in weed, I am convinced that float fished baits get dropped far less than legered baits when the water temperature is very low; a time when pike are more sensitive to resistance. I've proven it time and time again when fishing alongside anglers who are legering their baits and have frequently pointed out to them that a pike has taken their bait and is about to drop it. How did I know? I just kept an eye on their rod tips and would see their line tighten and tension the tip slightly, before falling back as the pike felt the resistance and rejected the bait. I emphasise that I am talking about cold water conditions, but in milder weather legering does not suffer so much from dropped runs as pike are bolting down baits and are less aware of resistance.

Armed with this useful knowledge, I cast out two pollan deadbaits, one either side of the narrow promontory which we fished from. The popped up baits would normally have been 'twitched', but there was a strong undertow on the lake which 'bounced' my baits along, albeit very slowly, and adding to their attraction in a similar way. Eventually, as contact with denser weed growth brought them to a halt, I would wait a further ten minutes and recast.

I love it when a plan comes together, and within an hour or so one of the baits was grabbed as the undertow inched it along, and the float was gone! Minutes later we waded into the ice covered margins to net an awesome looking pike which we weighed at 27 lb 9 oz! Before I'd had time to take it all in, my other bait was taken and I netted another stunning looking pike weighing exactly 22 lb which also took a popped up pollan. Sadly, my friend had just one run from a small pike on his baits which were legered on the bottom. Chances are that he might have caught those big pike on his bottom baits given enough time, but on short cold winter days when pike are not moving around much, you do need to provoke some action as fast as you can before you run out of daylight.

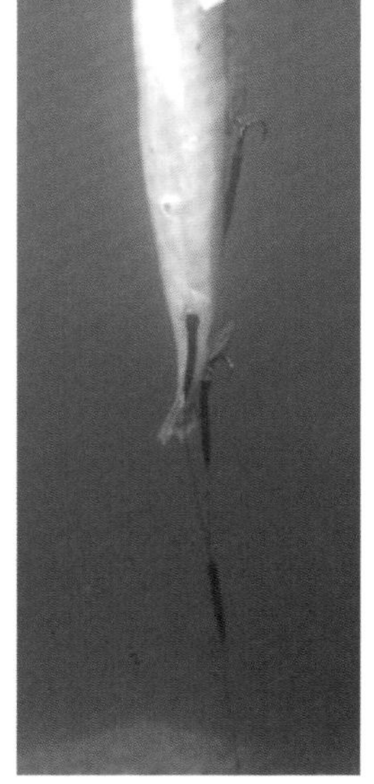

'POPPING UP BAITS MAKES THEM MORE VISUAL...'

With that lesson learnt, my friend said that he wasn't going to make the same mistake again as both of those pike beat his best for the water, not to mention beating my previous best from there either. On another visit a few weeks later we both fished in the same way with popped up baits, and he whooped me by catching the very same two big pike and another good one too, whilst I had to settle for a small fish!

Popping up a deadbait is a skill that the modern day pike angler must come to terms with in order to successfully tackle many pike waters as dense bottom weed is widespread, especially in clear water venues. Popping up baits makes them more visual and less prone to becoming lost in the weed. The end result is that the baits are found more quickly by the pike and the fishing becomes less frustrating by eliminating the retrieval of baits in amongst large balls of weed. I also think that a popped up bait gives off a better scent trail than a bait that is lying in amongst weed or silt, which will mask its scent to some extent. This also helps the pike to find baits more quickly - and that's what it's all about!

The method seems so simple to me now and could hardly be construed as high technology, and I

'...WE WADED INTO THE ICE COVERED MARGINS TO NET AN AWESOME LOOKING PIKE WHICH WE WEIGHED AT 27 LB 9 OZ!'

wonder why I never popped up my deadbaits back in the seventies. The frustration of fishing weedy venues like Cheddar Reservoir in Somerset and the St Ives pits complex in Cambridgeshire would have been eliminated, and I am sure I would have caught a lot more pike instead of shying away from such venues. It was only moving to South Lincolnshire that made me really come to terms with fishing in weed as most of the local venues are stuffed with it.

Popping up deadbaits started for me in the early eighties when I fished the Broads extensively with John 'Watto' Watson. I was air injecting them to make them buoyant but it wasn't easy or reliable, so I later progressed to John's preferred method of inserting chunks of polystyrene. We used to spend hours and hours during the evening before a session preparing popped up baits in his bath, but once we became adept at it we could knock up a suitable bait in seconds. We were not fishing in weed at the time but were both well aware that putting movement into our deadbaits was a useful ploy which encouraged pike to take them, a lesson learnt many years previously in our earlier fenland escapades. Popping them up makes the presentation even more effective and less prone to picking up debris and snagging wherever you fish, not only in weed.

'...Dense bottom weed is wide spread...'

Using polystyrene inside deadbaits later became frowned upon due to the potential for fish and other water creatures to swallow it. Sticks of balsa wood were an obvious alternative material which grew in popularity, although some anglers use foam sticks and polyballs, all of which have their uses with different types of deadbait presentations. Eventually anglers started to tie the buoyancy material directly to the trace so that it could be retained for further use. Originally mono was used for this purpose, then braid and eventually wire which is commonly used today to eliminate the chances of pike biting through it.

The rig I prefer for popping up deadbaits is very simple and not much more than a sliding float, a wire trace, and a weight to hold the bait down. The significant change from this basic rig is the addition of a balsa stick to provide the necessary buoyancy and a captive sliding wire link to retain it. It all seems very simple now, but went through various stages of development to arrive at it.

I have seen so many other different ways of popping up deadbaits, some of them being over complicated with unnecessary components, many being difficult and time consuming to rig up and some prone to tangles and potential bite offs. In comparison, the rig that I use is very simple and has hardly changed since I developed it many years ago. I feel like screaming every time a publisher asks me to write about it, and I have done so over and over again. The demand is there though, driven by tackle and bait companies to educate less experienced pike anglers, and at least I get a chance to emphasise the need for strong tackle and effective bite indication which are high on my own personal agenda for protecting pike from unnecessary damage.

Once again, I am not going to be tempted to describe rigs in detail just to fill a few pages. The Fox publication, *'Mick Brown's Guide to Pike and Predators'*, which is currently available, shows all of my predator rigs in depth and in the future there will no doubt be further publications showing the latest details. I would, however, like to discuss the popped up deadbait rig a little further to satisfy the curiosity of any new pike anglers, and to emphasise a few relevant points regarding how to use it to best effect.

As stated, I would always prefer to float fish my deadbaits, whether they are popped up or not, because the sensitivity of bite indication is, in my experience, far superior to that from a leger set up. Legering does have its place though and is a very viable method, even when the pike are rig shy, as long as the angler pays particular attention to minimising resistance. There are times when legering is the more practical method too, such as when long range fishing or when using multiple rods, and at night it's the only way to go unless you use a night float.

When I do leger a popped up deadbait, I minimise resistance by making everything as 'free running' as possible. I use a paternoster style leger link, which runs freely on the main line and which is normally about six inches longer than the hook trace. This enables the deadbait to be popped up by the length of the hook trace plus the additional length of the leger link. I can adjust the distance that the bait is popped up slightly, depending upon how much I tighten to the rig.

If the weed is exceptionally deep, I will make the leger link much longer to pop the bait up even higher. Even if there is no weed I will use this tactic of getting the bait well off the bottom if I want to get it noticed, maybe in low light conditions or in coloured water. This was the tactic I used when making the Angling Times video, *Better Pike Fishing*, with Matt Hayes at St John's lake on the Shimano Linear Fishery near Oxford. By fishing my baits at long range and high in the water on long leger links, I very quickly caught two cracking pike for producer Len Gurd's camera.

After a blank session on the previous day, we decided to make a fresh start the next morning on another part of the lake. On our arrival at daybreak we saw roach dimpling in the first light of the chilly February morning, but they were over eighty yards out into the lake. It was obvious to me that I would have to use a leger rig to reach the area, and hopefully there would be pike taking an interest in them. Float fishing was not considered as an option as its effective limit is about 65 yards for me. Even if I could get a bait out further than that, it would be difficult to see the float well enough to see bites register safely. I put everything into my casting and propelled out two popped up smelts on long leger links, dropping them right in amongst the dimpling roach. I tightened down as lightly as possible so as not to pull the baits down too far into the dense weed for which the lake is renowned. I then used a crafty dodge of 'tweaking' the line every now and again so as to give the deadbait a little movement.

Before too long I had a run which produced an 18 pounder which would have been good enough for the film we were making and which clearly demonstrated the point we were trying to make. Very soon afterwards, the alarm on the other rod screamed out and a real beast was brought to the net without too much of a struggle, typical of a late winter pike. It was clearly an 'upper twenty' which really stopped the show and gave the film the highlight it needed. At 28 lb 2 oz it was also a new fishery record! We'd certainly had a chance to make our point about popping up baits, and in style!

I hope that the reader is starting to realise that deadbaiting need not be a 'sit and wait' method. There are plenty of dodges you can use to provoke an interest in your baits. Another trick I use is to make the bait extra buoyant. Making a bait 'super buoyant' helps enormously when fishing in weed, encouraging the bait to pull upwards more forcibly to help straighten the rig out. To do this, I just add extra buoyancy so that the bait is really fighting to get to the surface. When using these 'super poppers' you will find that a four ounce leger weight is better than the standard three ounce weight, which is prone to being dragged along when tightening to the rig.

'Super buoyant' baits can be very beneficial in weed as there are two more big advantages. Firstly, you can release line after casting in order to make the bait shoot to the surface, before pulling it back down again to its fishing position. This gives you the confidence of knowing that the bait is not caught up in a patch of dense weed. Secondly, when the fishing is slow you can release line and make the deadbait shoot to the surface to get it noticed by any pike in the vicinity. They will often take it as it rises, the movement provoking them into attacking it. They might take it from the surface if you leave it there for a minute or so or they can also take it as you pull it back down into the weed. It's really exciting to see or feel the pike grab the bait.

'Super popper' techniques, like standard pop ups, can work just as well at venues where there is not a scrap of weed on the bottom. It's the visibility and movement that is important here. The visual effect is obvious but even the slightest movement will be noticed by pike as their prey is usually trying

At 28 lb 2 oz it was also a new fishery record!

A BALSA STICK PROVIDES THE BUOYANCY AND A WIRE LINK RETAINS IT.

not to move and give itself away. I'm convinced that another reason why popped up deadbaits are so successful is that approaching pike displace water which in turn creates micro movement in the bait, and as it wafts about it excites and encourages the pike even more into taking it.

If you are still not convinced that deadbaiting can be exciting, try fishing two leger rods with 'super poppers' on a mild autumn day on a weedy gravel pit, working them up and down through the water column and inching back a float fished popped up deadbait on a third rod. You just might start to see that deadbaiting can be very active and more effective than you could ever have imagined. You might also realise that there are one or two little tricks that more successful anglers use rather than just sitting and waiting for things to happen!

Weed is something that the pike angler has to live with and come to terms with. Fishing in weed is more likely to be associated with summer fishing, but with the milder winters that we get nowadays and the lack of severe frosts and prolonged cold weather, weed in many waters does not die back sufficiently and remains a constant problem throughout the year. If anything the situation is likely to get worse, but in most cases the deadbait angler can get around it, unlike the lure or livebait angler who can find himself frustrated by winter weed.

There is a positive side to weed as weedy waters tend to be clear and well oxygenated, making them perfect habitat for predators like the pike. They provide the advantage of cover for them to ambush from and the clarity of the water enables them to make the best use of their amazing eyesight. As much as we curse it, weed in most of its forms is the pike angler's friend.

Deadbaiting, and in particular the popped up deadbait technique, has been my 'bread and butter' method which has made me more money from pike fishing than any thing else. I have written vast numbers of articles on the subject, made several films and helped tackle companies develop and sell the associated tackle. It really has been very important to my business. Despite an upsurge of interest in lure fishing techniques, deadbaiting still has many more followers that any other tactic. It's no small wonder that manufacturers like Fox and Drennan see this as an important part of their business and produce the relevant tackle.

Although fishing for pike using a dead fish for bait has been a phenomenon of the late twentieth century, I am sure that anglers in previous times must have used this technique in some form or other. It wasn't until the second half of the twentieth century though that the practice became very highly tuned and developed, when pioneering anglers 'stumbled' upon its devastating effectiveness. The more recent practice of popping up the bait has taken the technique to an even higher level. It really is very simple and catches pike of all sizes from most waters, often singling out bigger pike. Even though I enjoy many other pike fishing methods, I still find deadbaiting exciting even after doing it for so long. Some pike anglers 'move on' to other methods which they perceive to be more exciting, such as various forms of lure fishing, and often see deadbaiting as old fashioned, stale and uninteresting by comparison, and some even believe it to be less productive. I don't burden myself with such thoughts and enjoy all pike fishing methods and use them all as and when appropriate. I always find deadbaiting interesting, but that's probably because I am generally busy and usually catching a lot of pike! It's only on particularly hard waters that you will find me sitting patiently and waiting behind deadbait rods for longer periods of time, when I know that's the best approach. I often feel that those who make such negative statements about deadbaiting have never really got to grips with it to arrive at such conclusions, but each to their own! I'll just carry on catching!

'I'LL JUST CARRY ON CATCHING!'

'Mind you, I did take a 27 pounder one morning when trolling a livebait to see what was in there!'

CHAPTER 12

I'm Your New Neighbour!

My clients were due to arrive in a couple of days time and I was feeling a little apprehensive as it had been very hectic getting my new lake ready for them in time for a pike tuition session. I don't do many such days, but in the late nineties I ran courses through one winter to help balance my books while other work was quite slow. That's how I like to do these educational days, just now and again and when it suits me, but I could never do it full time as it wouldn't offer enough variety for me.

I had made an arrangement with a private land owner to fish three of his lakes with the understanding that I could take clients there occasionally, and this group of four anglers were to be the very first. Before taking anyone there, I test fished the lakes myself to assess their potential. The first lake proved to be extremely weedy and a boat was the only way to fish it, but these clients wanted to fish from the bank so that ruled that one out. Mind you, I did take a 27 pounder one morning when trolling a livebait to see what was in there!

The other two lakes proved much easier to fish from the bank, but there was a problem that I never expected. There were hardly any pike in them! From one lake it was impossible to get a run, and the other lake would only produce a 'jack' or two in a whole days fishing. Why this was I had no idea as the lakes certainly contained plenty of roach which could often be seen priming at dawn and dusk. There were plenty of perch too which I caught easily on spinners, but very few pike. This could have been a scenario where there were few pike but some very big ones, but I didn't have time to find out. I had to think of my client's needs and they would want to catch fish rather than wait, possibly in vain, for a big one.

As they unloaded their tackle, I hid my concern whether a plan that I had just put into operation was going to work. What I had hurriedly done was to stock one of the lakes with a few additional pike to improve their chances of catching, but had I left it too late for them to settle in and become catchable?

These pike had been taken from another nearby lake where the situation was quite the opposite as there were too many pike in it. Unfortunately I couldn't get permission to take guests to that lake, but the keeper had been talking for some time about thinning the pike out and said it would be OK for me to take a few for stocking in my new lakes. I could come and get them at any time, but being rather busy and with just days to go before my client's arrived, I had not done so. I suddenly realised there were only three days to go, and in a last minute panic I went to try and catch a few. I managed to get five good looking fish in the five to nine pound range and a superb looking 12 pounder, and they were all swiftly transferred to their new home. I didn't feel that was enough, and from another session the next morning I acquired three more, two of them being singles but one of them a cracking 18 pounder. With just one day to go there were now nine new pike in one of the lakes, but I wasn't sure how long they would need to be in there to acclimatise and I knew I could have wasted my time. For good measure I prebaited the swims I planned to fish with about 15 lb of chopped herrings, most going into the lake with the new pike and a little into the adjacent lake where I had never caught anything.

The two lakes were within yards of each other with a small strip of land just the width of a footpath dividing them, and we could fish both lakes at the same time. I was interested to see whether the pike were doing well in their new home and at the same time, by fishing rods in the other lake, perhaps see what resident pike that one contained. Although such days are primarily for the benefit of my customers, I also use them to further my own interests by experimenting in ways such as this, not to mention any tackle testing I have to do at the time.

I now had four guests to entertain and show the basics of deadbait fishing. Some had done a little bit of pike fishing and others none at all. I explained first of all that the main problem with fishing this type of water is the dense bottom weed growth. I showed them how to rig up with popped up deadbaits and two of them sat content to watch floats and chat with me about pike. The other two were set up with light spinning rods and I had them working through a series of lures that would work above the weed without becoming snagged. It was actually a very pleasant morning as the weather was mild for the time of year, the early mist giving way to weak sunshine, and there was plenty of fun and banter as we chatted and drank coffee. We did need some pike though to make it complete, but I disguised the fact that I was worried about this working out as I'd taken the booking through an agent and it had cost them a lot of money!

There was no need to panic as a float soon came to life and an eight pounder was landed. As it crossed the draw string of the landing net, I could see the red blemish in its jaw where I had removed the trebles two days previously! As I explained the finer points of unhooking, I felt relieved that the plan was starting to come together.

Ten minutes later we missed a run, quickly followed by catching a three pounder after casting the deadbait back to the same area. It was clearly one of the native fish and although small, was very much appreciated by my client. It really is important not to spoil their enjoyment by devaluing their catches in any way, and for anglers in the early stages of their pike fishing, I realise that each pike is a big occasion for them and to be savoured. Furthermore, it's an opportunity to encourage them to appreciate every pike they catch and to learn to handle them carefully.

The pike was put back and the next few hours passed quietly. I then suggested that it would be a good idea for the anglers to change positions, with the deadbaiters now lure fishing and vice versa. I'd just been explaining feeding times, and how they can suddenly occur, when all of a sudden, as if on cue, runs on the deadbaits started to come regularly. The first was from a 12 pounder, recognised instantly as one of my stock fish. Then a couple of singles followed, one being a recapture of the first fish of the morning and the other was definitely another of the new residents. A fish was then hooked that was to be the highlight of their day and which fought long and hard, trying it's utmost to get into the overhanging willow branches on either side of the narrow swim. It was, without doubt, the 18 pounder which I had stocked two days previously but which now weighed a few ounces short of the magical 20 lb mark! For this party, it was a real show stopper and made me give a great sigh of relief to know that they were really happy with their day.

'It was, without doubt, the 18 pounder which I had stocked two days previously...'

This might seem a rather odd story to most, but as my business never provides a reg-

THE ALTERNATIVE - A TROUT WATER PIKE I DIDN'T SAVE!

ular income, it's a matter of living off your wits most of the time. When there are periods coming up when it starts to look like financial 'lean pickings' for a while, I will offer a few guided or accompanied fishing days, usually in the winter and at predictably good times for my customers. It may be a business but I would never want to let anyone's expectations down and I always do my best to ensure that they have a great day, even if I have to go to the extremes mentioned. Moving a few pike around in this way is not normally a problem and I have helped many fishery owners to relocate pike in their waters and always with good results, benefiting the waters losing the pike and also those gaining them. In many instances the pike removed have been saved from almost certain death because they have not been wanted, notably in trout fisheries.

It's all very well to declare that pike should be left in the fishery in which they originated, but in reality the world is just not like this. In commercial fisheries, carp fisheries, trout waters and many others, pike are often seen as a nuisance and the owners often want rid of them. Although we may not agree with this, we normally have no say in the matter, and without intervention I have no doubt that large numbers of pike would be killed. The situation is improving here and there, notably on larger trout fisheries, but not, it has to be said, with the welfare of the pike in mind. Realising the commercial value of allowing pike anglers to fish for them, many fisheries have become 'pike friendly' and tolerate their presence merely because of the extra revenue they produce.

I have come across many situations where water managers want pike removed because they are eating their valuable stock fish whether they are silver fish, small carp or trout. Since joining several trout clubs I now have some sympathy with this view, and although I would not agree with or condone the indiscriminate killing of pike, I can see that pike management is sometimes necessary and can be effective if sensibly monitored. The need to manage pike stocks varies from water to water and there is not, as far as I can see, an ideal blanket policy. It is all very well to have principals and opinions, but the only way to test them is to become involved where and when possible. Although my interventions might seem to be at an amateurish level, they are made because there is no one else to fight the cause of these pike and I have no problem with poking my nose in to do the best I can for them. I'll make no bones about the fact that if I can enjoy some special fishing and make some money from doing so, then that's even better.

In the fenland region where I live, there have been many opportunities to work with clubs and landowners to manage pike stocks and this has often given me a chance to explore and fish for pike in waters I would otherwise have no access to. Back in the Midlands I had very few opportunities, but one in particular comes to mind which might contradict the theory that pike rarely flourish when transferred to waters which are very different to those from which they originated.

On a cold January night, I transported a 23 pounder away from a large trout fishery where the water was absolutely gin clear. It had been caught by the fishery manager and he fully intended to bash it on the head as he had done recently with four 20 pounders that he had caught in an hour's fishing with a rusty old spoon. This was a magnificent fish and I had a chance to take it away or leave it to be killed. I borrowed a water container that just about housed the pike and went roaring down the motorway with water slopping all over the back of my van. It was kept in my bath overnight while I considered what I would do with it. Because I lived in the city I hadn't a clue, but having slept on the matter I realised I didn't have many alternatives and the next day dropped it into a local canal feeder reservoir of not much more than two acres in size. Even in winter the water was the colour of tea, but I knew it was full of roach and skimmers, and as it had no reputation for pike I doubted that anyone would catch it as no one fished there for them.

I told a friend about it and a few weeks later, as neither of us had caught this pike, we thought it would be fun to pass an afternoon to see if we could do so. Fishing with just one rod, I cast out a four inch roach livebait which was all I had. An hour later the float plopped under and I caught her! Despite her ordeal she looked magnificent and as though she had never been caught before. It was very different from the regular fishing I was doing at the time, travelling to the fens and broads and fishing for wild fish, but nevertheless an interesting diversion and a bit of fun.

The following winter was a tough one for me. Having left my full time employment as an engineer in a Birmingham factory, my recently self imposed employment in the building trade saw me going through a period with very little work, and I consequently became quite short of money. My long distance trips became few and far between but I had to keep pike fishing no matter what that meant. I fished a few local waters and didn't catch much from most of them, but suddenly remembered the pike in the canal feeder. I wondered if she was still there as it was possible for her to swim over the inlet sluice when the water level was high and get out into the main canal. Nevertheless, I decided to have a session.

It was all very casual and another bit of fun, and I was interested to see if there were other pike in there too. As there was a tow path all the way round, I had the great idea of 'walking' a float fished suspended livebait around the feeder in such a way that I covered every square metre of it. It actually turned out to be quite challenging, dropping the livebait in the margin, walking to the opposite side while letting out line and then gradually inching the livebait back to me. With the mono line being

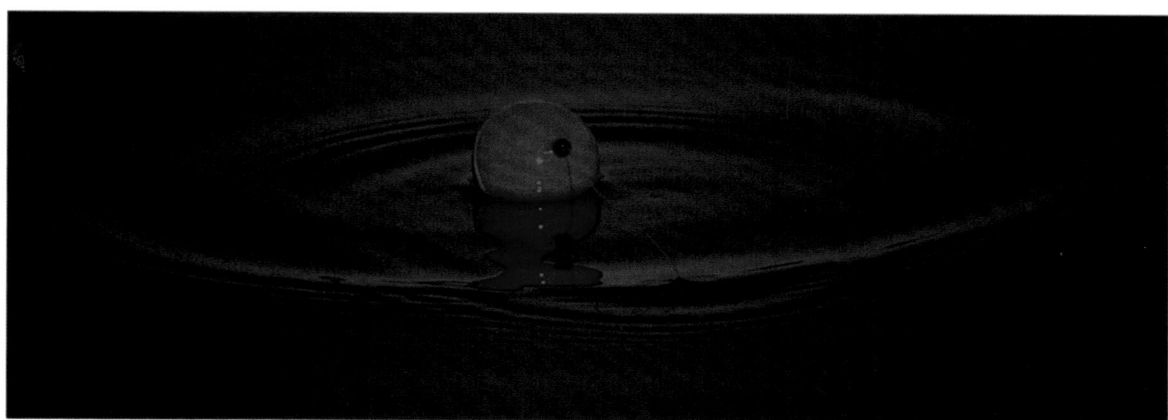

'...GRADUALLY INCHING THE LIVEBAIT BACK TO ME...'

Pic: Bob Jackson

'Despite living in muddy, shallow water for a year, she was in fantastic condition...'

greased to stop it from sinking, it was easy to keep in close contact with the float. When it was almost back, I would let out line again and walk to another bank and do the same again. In essence I was 'walk trolling' the livebait and it must have seemed very amusing to anyone passing by. I might have only done this once, purely for fun, had not something happened on that first visit. Although this was in the winter time, I had a 'take' just on dark which proved to be a very large eel that, to my annoyance, shed the hook as it writhed on the surface. This prompted me to have another go as it had added to the interest of the venue.

The canal feeder was only a few miles from home and it wasn't costing me much to get there. Although I wasn't catching anything, I started to fish there quite regularly, partly because I couldn't afford to go anywhere else but mainly because I had developed an unexplainable fascination for the place. Eventually this became an afternoon ritual where I would nip down there for two hours, get in a bit of fishing and be home for tea. Before long I had notched up a couple of dozen short sessions and caught nothing, but as I had other things going on in my life at the time I was quite happy with the situation. It was what fishing is about for most anglers, a little bit of escapism from the cut and thrust of everyday life, no more and no less.

I enjoyed fishing there most of all when darkness approached and the water was lit up by the orange glow from the street lights. For some reason, probably because my dinner wouldn't be ready for a while, I often stayed well into the dark. By keeping the float moving I knew that if I had a 'take', I would feel it even if I couldn't see it. One evening whilst standing on the dried up inlet from the main canal, I was

Pic: Mick Rouse

I'm pretty sure this 26 lb 4 oz pike originated from a large trout reservoir!

thinking about giving it another few minutes and then going home, as I drew the float back to the brickwork ledge where I had previously contacted the big eel. This was the deepest point in the feeder reservoir, being about five feet or so whilst most of the other water was only about three feet deep. I was in no rush to lift my bait from the water and stood for a while in the darkness thinking more about my evening plans than anything else, when the 'bung' shot under with an almighty 'plop' as my live crucian was grabbed. A few minutes later I slipped the net under the 20 pounder which I had rescued from the trout reservoir over a year previously. Despite living in muddy, shallow water for a year, she was in fantastic condition, and although down slightly in weight, her appearance was still that of a stockily built trout water pike!

My little escapades are nothing compared to the scale at which pike are removed and stocked in commercial situations. There have been lots of instances of big pike being used for stocking fisheries so that they can be caught by anglers on a commercial basis. In principle, I can't see anything wrong in doing so if done properly, after all we do so with most other species, and we wouldn't have the great carp, tench and catfish waters that we have today without such management. Doing so with pike is not that easy though and rarely works well as they will not tolerate being caught as repeatedly as other species do. If the fishing is properly controlled to prevent over fishing from happening it can provide good sport, but the angler must not kid himself that this is a natural situation.

Such a water was the so called 'Forgotten Lake' in Suffolk which was set up as an £800 a year syndicate. In reality it wasn't 'forgotten' at all and there was a lot of hype spouted about it. I was tipped off that the fabulous double figure bream and 20 lb plus pike that were 'discovered' in the lake had actually been netted and transferred from a large trout reservoir. Whilst working closely with Angling Times in the mid nineties I had an opportunity, along with other well known pike anglers, to have a day's pike fishing there.

My boat partner was Mick Rouse from Angling Times and we arrived on a glorious October morning. I quickly realised that I was in the position that my own clients were often in and was fishing for stocked fish. Lots of pike were caught on all sorts of methods and in particular with livebaits and lures which most anglers were using. I fished lures too, but because the venue was so much like the weedy waters I was used to, it screamed out to be fished with a popped up smelt deadbait, deep down in the weediest areas. If I remember correctly, there was a low 'twenty' caught on a livebait from the other boats amongst large numbers of smaller fish. Mick Rouse and I took our fair share on lures, but the highlight of the day was the two runs which came to my popped up deadbaits, producing a brace of 26 lb 4 oz and 21 lb 4 oz. I almost achieved the 'treble' when I dropped off another 20 pounder which had taken a surface lure, my old favourite Jitterbug. These stocked pike were obviously fitting in very well, and because it was a large water fished only by a small syndicate, they did well for a few more years before the pike population reverted to its natural level as supported by the available prey fish stock.

I can see the sense in stocking larger lakes with unwanted pike as they are not so easily persecuted in a bigger water. It might not necessarily be a good thing for the water though as they may quickly eat their way through the resident prey fish, but that is for the water's owner to take into consideration. One thing I do not like are small stocked commercial pike fisheries which are fished on a day ticket basis, where pike are so hungry that they become easy to catch and are caught over and over again. When given a chance to become involved with such a fishery, I initially agreed so that I could see this at first hand rather than make assumptions and there was talk of a deal whereby I would have some control over how the water was fished.

The water was the Baston Fen Pike Fishery which was set up in a six acre gravel pit which used to be a stock lake for the nearby trout fishery and then later run as an unsuccessful carp fishery. The new owner had acquired pike of all sizes from far and wide and had stocked eels, zander and catfish too, having the relevant paperwork to cover them. The idea was that I would help him promote the fishery in exchange for free fishing initially. I agreed to do so, but told him that I doubted whether it would last more than a season or two because the pike would not tolerate excessive handling. I urged him to regulate the numbers of anglers and ensure that they were fully equipped to catch and handle the pike safely. In this respect he was onto a 'loser' from the start, because the inadequate standard of handling when acquiring them had resulted in them being tatty looking specimens from the outset. The biggest pike I caught when I test fished it was a 26 pounder which took a jerk bait. I was gutted that it had clearly been a magnificent fish at one time, but poor handling by the netsmen had left it with bodily blemishes and a damaged tail. Even before it opened to the public I felt uneasy about having more to do with the venture, but couldn't stop it from going ahead and was only able to watch the outcome from the sidelines. Two seasons later it was all over and the water was once again up for sale!

How much merit one places on the capture of stocked pike is for the individual to decide. When other species like carp are stocked it doesn't seem to matter to the anglers who fish for them, but serious pike anglers tend to hold very different views I've noticed. Smaller stocked pike are neither here nor there, and they can become the specimens of the future in waters that are able to absorb them. I've known many 'jacks' which have been rescued from waters where they were not welcome, grow into 20 pounders a few years later in their new homes. Fishing for stocked 'big pike' is another thing though, but pike anglers quickly descend upon these waters as soon as they hear about them. Such fish are usually caught very quickly, often the next day! Many anglers have added a 30 pounder to their notoriety on the capture of stocked fish, but that's their business. If they get pleasure from doing so, it's not doing any harm as long as they don't try and kid anyone otherwise. It's better than seeing these pike bashed on the head at the fishery they have come from, and at least anglers have the pleasure of seeing them. It's up to the individual to decide what such a capture means to him, and at the end of the day there are much bigger issues in pike fishing to worry about!

'...I finally 'chinned' her, getting a firm grip and taking care to avoid the trebles.'

CHAPTER 13

What Lies Beneath?

We'd trolled the river for over a mile, and despite conditions seeming pretty good had only taken two jacks in the process. It was well into November and recent rain had added a nice tinge of colour to the water, and with its temperature dropping below ten degrees centigrade, it just had to be time for some bigger pike to show up! I was feeling pretty confident!

'Here they are!' I shouted to Jan, making sure I was heard above the drone of the outboard. 'Any second now' I added, as I checked my lure was vibrating well and the reel's clutch was adjusted correctly. Thirty seconds or so later, my rod rammed round and held there for a while as I stopped the boat to tussle with a lively pike which thrashed the surface to foam in a violent display of anger. After several attempts, I finally 'chinned' her, getting a firm grip and taking care to avoid the trebles. I used both hands to prise open her jaws while Jan easily extracted the lure with a pair of long nosed pliers.

'She's been feeding well' I commented as I swung her back into the river, levelling her off and waiting until she pulled from my grip in a great swirl, soaking my arms and face as she powered back into the deep water beneath us. It was a great start to a day which would produce several more such pike - and all thanks to the aid of an echo sounder on the boat.

Twenty years ago it was quite unusual to see an echo sounder on a pike angler's boat. They were considered a luxury item and the benefits had not been widely realised. The models available then were pretty sophisticated for their time, but have since advanced much further, featuring colour screens and higher resolution which shows much better detail. They are also referred to as fish finders or sonar units but these are all the same thing; a device which is used to send ultrasonic frequency signals from the boat to the bottom of a river, lake or sea bed. The signals are bounced back, and as well as the bottom contours, anything else that gets in the way is also interpreted and presented on the screen, showing its distance beneath the boat and an indication of its size. In other words, you can easily see a picture on a scrolling screen of what lies beneath you. Of particular interest to the pike angler are the bottom contours, any snags and structures, shoals of prey fish and individual larger fish.

I find this fascinating, and I enjoy a day's boat fishing even if I don't catch very much as the sounder makes the day interesting and informative. The fact remains though that I usually do catch plenty of fish as a result of using one. How many anglers could tell you that they know every depth and contour over miles and miles of their local rivers for example? Imagine the benefits of knowing this! The sounder picks up fish too, showing larger ones individually and smaller fish in shoals when they are packed densely enough. These facts offer a great advantage to any pike angler, and in my work which is all about catching pike, this is a major benefit.

Echo sounders are commonplace on pike fishing boats nowadays, but opinions about their use vary. Some regard such technology as making the sport too easy, not proper fishing, or even bordering on cheating. How far should we go in introducing such technical wizardry into helping us to catch pike?

I think that many 'anti's' come from a traditionalist background and are quite happy to catch what they do by watercraft alone. Others seem to be quite ill informed about what this equipment can do. The former are entitled to their views, although I think I could convert them if they spent a day afloat with me. The latter, I just don't have time for.

For me, sonar has helped to catch considerably more fish than I would have without it, but I am certainly not emptying waters or catching what I would consider to be 'too many'. Far from it! More than anything else, it has made my fishing a lot more interesting and given me a better understanding of fish behaviour and the topography of venues than would be possible to amass in three lifetimes without it. Indeed, the knowledge that can be acquired in a single day can be mind blowing, but you still need the skill to use it to your advantage.

There are many other features on echo sounders which can be useful, such as a zoom facility which shows finer detail when required. It is also possible to interpret bottom hardness and some units have split screens to show multiple information in more complex situations. There are even alarms to warn you of shallow water or the presence of fish. If you are a technophobe you can play around with it all day, but I mainly use the basic features and like to get on with the fishing!

Echo sounders are at their most useful on larger venues where there are vast expanses of water in which to locate fish, but they can make fishing on smaller venues interesting as well. A medium sized pit I once fished was full of features: shallows, bars, weedy bays and an island. When checking it out with my echo sounder on the second season I fished there, I located a hole of almost 19 feet deep in a fairly flat bottomed surrounding area with an average depth of about 13 feet. Man made pits frequently have this type of 'sump hole' feature, where water was pumped out from during the excavation. They are usually located adjacent to a nearby water course if you are looking for them.

On a very cold February day, Jan and I decided to fish baits in 'the hole' after pre baiting it a few times at the end of each of our last few visits there. It had to be fished from a boat as casting from the bank was very difficult due to overhanging bushes. Casting accuracy was vital too as the hole wasn't particularly big, probably just big enough to drop a Transit van into.

There was just enough room for two baits in the hole. Jan cast a paternostered livebait to the right hand side, whilst I cast a large herring to the left. Five minutes into the session Jan was away on the livebait and a jack came on board sporting a severe gash across its flank which looked quite recently inflicted. Another half an hour passed and I started to get fidgety as my bait hadn't been taken, and neither had my other two float fished deadbaits which I'd cast to the other side of the boat.

After weighing things up I decided I might, just might, not be quite in the hole, so I tweaked the bait towards me by a few feet and released the line. The unweighted pencil float stood up vertically, clearly indicating that the bait had now dropped into deeper water and I was beginning to think I should reset my stop knot depth by a couple of extra feet or so.

There was no time to do so, in fact no time for anything, as the float slid away and down into the hole! My rod bent right over when I struck into the fish but it didn't budge, almost as though I was snagged in weed. With the rod still arched right over, the very weighty pike thumped hard once or twice and then plodded away as it left the hole, pulling the boat round in the process. Jan quickly wound the other rods in and we held our breath as I inched it towards the surface of the cold, clear water. Soon its bulk was revealed, and it looked a good 'mid twenty' without any doubt, but its true size wasn't apparent until it rolled onto its side in the landing net. It was very fat indeed and well padded out with spawn. Our best pike from the lake up to that point was a 23 pounder, but the monster in my net pulled the scales eight ounces past the 30 lb mark! It was, in fact, the 23 pounder which we'd caught in a different part of the lake on a lure in the previous season. She'd put on over seven pounds in a year!

'...15 FT OF WATER AND 8 FT OF ROACH. THERES GOT TO BE PIKE NEARBY!'

The capture of a 30 lb pike from a new water is the sort of success that would delight any pike angler, but for a consultant in the tackle trade it is a real boost to business. My then current sponsors, Shimano, gained plenty of mileage from being able to use it in articles and brochures to promote their tackle. For me it was another dream come true, to catch a 'thirty' and then be well paid for doing so! Around that time, in 1998, I started to realise that I had turned my obsession with pike fishing into a way of life that, if I was sensible, would make enough money to pay my bills and pay for my fishing too. It was certainly heading that way. I'd really got things worked out now!

Of course, I might have caught that 30 pounder without the aid of an echo sounder by casting anywhere in the lake from the boat. After all, boat fishing allows you to move frequently and to use very effective methods like trolling livebaits which enable you to cover a lot of water. Nowadays though, I would feel 'undressed' using any tactics without an echo sounder on my boat as it really is 'fishing blind' without one, and in my view a poor second best.

I might even have caught it from the bank, but I would be fishing blindly again, taking considerably longer to find useful features like the deep hole. In fact, I probably would never have found the hole at all due to the difficult nature of the bank nearby making casting awkward.

'... THE MONSTER IN MY NET PULLED THE SCALES EIGHT OUNCES PAST THE 30 LB MARK!'

Why should the pike be in the deep hole anyway? After all, it is free to roam far and wide. I do realise this, and a follow up to that story told me a lot about just how much pike can roam around in the course of the day.

Returning to the lake the following season, fishing the deep hole became a regular thing from the bank once I'd worked out how to do so. From a point on an opposite bank, I found that a full blooded cast with a leger rig and a well prepared and streamlined bait would just about reach the hole or be very near to it. To get such range required using the stiffer rods I was developing for Fox at the time, and the use of a four ounce leger weight instead of my normal three ounce weight to give me vital extra yards.

Although I try to take things as seriously as I can, I will admit to the occasional fiasco. One day, when trying to power a deadbait out to the deep hole, the small piece of herring tail came off the hooks, flew high in the air and landed in the water just down the marginal shelf in front of me. The rig made it to the deep hole but obviously without the bait! After enduring a ribbing from Jan, I re baited and got a second bait successfully into the hole. The day progressed with a couple of fish on the other rods, but the bait in the hole never moved. Half an hour before darkness it was finally taken, and a 29 pounder was soon on the bank being unhooked. Apart from the herring bait I'd caught it on, which was still hanging from its jaw, there was another herring showing in its throat entrance. I teased it out and it was the piece of herring I had cast off at the beginning of the day! That pike had, at some time during the day, been within ten feet of the bank, and literally under our feet. I could most likely have caught it by just dropping the bait in the margin! After events such as this, I often go home wondering whether I know anything at all! Such unexpected happenings like this bring me down to earth, but are useful in the process of continually examining and re assessing what I think I know. Knowledge gained through the use of an echo sounder combined with my practical results brings me closer to the understanding of pike I'm looking for. To quote the great British economist John Maynard Keynes, 'When the facts change, I change my mind.' I couldn't have put it better myself!

When fishing bigger waters, echo sounders really come into their own, and I know that most experienced pike anglers will agree with this. Just look at the boats at the pike events held on trout waters like Chew, Blithfield, Rutland and Grafham, or boats out on big natural waters like Windermere and the Western Irish Loughs. Almost without exception, every boat will have an echo sounder set up. Even when bank fishing such venues, my tactics will usually be based upon what I have learnt about the bottom contours when fishing them previously from a boat, and I'll use this information to position myself where I think is favourable for the time of year. I will have gained knowledge about depths and the nature of the bottom terrain I am casting into, and in particular whether there are snags. Features like sunken tree stumps and boulders are great for attracting pike but deadly for snagging up, and knowledge of their whereabouts gained from an echo sounder is invaluable. The implications can be disastrous if the angler should 'snap off' on such a snag when playing a pike or have to pull for a break when snagged on one, leaving a baited trace for a pike to swallow later. How you come to terms with such swims is for you to decide, but at the very least you should be using the strongest line possible and trebles which will bend before the main line breaks. Typically this could mean using 50 lb breaking strain braid, which will easily bend most trebles well before it breaks.

'...There was another herring showing in it's throat...'

In the UK, even our biggest waters are tiny compared to many in Scandinavia, mainland Europe and North America. My travels have taken me to many of these wonderful places to fish waters that are so daunting, you know instantly that you would never get to realise their potential if you fished them for a lifetime. Some of them are so large that they are actually frightening when the wind picks up and the waves start rolling, and many times I've thought better and come back in quickly. At other times I've not even chanced going out!

On calmer days, to be out on these vast waters is simply a pleasure in itself, giving you a great sense of freedom and the feeling that it's just good to be alive. Trolling through the night on the massive Lake Mjosa in Norway for its pelagic pike and ferox trout with my fishing buddy Matt Hayes, is an experience I will always savour. It really is a huge piece of water, and at 362 square kilometres in area it's almost the size of the county of Rutland! We caught pike to 20 lb and double figure ferox trout by fishing just three feet deep over water which was up to 600 feet deep, and the echo sounder was vital for locating the shoals of freshwater smelt which

'Trolling through the night on the massive Lake Mjosa in Norway for its pelagic pike... is an experience I will always savour.'

they feed upon. The sounder also helped us work out the feeding cycle of the predators, which was based upon the movements of the prey. The prey would drop into deeper water during the daytime, typically from 200 to 300 feet down in the black abyss beneath us. Night time in Norway in the summer is a short lived affair when it barely gets dark at all, and as the light starts to fade, the prey fish gradually drift up near the surface to feed, and any stragglers which stray from the main shoals are in danger of being picked off in the upper layers by the predators. When a trolled bait was taken, we would never know whether it would be a trout or a pike, and sometimes even a perch. It is fascinating fishing and not pike fishing as anglers in the UK know it to be, but pike can adapt to all sorts of different environments and an echo sounder is invaluable in helping to understand the mysterious world of the very deep water they inhabit.

The echo sounder is also vital from a safety point of view on larger waters. Some are predictable but many are not, and you cannot take anything for granted as it's very easy to get into serious danger. I could illustrate this point with quite a few examples, but to avoid too much embarrassment I will offer you just two. First of all I will give you a good example of why you should not get over confident! Most big waters have been charted and it's quite easy to pick up a map showing depth contours and positions of hazards such as reefs and islands. That's all very well if you are interpreting the chart correctly!

On Lake Asnen in southern Sweden, Jan and I were heading out at dusk to reach the deep water trolling grounds for a night session. On this occasion we didn't have an echo sounder as we had only stopped off on our way to another venue where we would be fishing from a fully equipped boat. By courtesy of the Swedish Tourist Board we had blagged a couple of days on Asnen where we were provided with a basic boat and engine but no sounder. We had to rely entirely on the chart given to us by the boat hirer who warned us that we would have to negotiate about a mile of dangerous rocks and reefs before we reached open water. Feeling rather over confident, I steered a meandering course around rocks just beneath the surface, some marked with hazard markers but others not because rough weather had washed them away.

Jan kneeled in the front of the boat and kept me informed of any approaching underwater danger, but thinking more about the fishing and less about safety, I didn't really listen when she said we were going into shallow water. 'According to the chart we couldn't be' I replied with a hint of sarcasm. I really should have listened when she said there were now some big rocks just under the surface, but it was too late to take any evasive action when she ducked down in the boat and yelled 'we're going to hit the f******* rocks you idiot!' Crash, bang, crunch – you know the rest!

I got away with it that time, but came even closer to a very serious disaster on Clear Lake in Canada. I'd been exploring the predator potential of the lake with Martin Founds from Angler's World Holidays, and by the time we'd decided to stop fishing we had travelled five or six miles down the lake. Powering back in a 16 foot aluminium boat with a 30 horse power engine can be quite exhilarating, and you can really get some speed up and cover the miles in no time at all. We had an echo sounder which indicated that the water was typically from 25 to 35 feet deep, and speeding down the middle of the lake we expected a smooth journey home. Wrong again! All of a sudden there was an almighty bang as the boat slurred to a halt and the engine flipped off its mounting clamps! A reef had appeared from nowhere and we were going too fast to see it coming! Luckily we managed to get the engine back into position, albeit with some damage to the boat's transom and its mountings. We had been very lucky, and another lesson had been learnt the hard way!

To avoid danger when fishing on these vast waters, you would be well advised to also have a GPS (Global Positioning System) on your boat which you can use to mark a safe course. I have one fitted on my Orkney Fastliner, but when travelling abroad I often have to rely on other people having one. Working from signals sent from satellites, a GPS can pinpoint your position within a few metres. This has not always been the case, and a few years ago when military security was a big issue, they were about as accurate as a tabloid journalist, but accuracy today is considerably better and very reliable. (GPS that is – not journalists!).The GPS has many other major advantages for anglers such as marking the positions of good fishing areas and enabling returning to them quickly and accurately on future occasions.

It was on the Baltic Sea when fishing with Anders Forsberg in his 21 foot Buster that I realised the true value of a GPS. From years of fishing the waters around Vastervik, an area of dozens of square miles, Anders had marked the positions into his GPS of most of the best fishing spots and had a good working knowledge of the best times of year to fish them. Good swims were typically from a mile to five miles apart! It was a real 'eye opener' to proceed at high speed, propelled by a 100 horse power engine, to reach a fishing mark, quickly pinpoint it, drop the anchor and catch a pike within minutes, often on the first cast!. Being well out to sea with the shore but a thin line in the distance, and to drop straight onto some pike, is just mind blowing. To power up the engine and head for another mark several miles away and do the same again, opened up a world of pike fishing that I had never dreamt possible. Nearly 15 years later, this approach is now seen as standard on the big European and North American pike waters, and accessible to anyone who can afford the equipment.

GPS is undoubtedly an invaluable aid to safety too, and nowadays I would be reluctant to fish some of the more dangerous venues I've tackled in the past without it, especially when fishing or travelling in the dark. It's reassuring to know that I can get safely back to my launching place as it's very easy to get lost, even on waters of a modest size. This can be very frightening when a storm comes up, or just as disturbing when a big mist comes down.

I was trolling for sea pike off the southern Swedish coast with Thomas Søbirk, along a 'drop off' line where a big river entered the sea. Towards dark, a big mist came down and we lost sight of the shore. We now had to find our way back from the deep water of the open sea to the safety of the estuary, negotiating our way through shallow rocky water. We had a journey of about a mile ahead of us, but we couldn't even see a distance of three feet! With me hanging over the front of the boat looking for rocks, Thomas gingerly inched the boat along. Once we had reached the shallow water rock line, more by luck than judgement, we couldn't run the engine any longer and risk smashing the propeller, so we took an oar each and pushed the boat in what we 'thought' was the right direction.

Two hours later we hit land - but we were not in the river mouth! Was it to our left, or was it to our right? It could have been in either direction so we took an intuitive guess. Luckily we got it right and reached the river entrance another hour later after using the oars to push the boat through the mist in seemingly endless shallow rocky water. Had we have gone the wrong way, the next town is 20 miles away! From that day on, I never take risks on dangerous waters by not having GPS on the boat.

When fishing these huge waters, it's obvious that the fishing will be difficult to come to terms with on occasional short visits. You need to be aware from the start that you are unlikely to get more than a glimpse of the potential of such a water or understanding of the habits and movements of its pike. At least by using an echo sounder you can position yourself in favourable areas where you might, in theory, expect to find pike at a given time of the year.

'...EVEN THE WORLD'S LARGEST WATERS CAN BE TACKLED WITH THE RIGHT EQUIPTMENT...'
PIC: THOMAS SØBIRK

Spring is probably the easiest time to find pike on these big waters when they venture into shallow weedy areas to spawn and then hang around to attack prey fish when they come in to do the same. The timing can be very critical though, and on pre arranged trips you can easily be too early or too late.

With the echo sounder you should be able to find the shallow bays and work out their extent, and also locate the shelf where they drop into deeper water; a useful place to try if the pike are not actually in the bays. If they are in neither position, you have little option but to troll the open water with lures or deadbaits to try and find them, and this is rarely easy as the fish could have moved miles away from the spawning bays and returned to their regular deep water feeding patterns.

Where they will be depends largely upon the movement and location of their food supply. Faced with thousands of acres of water deeper than 30 feet, and often down to hundreds of feet, most anglers would be totally daunted. It can be like looking for a needle in a haystack, but the echo sounder

BIG PIKE LIKE THIS ONE FOLLOW THE BIG PREY SHOALS.

helps locate their prey and tells you at what depth they can be found. It's a good start, but by no means always the answer and this fishing is rarely easy!

I've used examples from fishing huge foreign waters to show that even the world's largest waters can be tackled with the right equipment and a big boat with a powerful engine. My work has given me just a taste of it and I wish I was a much younger man with a private income and plenty of time on my hands. That will never be the case, but I still enjoy exploring more modest sized UK waters and would never feel dissatisfied or frustrated in doing so as they also have plenty of challenges to offer. Waters like Rutland and Grafham are big enough when you fish them and certainly don't seem tiny after a while, even though they may be by comparison.

Our UK river systems are also quite extensive, although small compared to continental river systems, and I thoroughly enjoy fishing them from a boat. I particularly like fishing on the Severn and the Great Ouse as they are so interesting, and even smaller rivers like the Warwickshire Avon and the Nene I find fascinating too. Although they are not likely to throw up a big pike very often, they do provide some interesting fishing and reliable sport. I'm drawn back to these rivers time and time again, and from my business point of view, I get plenty of action for testing tackle and bait. Even if I had all the time in the world on my hands, I would still fish for smaller pike in interesting venues and not solely for big pike. I've picked up my share of bigger pike along the way, but haven't got the mind set of the 'big' pike chasers who fish exclusively for them every time they go out. I do admire their dedication though, and good luck to them!

Understanding the relationship between pike and their prey is vital to succeed at catching pike, and the use of an echo sounder unearths so much beneficial information. Facts emerge which you could not discover easily in any other way. On big stillwaters you might have to be content with finding the sort of features which attract pike, although you can sometimes find prey shoals but on most of the rivers I fish though, it's easy to find prey shoals in the winter and this gives a big advantage. Prey fish can gather so tightly that it is not unusual for there to be several miles between big compacted shoals, and there are no prizes for guessing where the pike are! On my way between the 'hot' pike swims, I often pass bank anglers fishing swims that are totally devoid of any fish at all. I'll often stop and have a chat with them and mention this fact, especially those with dry nets!

When searching for bigger river pike, I do like to fish close to bream shoals in the substantiated belief that big pike are attracted to them. I've learnt to distinguish between roach shoals and bream shoals on the sounder screen, and my suspicions of the presence of bream are frequently verified as I mis hook quite a few of them on jigs when fishing the areas which I suspect hold them. They are often seen topping at dusk in these swims too, confirming my suspicions. Shoals of prey fish, even big bream, can be very tightly packed though and it is possible to be fishing just outside of the area. You need to be very open minded when searching a river with your echo sounder as it is very easy to miss prey fish which are tucked in very tightly against the bank. Whether they are roach or bream, I'm not happy unless I'm fishing amongst them. Of particular importance though is the revelation that long sections of any river can be totally devoid of any prey fish, and this vital knowledge tells me why it is wise to keep moving when pike fishing, and the importance of leap frogging the rods when I'm bank fishing.

I have also learnt a lot about the movements of prey fish in river systems which is obviously relevant to catching pike. The echo sounder has revealed to me that prey shoals are often 'on the move', not always in one direction either but frequently going back and forth along a section of river. This might explain how during a bank fishing session you can get bursts of runs at different times. This fact should give some encouragement to bank anglers as there's a chance that prey fish might pass through their swim at some time, and hopefully the pike which are following them as well. Then again they might not, and this is where an echo sounder takes away any doubt and offers a boat angler a big advantage.

Pike are naturally interested in prey shoals, and finding them is an important part of my pike fishing. In particular I enjoy the combination of trolling to find pike and then anchoring up to catch them in a more relaxed manner. Trolling is about more than catching pike; it's about finding prey fish and learning about the water. Densely packed prey shoals often give themselves away when I'm trolling as I frequently feel my lure 'banging' into them when there are too many to get out of the way in time. I love to find a big shoal of prey fish and really enjoy dropping the anchor near to them, putting out some live and deadbaits and putting the kettle on! I never get tired of mentioning these special times when it feels good to simply be out fishing, but when anchored in a swim which I have discovered through my own efforts and which has great potential, the contentment is beyond description.

Once you have a big boat, echo sounder and GPS, you can tackle even the biggest waters with success, given enough time to work it out. Such investment could not easily be justified by British anglers and most of us have to dream and drool over what it would be like to fish these waters on other than brief holiday visits. On a more modest home based level though, there is still immense pleasure to be gained from boat fishing with the aid of an echo sounder, and I rate this piece of equipment as one that has revolutionised pike fishing the most fishing during my lifetime.

CHAPTER 14

Chase Me

'...AS I LOVE TROLLING, I DO SO EXTENSIVELY...'

Trolling for pike with lures is nowhere near as popular in the UK as it is elsewhere around the rest of world, and consequently not so well developed here. In the lowlands of England in particular, we have comparatively few waters big enough for trolling to encourage anglers to spend money on boats and the associated equipment, although there are signs that it is becoming more practiced. In England most trolling is carried out on big rivers and large reservoirs, although there is no reason why smaller waters cannot be trolled with some advantage. Local by laws and club rules often restrict the practice, but there are enough opportunities for the keen troller to find somewhere to fish and enjoy his sport if he looks hard enough. Because trolling is not widely practiced, my work in the tackle trade and media has not involved a great deal of related tackle development or writing work, but as I love trolling, I do so extensively as a self indulgence rather than to make money in my business!

When Matt Hayes and I joined the Blithfield Trout Fishing Club, our thoughts were largely focused on enjoying the spring and autumn fly fishing for pike, fitting in a bit of trout fishing in the warmer months. However, one of the perks of being a member is that you are allowed to fish for pike for two days in March with lures, just before the trout fishing starts. We, of course, were not going to miss that!

We were there at daybreak on the first day, and I must say with a quite philosophical approach to the fishing and were going to enjoy it regardless of what we caught. The weather was absolutely perfect, being mild for the time of year and with just a light wind. We had both fished there before as members of the winter pike fishing syndicate and had both caught 30 pounders, but the fishing had always been very patchy and quite difficult to get to grips with. We hadn't done too badly though, and up to that point all of our bigger fish had been taken by casting our lures. We had caught plenty of pike by trolling them, but had never taken any bigger fish in this way.

One thing we had noticed was that many bigger pike were caught by anglers who had very little lure trolling experience, and who were fishing their lures at mid water and above, whilst those who were carefully following the bottom contours with their lures, as we tended to do, were not getting the results one would have expected. It eventually became clear that these trout water pike did not follow the rules as we knew them for most other waters we had fished. Taking this into account we decided to mix up our fishing this time, sometimes trolling our lures near the bottom and at other times running them much higher in the water.

Our first trolling run took us through the deep water along the clubhouse bank, then past the 'hump' at the entrance of Nine Acre Bay, finally skirting the drop off in front of St Stephen's Bay. Running Manns 25+ deep divers, we could flirt with the bottom contours in depths from 20 to over 30 feet by controlling the amount of line we had out and the motor speed. It seemed the right thing to do as it had worked for us on other waters for bigger pike over 20 lb, but once again on Blithfield we ended up catching nothing.

As we turned to start a new run, parallel to the causeway road and bridge that divide the upper and lower sections of the reservoir, we changed to Rapala Super Shads which run at a depth of 10 to 11 feet or thereabouts. It didn't seem to be the right thing to do while the water was still very cold and the

Pic: Matt Hayes

'Weighing exactly 34 lb – it was a monster...'

fish being laden with spawn, but we'd seen it work for other anglers too many times to ignore the fact that the Blithfield pike will come up and have them.

By the time we had almost covered the full length of the causeway and were thinking about making the turn at Watery Lane corner, my rod arched round. It wasn't a ferocious bite and there was no lunging or head shaking, the rod simply pulled round and stayed there! It was almost as though I had hooked a snag, but as we were over more than 20 feet of water I knew that wasn't possible and it would be a big pike!

I was quite surprised that, even after catching a lot of big pike, I could feel a little bit of shaking in my knees, as Blithfield has a reputation for monster pike and there could have been anything up to, and above, record size on the end of my line. It wasn't a great fight, just a lot of wallowing deep beneath the boat, and it didn't take long to bring her to the surface. Firmly focused on making sure she didn't panic and throw out the lure, I looked on in awe at the bulk of the pike as Matt slipped the net under it. It was one of the fattest pike we had ever seen!

We were only 30 yards from the shore, so I asked Matt to get everything ready for weighing and photographing it whilst I held onto the landing net and allowed the breeze to blow us conveniently into the shallow margin. There's no way I can describe how these moments make me feel. It's only a fish for goodness sake, but for some reason the capture of a special fish like this fills me with a very warm, almost smug, glowing feeling. Perhaps it's because it happens so infrequently after putting so much effort into my fishing that it's more of a release of tension than anything else.

The boat touched the shore and Matt jumped onto the bank, taking his camera and weighing gear with him, and he pulled the boat further onto the soggy margin to secure it. I followed swiftly behind, struggling with my heavy prize, being very careful not to let it roll in the net and snag the trailing treble of the lure in the mesh. She was quickly unhooked, and only then did we realise what a superb fish we had caught. Weighing exactly 34 lb – it was a monster but there was no time to admire her, we had to get her back into the water as quickly as possible! As she waddled away across the shallow margin and back towards slightly deeper water, she paused for a while and we made the most of looking at her vividly mottled back of many shades of brown and green, dappled with hints of yellow, silver and orange which blended perfectly with the bottom. We couldn't wait to start trolling again, but for the rest of the two days we didn't have another bite. That's not unusual at Blithfield!

PIC: STEVE MARTIN

'...IT'S BEEN VERY SUCCESSFUL FOR CATCHING OTHER PREDATORS LIKE PERCH...'

Trolling with lures is one of my favourite pike fishing methods. In fact it's a method I love for many other species too and it's been very successful for catching other predators like perch, zander and chub. Further afield I've caught more unusual species when trolling in freshwater like Asp and Walleye, and in the sea I've taken species like Cod, Sea Trout and Striped Bass.

Trolling is very effective because predatory fish naturally chase their prey, and the technique, skilfully performed, puts the bait which represents their food in their 'strike zone' for long periods of time. This is a great advantage in the presentation of the bait. The boat does most of the work, eliminating the need for regular casting which can become very tiring throughout a long day.

In this instance I'm talking about trolling with lures, but trolling can involve pulling any bait behind a boat, whether natural or artificial and whether under engine power or by oar propulsion. This chapter is mainly about trolling under power

A pike of 22lb 13oz taken on a large trolled fly.

with lures, but it's worth mentioning other methods as they are very useful in different circumstances.

Trolling livebaits or deadbaits fished beneath a float, is a tactic I use a lot and is covered in more detail in another chapter. The boat can either be rowed, or propelled by an electric motor which ideally has a variable speed control. Float trolling of fish baits is, I feel, a better option than lure trolling in very cold weather when a more delicate bait presentation is essential to tempt lethargic, torpid pike which hug the bottom. Livebaits usually out fish deadbaits by a considerable margin and I find that float trolling deadbaits is better when the pike are more active and will chase more freely.

Deadbaits can also be trolled without suspending them under a float, trolling them in a similar fashion to lures without any weight on the trace when working the bait shallow, or with suitable weight on the trace to take the deadbait deeper where necessary. The bait can be anything from a small roach to a full herring or mackerel and each has its moment dependant upon the pikes mood. For winter trolling I find smaller baits more successful whereas in the milder months you can have great fun trolling baits as big as you can manage. Unfortunately bigger baits, as always, lead to quite a few missed bites and a few pike dropping off. That's why I prefer to troll smaller deadbaits with this technique. Small baits are also useful for 'wobbling'; another deadly tactic to try at times and there's no need to re rig to do so. If I miss a 'hit' on a trolled deadbait, I'll stop the boat and use the same bait to cast around the area for a few minutes. If I'm getting quite a few 'hits' in a particular area, I'll stop trolling altogether, anchor up or put out a drogue, and wobble the bait for a little longer.

You can also troll using pike flies and I do so quite a lot, not only on my fly rod but at times on a small spinning rod. I have made lots of my own trolling flies of different sizes, some buoyant for surface trolling and others weighted for fishing deeper. Some are also suitable for casting but most are dedicated trolling flies. The best fun I have ever had with flies has been with my 'monster' patterns. They are over a foot long, mainly constructed with Christmas tinsel materials and have up to an ounce of weight built into them. They feature a tandem hook system which consists of a large single hook at the head and a big treble inside the body. They often bring amusement to those that see me using them, but they can laugh as much as they like as I've caught several 20 pounders trolling them and a 28 pounder when casting one!

Trolling can be a very useful way of finding concentrations of pike and prey fish. You can enjoy the trolling and then benefit from using other methods once a good swim has been located. I quite like to take an occasional break from trolling and anchor up to cast lures or wobble deadbaits, or even put out livebaits or static deadbaits. Shutting the engine off will disturb the swim less, especially if it is shallow. I really enjoy the 'take' when a pike slams into a cast lure or deadbait, not to mention the 'follows' you often see if the water is clear and which you don't see when trolling. As far as I'm concerned, trolling is much more than just pulling a lure behind a boat and is part of a very versatile pike catching system.

I'm happy to go trolling for pike at most times of the year, although I do not troll when the water temperature is unsuitably high and catching them could exhaust them. Other species like perch and chub make good alternative trolling targets at these times. I really enjoy trolling for pike in the early spring and the autumn when they will slam into lures with great confidence and aggression. The unprepared could find themselves with a broken line at this time, so it's vital to use one which is strong and reliable and to set the reels clutch to give line as necessary.

Winter trolling with lures is a very different affair and usually requires a much greater degree of precision to tempt pike, but nevertheless can be a deadly tactic on some waters. In winter I often use thinner lines which permit better presentation, especially in deeper water. They create less of a bow in the line which enables the delicate bites associated with cold water to be better detected. Fortunately pike do not fight hard in cold water, and provided snags are not an issue, lighter lines are a better way to go, albeit within sensible limits.

Readers might be surprised if I mention that I do a lot of trolling with lures in the dark. It's something I seem to do more with each passing season and that might just have something to do with how successful it is! Fishing with lures in the dark, whether trolling or casting, has showed me just how effectively pike can detect prey if they need to, regardless of whether they can see it or not. When pike are hunting blindly, as at night, it is commonly accepted that they rely upon on their lateral line sensors to detect vibration from prey, and many lures have inbuilt rattle features which are said to emit vibrations at frequencies that pike will recognise and home in on. This is, of course, useful at any time of the day or night, but night fishing must offer the definitive proof regarding whether this is really true.

'...I WAS SOON CHINNING AN 18 POUNDER ON BOARD.'

'The Crestliner is kept on a trailer at home, and is ready to go anywhere at short notice.'

When testing new lures for Fox International, I was running a prototype XDD (Extra Deep Diving) Raider, closely following the bottom in 13 feet of water in an area where I had picked up a stack of prey fish on the echo sounder. It was a very cold, pitch black, November night and we had already taken two doubles and a couple of smaller fish. Having taken a pike of 25 lb 10 oz for a client when trolling a Raider XDD at night very recently, I had convinced myself that the rattles in these new lures were contributing highly to their success. I wanted to prove it though!

Knowing that there were pike in the swim and that they were active, I thought it would be a good time for experimentation and to try a lure without a rattle to see if it really made a difference. I chose an old favourite, an 18cm Rapala Magnum which is made for high speed trolling, and because of this has a very gentle wobble and a barely discernable vibration - and it does not have a rattle! The first run through the swim with the Magnum saw my rod pull round and I was soon chinning an 18 pounder on board! Once again I had proved to myself that it's wise to question everything I think I know and not become too entrenched in dogmatic thinking. I'm beginning to think that rattles are not always necessary as pike are fully aware of our lures when in feeding mood. I think rattles could play a part when trying to attract pike from greater distances or those which are resting, possibly deep in weed beds. I'm always aware that the hooks on lures clatter about quite a lot too, which might help attract pike at any time.

When trolling lures, we must run them past many pike which do not attack them. If you troll three or four miles of river without a 'hit' where there are plenty of prey fish on the sounder, this must almost certainly be so! When I identify such a situation, I know I need to run my lures more precisely, varying my approach until something works to tempt a few into making an attack. What I have said elsewhere about feeding and digesting periods and the effects of prevailing conditions still applies, and I accept that sometimes I am trolling for uninterested pike and will have to work that much harder to catch something. Trolling can seem very easy when you are catching, but I think we pass over so many pike that we do not catch, and with that being the case, a skilled troller can potentially catch many more pike than the casual troller who puts little thought into it, simply covering as much water as possible in the hope that something will grab his lure.

After several decades of trolling on all sorts of waters, and for many different species, I think that it is a method which requires as much skill as any other, although I often hear remarks suggesting the opposite. Trolling can be very easy at times, it's true, but then again so can any other method. It usually requires a considerable degree of application, and when carried out seriously with the right equipment can be extremely challenging. Apart from the pike you catch, covering large expanses of water can arm you with considerable knowledge about the nature of the venue and the location of its pike and prey, which will eventually be useful if you fish there again and regardless of the method you choose. It is vital then, to get the boat prepared efficiently and have the right equipment on board.

Pic: Paul Reeves

'The petrol engine gets me to places quickly whilst the electric can then allow me to troll quietly.'

At the time of writing I have four boats, all of which I use for trolling. Two of them are 'every day' small rowing type boats which can be used with an electric motor, and I use these on small waters where lure trolling is a good option. Most of my trolling though is on bigger waters where I use either my 14 foot Crestliner Sportsman or my 16 foot Orkney Fastliner. The Crestliner is kept on a trailer at home, and is ready to go anywhere at short notice. The Orkney is currently kept in a boat yard on a local river, but can be retrieved at any time for use elsewhere. This gives me plenty of options to take a suitable boat wherever I want to troll.

The bigger boats can be used with a petrol or electric engine, and this is a decision based upon where I am fishing. If necessary I can have both a petrol and electric engine on these bigger boats. The petrol engine gets me to places quickly whilst the electric can then allow me to troll quietly. In practice, on most of the venues I fish, the petrol engine alone is suitable. It might sound rather grand having so many boats and engines, but the whole lot is probably not worth much more than a decent second hand car, and the collection has been built up over 20 years or more.

Kitting the boats out can be as elaborate or as basic as you want it to be. My boats also have to be used for all sorts of other fishing ranging from fly fishing for trout to float fishing for tench, and are not dedicated lure fishing boats as such, but do have the basic essentials of echo sounders and trolling rod rests. My Orkney boat is also set up with a GPS (global positioning system) to accurately pinpoint my position and a downrigger which is useful for trolling small lures at greater depths than they would troll on a 'flat line'. Other than the tackle and lures, I'm ready to go trolling!

The rods and reels are the same ones that I use for bank fishing, some being fixed spool set ups and others multiplier set ups. I have built up a big collection of rods and reels and have my own preferences of where and when to use different types. I use stiffer rods for trolling (or casting) bigger lures, high resistance crank baits and jerk baits, and these are better matched to multiplier reels. On the rest of my lure rods I prefer fixed spool reels, and the smaller the better to minimise weight. A recent addition to my trolling tackle is a reel with a 'line counter' facility. Knowing exactly how much line I have out takes a lot of the guesswork out of the fishing, and once you get familiar with it, it enables accurate repetition at times when trolling at a precise depth is important. All of my reels are loaded with braided main line for the benefit of its minimal stretch properties which makes bite indication and setting hooks really positive.

I prefer to troll one lure at a time, especially in winter when precision is required and I am making regular adjustments to closely follow bottom contours with the lure. When trolling bigger waters, with the lures running well off bottom and minimal chances of snagging up, I don't mind fishing a second rod which I set in a locking rod holder. If 'hits' are few and far between this helps in the search as I can work two different lures to compare different options such as colours and running depths.

Before going any further, it's worth looking at the types of lures I troll. In actual fact, it's hard to think of any lures that I don't troll. Where and when appropriate I troll lures at all depths ranging from those that splash across the surface to those that scrape the bottom. Some lures are designed specifically for trolling such as those with large, shallow angled diving vanes. Such lures usually create considerable resistance during a retrieve and they would be very hard work to crank in by hand. There would not be enough time to get them to dive to their working depth on a cast retrieve, so trolling them is by far the best and, sometimes, the only option and usually what they are designed for.

Trolling surface lures can be great fun. You might be surprised that pike are not usually put off by the boat's engine, and I rarely troll my surface lures too far behind the boat. It's very exciting watching the lure making its wake across the surface and then to witness just how far a pike will open its jaws to engulf it! Where boats are a regular feature on a waterway, pike seem even bolder, and we had great fun trolling along the smaller shallow drains of the Middle Level system behind our 22 foot cruiser when we owned one. The engine's wake and the boat's disturbance were considerable, but pike would regularly snatch surface lures even in just three or four feet of water.

At the other depth extremity I will troll jig style lures, bouncing the bottom with them, and by working in conjunction with the echo sounder I can get them to very accurately follow bottom contours. In the very coldest water conditions, when pike stay close to the bottom, this has worked very well because the lure can be put right on the pike's nose. Jigs often need to be worked at a snail's pace, and even worked 'on the spot' at times. When using a variable speed electric trolling motor this can easily be achieved, provided there is not too much wind. This has worked very well in coloured water and at night too when, ostensibly, I am fishing for zander, but good numbers of pike are regularly caught as well.

In between the surface and the bottom, there are so many different lures that can be trolled at various depths, and the skill is in determining which ones to use. This can only be done with any accuracy after considerable experimentation, and you can eventually get to know what works on the waters that you fish regularly. This knowledge gives you a good starting point and a degree of confidence when moving on to tackle new waters. A list of the names of the mid water lures I troll would be very lengthy and really of no benefit as they are related to the waters I fish, but include crank baits designed to run at different depths, spoons, spinners, spinnerbaits, soft plastics, swim baits and even jerk baits. Rather than listing my favourite lures (you will eventually have your own) I think it would be more useful to describe how I decide which lures to use, or at least which ones to try. I ask myself five questions when selecting a lure, whether for trolling or for casting.

1 – What depth do I want it to work at?

This is the most important consideration for me. It is vital for the lure to be fishing in the 'feeding zone'; above it or below it and your chances of catching are reduced or even eliminated altogether. Fortunately in mild weather, the 'feeding zone' is quite wide and running depth accuracy may not be so critical. In cold water conditions however, the 'feeding zone' will be narrowed dramatically and more precision is required. In typical lowland waters it can be vital for the lure to be hugging the bottom contours at this time when pike frequently refuse to rise very far from where they are lying. In deeper waters where pike may be 'suspended', it is possible to be trolling too deep and below them. It is important to get to grips with the vital point about lure depth. Get it wrong and everything else is irrelevant!

'...YOU CAN EVENTUALLY GET TO KNOW WHAT WORKS ON THE WATERS THAT YOU FISH REGULARLY.' THIS COLOURFUL RIVER PIKE WOLFED DOWN A RAIDER XDD.

2 – How fast should I retrieve it?

Speed can be important but I put it secondary to depth. There will be an optimum speed range to suit the conditions, but for most of the time unless it is really cold, the range can be quite wide, and when in the mood pike will often take lures trolled at surprisingly high speeds. When it is colder though, the speed range is narrowed and you often need to get it spot on, usually needing to troll very slowly. The trolling speed can be varied by controlling the engine speed although, due to the effects of wind and current, this isn't always as easy as it seems when trying to troll very slowly. A useful trick is to drag a drogue along the side of the boat, attached by a short rope to a rowlock, creating resistance and slowing the boat down. It is very useful to know your actual trolling speed and ideally you should use an echo sounder that has a built in speed gauge which works in conjunction with a suitable transducer mounted under the water. This enables you to accurately repeat a successful trolling speed when it is critical. Varying the trolling speed is important until you find what they want on the day.

3 – What colour should I use?

This is something I never like to 'second guess' as I am often very wrong! What I do know is that a particular colour can often be deadly and can out fish every other lure I have with me, and that's the one I'm always looking for! It helps enormously to have lures in a wide range of colours but this can obviously become expensive. To help you to decide which ones to buy initially, many lure anglers use a rule of thumb which suggests that natural colours often work better in clear water and brighter colours work well in coloured or stained water. In doing so, we are assuming that pike take lures primarily by sight, but after catching so many in the pitch black of night I think that other senses are at work as well and colour isn't always the prime factor.

4 – What sort of action does it need?

This is another contentious issue. I used to favour a 'wild' action in milder conditions and a more delicate action in cold water, but experience now tells me that you need to have an open mind about this. I am increasingly beginning to think that lures with a wild action can sometimes deter pike from taking them and I am very careful how I use them, but you can't neglect trying them. Jerk baits, especially those with a subtle gliding action, can produce devastating results when trolled, just as they can when cast, and are well worth trolling in clear water.

'...I INCLUDE CRANK BAITS DESIGNED TO RUN AT DIFFERENT DEPTHS...'

Whatever type of lure you are using, its action can be modified to some extent by working it with the rod. Sometimes a 'ripping' action, pulling the rod against the lure, can provoke a following pike to take the lure as it speeds up momentarily and its action changes. This works particularly well with spoons. Lures with diving vanes will suddenly run deeper as you do this and that might make all the difference. Dropping the lure back, by slackening off the pressure on the rod for a few seconds, can also make a 'following' pike grab it. For example, jigs will often be taken as they fall deeper when dropped back. Crank baits can be taken as they rise when slowed down. It could be that doing something different is enough to create a 'trigger' which provokes an attack. There are no hard and fast rules about this, and if there was ever an area where trial and error had a lot of mileage, this is it. When trolling, I am never surprised when a take comes immediately after doing something different to the lure with rod action.

Trolling with other anglers in the boat can be very useful as you can compare each other's results. Such comparisons often highlight the fact that success is not entirely down to choice of lure and may be affected by the way that the angler is working it. When using similar lures, I have many times known one angler to be catching whilst the other one isn't. Most times the successful angler doesn't know or realise what he is doing differently as the difference can be quite subtle. It could be due to the way the lure is being worked, but it is also worth examining very closely the difference in tackle and how it's used. It's vitally important to remember, for example, that thinner lines run deeper, and when trolling, the more line you have out the deeper the lure will run. The weight or length of the wire trace can have a surprising effect on the way a lure is presented, especially with smaller lures. These details can result in differences in presentation, and I am always thinking about this and never carry on blindly doing the same thing when I am not catching.

'I EXPECT TO CATCH IF I HAVE GOT IT RIGHT'

5 – What size would be best?

As when bait fishing, to make life as uncomplicated as possible I mostly use lures of a manageable size, normally being between five and seven inches in length. There will be plenty of times when pike will take a considerably bigger lure and times when a much smaller lure is needed, but other than in specialised situations I rarely find that I need to veer away from my preferred size range. Where pike are feeding predominantly on large prey, it's clearly a good idea to use much bigger lures such as Bull Dawgs and there is logic in using them on very big waters where the nearest pike might be 50 yards or more away from your lure, giving them a better chance of seeing it and enabling them to sense the greater disturbance it will be creating.

When trolling in Finland with professional boatmen, they worked upon this principal and trolled with lures which were typically 15 to 20 inches long, and it was most apparent from the battered appearance of their lures that they had seen a lot of attention. The heavy weights used on their downrigger set ups were also well chewed up from being attacked by pike in deep water. A similar thing had also happened to the large metal 'flashers', which they rig, either singly or in tandem, on lines trailed behind the boat to attract salmon to their lures! There is so much we still have to learn, but it is clear that fishing for pike demands that we keep a very open mind and try and match what we are doing to the prevailing situation. I have my preferred size range for lures, but occasionally try larger or smaller sizes when attempting to improve my catch rate or when struggling to catch at all, finding occasionally such a change to be necessary.

If I have considered all the points I've mentioned and are still not catching pike, it's difficult to know whether it's because I am doing something wrong or simply that I have not passed over any feeding pike yet. The only time this really concerns me is when the echo sounder tells me I am going over prey fish and not catching. With a very good likelihood of pike being with or near to them, I expect to catch if I have got it right. Provided that continual trolling over them does not spook them, I make changes until I catch one and it's very satisfying to work it out. I'll admit that there have been plenty of times when I've given up with the lures, but a livebait or deadbait has done the business! Every method has its day, and that's why my boat is nearly always set up for a multi method approach.

'...AND VERY QUICKLY CAUGHT FOUR PIKE TO 24 LB 10 OZ ON DEADBAITS...'

I particularly enjoy 'plotting up' in a swim and using livebaits and deadbaits after locating pike or shoals of prey fish by trolling lures. I get the best of both worlds, and when the runs dry up with fish baits, I can move on and troll lures again until I find another good area to stop in. Anchoring in such swims to bait fish gives me time to relax and make a hot drink or a snack. The fishing isn't all about 'the catch' and these simple things give me great pleasure. There's nothing I can imagine better than sitting quietly and drinking coffee, watching my floats in a swim that I suspect holds some good pike and knowing that there's plenty more swims to be explored when I have finished in this one. The fish baits will often catch pike which have not taken the trolled lures, and before moving to another area I always troll the swim again after it has had a rest or the bait fishing has stirred the pike up.

Trolling on bigger waters can see the boat taking a random course, which is not an efficient way of covering the water. When faced with this situation, I make good use of my GPS and troll in a grid fashion, keeping a close eye on my course shown on the screen to ensure that I take parallel runs and do not cross over previously trolled water. On the GPS I can mark places where I have caught fish or where I have missed bites with the intention of building up a picture of where there are congregations of pike. Without the GPS you may think you know where you have trolled, but believe me you will be well out in your assumptions unless there are positive markers in the water such as buoys or rocks. Once I have plotted the positions of enough pike, and if the GPS indicates that they are tightly packed, I will anchor up in the middle of them and fish baits around the boat. On my first visit to Llangorse lake in South Wales and knowing next to nothing about the water, I grid trolled for the morning using my GPS and pinpointed an area right out in the middle of the lake where I'd missed a few bites and caught a couple of single figure fish. I anchored up appropriately to the GPS co-ordinates and very quickly caught four pike to 24 lb 10 oz on deadbaits. I dropped back into the same swim the next morning and took five more on deadbaits to 23 lb 8 oz. The system works!

On vast Scandinavian waters, Matt Hayes and I have used GPS effectively to track down good trolling runs for pike and big trout, several miles away from our launching point. We have been able to quickly go back to them later and start catching straight away instead of wasting valuable time searching for them again. GPS is a great piece of equipment, although the better ones are very expensive.

How does a pike take a lure?

A lot of what we conclude about how pike react to lures is only supposition as we rarely see their response, and our observations are mostly based upon seeing pike at close range when they follow or grab our lures after casting them. To try and learn more, I have tried trolling lures in clear water as close to the boat as possible to watch pike in action and to try and get a better look at how they approach and grab lures. This has wasted a lot of fishing time but has been great fun and quite an eye opener. You often hear statements that pike take lures in a particular way, but from my observations you can never be sure how the next pike will react.

The main thing I have noticed is that the attacks can vary so much in terms of the angle they approach them from and the amount of effort they put in. Sometimes they take small lures so quickly, it's hard to see what has happened as the lure disappears in a flash. On another occasion though, a lure of similar size might be stalked by a pike only inches away from it and then it will nip gently onto it, holding it on the end of its snout without making much effort to swallow it. Lures near to the surface are often engulfed with the pike's mouth open so wide you can see its gill rakers and throat entrance.

Bigger lures are usually clamped onto from the side, but at other times inhaled well into the mouth and taken right back if they are made from a soft material like rubber. Large flies are inhaled in the same way. It almost seems as though the pike knows how hard or how soft its target is and reacts accordingly, making split second decisions. More regular sized lures can be attacked in many ways, even on the same day. They can be attacked from either side, from underneath or from the back. Sometimes the pike will nudge it first before taking it and at other times it will run underneath or to the side of it, seeming to be getting a better look at it, and then tracking around it and grabbing it from another angle. So, how does a pike take a lure – any way it feels like!

'... I SETTLED FOR A PICTURE OF HER FAT FRAME FILLING THE BOTTOM OF THE BOAT...'

CHAPTER 15

Getting To The Bottom

It was a warm May evening as I slowly trolled the 'drop off' in my small aluminium boat, inched along by my electric motor. I wasn't trolling livebaits as you might think, even though the gentle pace I was travelling at would have been highly suitable. I was trolling a soft plastic lure known as a 'jig', which is ideal for trolling extremely slowly or even 'bouncing' on the spot when stopping the boat for a while. It's a great presentation for lethargic pike, but can be effective at almost any time.

I wasn't expecting the pike to be lethargic in May, quite the contrary, but I needed to go slowly to feel my way over the weedy bottom, gently teasing the jig away from it when it I felt it touch. The single upturned hook rarely snags, but when it does a quick snap of the rod tip usually clears it, although I usually check it for weed every now and again anyway, it takes but a second or two. Most times I can tell when the jig is running true. It's hard to explain, but when its tail is rippling perfectly it transmits a feeling of 'electricity' through the braided line and into my finger on the spool lip.

The water I was working drops away from a seven foot deep plateau into 15 feet, and is a great area to fish for pike that wait for the prey fish to come over the ledge from the shallows as darkness approaches.

A fierce tug at the jig saw me strike instinctively and the seven foot rod was buckled into an alarming curve. I quickly disengaged the anti reverse lever to allow the fish to take line while I 'back wound' the reel. For fish like pike which don't often fight too frantically, I prefer to back wind rather than use the clutch as doing so allows me to have the clutch set really tight to get a good firm strike.

A great fight followed but the tackle was well up to it. She was bundled into the landing net with a lot of swirling and splashing, but not before my little boat had been turned around and around as I guided the pike to safety. I heaved her on board, with the boat rocking and rolling all over the place and disturbing the calmness of the lake. I then quite easily removed the six inch shad jig from the corner of her huge jaws. It was a favourite pearl and chartreuse Action Shad. One of the great benefits of jigs is that they 'hook up' well, but the single hook is usually so easy to remove with minimal danger to pike or angler. Quite frequently I can remove the jig without the need for forceps.

The jig was already battle scarred and ripped, but it's quite easy to repair them with a hot blade or glue. I'd have to repair this one as it was my last in that colour, but that job would have to wait till I got home as the pike needed weighing and returning quickly.

In other chapters you will read of me taking fish to shore or finding someone to take a few pictures, but I only do so if I know the pike will be safe. In the water temperatures of May this is not a good idea, so I settled for a picture of her fat frame filling the bottom of the boat, but feeling happy that she would be back in the water as soon as possible. A 26 pounder on a jig is a fantastic catch and I would have loved a better photo to remember it, but her welfare had to come first.

How fishing with jigs escaped the attention of British anglers for so long is quite unbelievable. Although jigs have been widely available in other countries for several decades, it has only been in the last ten years or so that British anglers have 'discovered' them. At least they have made up for lost time by using them extensively, and with devastating results. Indeed, my heaviest pike, which weighed 35 lbs 2 oz, was caught using a six inch long, twin tail jig, something I would have been quite surprised about at one time and classed as a fluke.

For the uninitiated, a jig is basically a soft rubber lure, usually fish shaped, and which owes its enticing movement to its flexible body and weighted head. This weight may be permanently built into the lure or may come in the form of a separate 'jig head', which is usually moulded from lead around the hook shank. Jigs come in many variations, and amongst the other styles that I commonly use are 'twin tails', which resemble frogs and also various types of 'worms'. They all come in a very wide range of sizes, from miniscule to massive. These extremes are not designed with pike in mind, although some of them can be pressed into service. The ones I use mostly are intended for pike and are typically from four to eight inches in length. Many have interchangeable heads and bodies resulting in a very versatile system. For example, it is possible to fit a lightweight jig head to a large body for fishing a large bait in shallow water, and a heavyweight jig head to a small body for fishing a small bait in deep water, and every other permutation in between by using the different sizes of heads and bodies available.

The weight gives the angler a great deal of control and 'feel' of the jig's flexible movements, and by working the jig in various ways, a good angler can make such lures really 'sing and dance'. They can be either 'bounced' along the bottom or, alternatively, retrieved at various depths, and both of these presentations have their uses; certainly in my own fishing. The range of their usefulness is so great that I rarely go pike fishing without at least a few in my tackle box, and whilst they have been devastatingly effective for pike, they have been even more so for zander and perch.

Jigs can also be trolled as I have previously mentioned, and when used in this way, in conjunction with an echo sounder, you have a deadly fish catching combination, using control of line length and boat speed to precisely follow the bottom contours. Small depth variations of a foot or so can be catered for by lifting or lowering the rod tip, but more dramatic changes in depth need a quicker reaction. Sudden depth increases require the angler to open the bale arm of the reel to let more line out under a controlled descent, whilst entering shallower water requires a quick retrieval of line. The exact amount of line that is let out is arrived at by feeling for the bottom, and is much better performed on a hard bottom than one which is muddy or weedy. The guy who is driving the boat always has a big advantage by being closer to the echo sounder, and is able to react more quickly to contour changes than his boat partner. The angler in the front of the boat will have an advantage too because his jig will enter the swim first, and pike will see it first! A good boatman will continually keep his partner informed of depth changes, and like most boat fishing, it is all about team work!

'PIKE TEND TO HOLD ONTO JIGS FOR QUITE A WHILE BEFORE REALISING SOMETHING IS WRONG.'

I have reaped the benefits of jig fishing for more than a decade, and have done so very successfully on waters ranging from small rivers to huge still waters, but jig fishing is not without its problems. Where they are being used to bounce along the bottom, occasional snagging is inevitable. It can be a problem anywhere, although some waters will be worse than others, notably rivers. After a while you will discover how to feel the jig over the bottom terrain, recognising the difference between a snag and a bite. Pike tend to hold onto jigs for quite a while before realising something is wrong, when compared to a hard bait. For this reason I don't strike immediately, but 'move' with the pike for a second or two until I am absolutely sure it is a pike and I have not hooked a snag. Most times it is obvious, but once in a while this 'delay technique' saves you from driving the hook into a piece of sunken wood and getting snagged. By using a braid line of a suitable breaking strain, you can normally pull the jig free before the line breaks, even if this means bending the hook slightly. When using my technique of 'going with the bite', the realisation that it is a snag usually prevents me from pulling hard into it, and it is then usually a matter of shaking the rod tip and the jig will come free.

'...I WOULD SYSTEMATICALLY EMPTY SWIMS...'

When fishing jigs in very snaggy waters, like the middle Great Ouse or the Severn for example, trying to get them free can be a very regular occurrence. It's only when jigging that you realise just how many sunken branches there are littering the bottom of some sections of our rivers. It's not all bad news though, as snags are features which often mean that pike will be close by! When boat fishing, if I can't 'shake' the jig free, I have a small grapple on a rope which usually pulls the snag up from the bottom or clears the jig from it. It's usually a tree branch and often a lot smaller than it first seems.

I obtained my first jigs over 20 years ago, and I was not alone in totally missing the potential they offered for UK pike fishing. We thought that they were an American gimmick, used for walleye and bass species. They were certainly used in this way, but they were definitely no gimmick! They were without doubt, a very effective lure, capable of out fishing all other types of lures in many situations.

My big initial mistake was in discarding the jig heads, and rigging up their rubber bodies on trebles. I caught lots of pike this way, but in all honesty, this approach offered no benefit over other lures like spoons or from wobbled deadbaits. It's easy to overlook a better option when you are catching well with your existing methods, and this seems to be why it took so long for the penny to drop, although lack of availability of jigs was holding back progress too.

In the nineties I caught quite a few pike with jigs, but at the time it was just another method, and with other types of new lures coming to our attention on a regular basis through the efforts of importers like Andy Lush, I guess I just wasn't aware enough to realise what jigs were capable of. Other lures seemed more exciting, like spinnerbaits and jerk baits, and most of us were just not seeing the possibilities before us.

This all changed during a zander session, around the turn of the century, when I got bored with watching motionless deadbait floats on the Middle Level drain when fishing with two friends. With nine deadbaits out between us, we hadn't had a single run all day, but that wasn't unusual though for that venue. I got fed up, reeled in, and went off with a lure rod and a landing net. To save a long story, in the next hour I caught a zander, a pike and three perch over two pounds – all on a four inch Action Shad jig in pearl/black colour. The fact that they were not big fish didn't really impress anybody, but so fascinating did I find the fishing that I went back two days later and was rewarded with five pike to 10 lbs, three more good perch and four zander to 13 lb 6 oz! All came to the same four inch Action Shad!

Around the same time, my fishing buddy Matt Hayes was having great success with the very same jig patterns in the West Midland rivers, and our endless telephone conversations only served to fire us up more and more into exploring this fascinating and productive method. Suddenly, we were into 'jig'

'After catching pike to over 19 lb on it, I knew I had to step up the tackle...'

mode and took the jigs everywhere, drains, rivers and stillwaters, and as our understanding and enthusiasm grew, we started catching at a rate that staggered us. The method was mobile, which suited us, and was often instant. Just a couple of casts around a feature like a bridge support, a moored boat or a sunken bush, would be enough to tell us if there were any 'takers' at home. Friends soon came on board when they realised what we were catching, and the whole business suddenly escalated out of hand.

At first we kept our success with jigs close to our chests, but I'm sure that others must have been quietly reaping the rewards too. To keep it under wraps for as long as possible on my local river, I would conceal the fact that I was jigging, and would try to give the impression that I was deadbaiting by casting a couple of floats around my swim. Very often there weren't even any baits on the hooks! When other anglers were well out of sight, out came the jigs and jig rods. The first rods I tried were far too flimsy, but with specialised jig rods not being easily available in the UK at that time, I had to start somewhere. Great fun was had with a little five and a half foot long Shimano Sedona rod which I'd picked up when filming in Sweden. It was only made for casting lures of two to seven grams, and I was well under gunned. After catching pike to over 19 lb on it, I knew I had to step up the tackle as the tip was literally at the reel when playing pike of even half that size! Without the other anglers knowing what we were doing, my partners and I would systematically empty swims, putting 53 fish in our nets on one occasion in a haul which included pike, perch and zander! We soon realised how jigs can be incredibly effective on waters where predators hadn't seen them before. This was also a time when UK anglers were 'discovering' that zander could be caught on lures; something thought to be difficult just a few years previously. Nowadays, lure fishing is the first tactic that many consider when fishing for zander and jigs are often their first choice.

A FEW OF MY OLD FAVOURITES. THE TWIN TAIL CAUGHT MY 35-POUNDER!

Had Matt and I realised what was going to happen when we showed jig fishing in one of our TV shows, we could have been rich men today if we had capitalised on how the sales of jigs were going to go through the roof. Once again, we missed the boat by neglecting a business opportunity and going fishing! Others were much shrewder though, and all of a sudden the market was awash with jigs of every description.

I think that many 'big pike' anglers dismissed jig fishing as a 'small fish' method at first. To be fair it is not a selective method and seems to produce fish of all sizes, and on most waters small fish tend to outnumber the big ones. Indeed, of the vast numbers of pike I had caught on jigs at that stage in the proceedings, most were small, although there had been a couple of 'twenties' amongst them. Catching small pike has never bothered me, and the sheer joy that this style of fishing brings only serves to reinforce my philosophy of enjoying the fishing above everything else. I don't mind catching loads of small pike, especially if I understand that this is all the venue contains. Catching lots of small pike helps me to perfect my techniques and improves my confidence with a method, and the only difference between catching large and small pike is usually the venue. I'm convinced that all methods can produce bigger pike when the angler is fishing them sensibly at the right venue.

My learning days with jigs were on the fen drains and rivers, catching hundreds of pike, perch and zander, but as I took them successfully to other rivers and then gravel pits and reservoirs, I knew this was a very special and effective method I now had at my disposal. Little did I know that an insignificant looking jig would soon be going to catch me a new personal best pike!

My big day came in November 2001 when I was fishing Blithfield Reservoir in Staffordshire as a member of the recently formed pike syndicate. It started badly for me as I had a seriously bad stom-

'JAMES GARDNER UNHOOKED IT AND WEIGHED IT, AND PRONOUNCED I HAD JUST CAUGHT A PIKE WEIGHING 35 LB 2 OZ...'

ach problem and almost didn't fish. As dawn broke, I joined the other dozen or so hopefuls who had each claimed about five yards of bank space in the famous Watery Lane corner. Ever since pike had been fished for in the reservoir, going back to the early pike trials of the eighties, this was the prime 'hot spot'. If a big pike was going to be caught, it would probably come from this area!

We started fishing in the grim pre dawn gloom, and most of the anglers who crammed into the 'hot' area, were well aware that it was not going to be easy. They also knew that the swim could produce, for some lucky devil, the fish of their dreams. Lure fishing was the only method allowed, and with the water being really murky and visibility being almost at zero, I decided that fishing with a jig would be a good opening option. I had no doubt that pike could detect lures in coloured water, and was also aware that at dawn they could be active. I was overflowing with confidence with jigs as I had been really bagging up with them for some time on my local waters, and started casting and searching the water in front of me.

Trout water pike spend a lot of time lying on the bottom and then strike higher in the water when in the mood to do so. My plan was to start by fishing for any inactive pike lying on the bottom with my jig, but watching the other anglers around me and seeing how the pike responded to their jerkbaits, spinnerbaits and crank baits being fished higher in the water. I was doing something totally different to everyone else and I knew it was a gamble.

By the time we had been fishing for two hours, no pike had been caught. Suddenly the intense concentration of the eager anglers was broken as one of them hooked into a fish on a crank bait worked at mid water. When everyone around me rushed down to see it being landed, I saw a chance to cover fresh water with my jigs as the others left their fishing positions. Watery Lane corner is a fantastic 'hot spot', but with anglers crammed in there to fish it, you each have no more than a couple of yards either side of you to cover. With everyone else now out of the way, I grabbed the chance to cast into the adjacent swims! As everyone was returning to recommence fishing, I felt the tiniest tap on my rod tip which, unless I hadn't been jig fishing extensively for the last couple of months, I might easily have overlooked and not struck into it. I did strike, and set the hook into what felt like a brick wall!

There were some 'big names' there on that day, including top lure angler Derek Macdonald who had been fishing close to me. He was returning to his swim having just videoed a 20 pounder further down the bank. I can distinctively remember turning to Derek and saying 'don't put that camera away yet mate', and then immediately focused on playing what was now clearly a very heavy pike. The fight was not dramatic, just dogged and powerful, and we never had a glimpse of the fish until it came up into the shallow flooded grass margin. Due to the coloured water, all we could see in the grass stems was the back of a pike that was so wide, someone, I think it was Nev Fickling, remarked that I was just about to land a personal best. At this point it surged away into the deep water, and I knew that this was not a time to be distracted by the friendly banter of the crowd that had gathered around me. I focused intensely on ensuring that I kept in touch with the pike, and didn't give it a chance to shake its head and throw the jig out.

When it was safely in the net I must admit that, had I been on my own, I would have held it in the net in the margin for five minutes or so to gather my thoughts and overcome my disbelief of the monster I had just landed. The Blithfield lads are a great bunch, and seeing the state I was in they literally took over to deal with the fish. James Gardner unhooked it and weighed it, and pronounced I had just caught a pike weighing 35 lb 2 oz, to which I replied that it had beaten my previous best by 11 ounces!

The pike was swiftly returned, but everything went so quickly and smoothly that I didn't really have a chance to take a good look at it in close detail. These trout water pike can be very fragile and require minimal handling and a quick return. It must be said that the one I had just caught was not at all fat, it was just a very big fish. Fortunately Derek filmed the whole of the proceedings, and from the awesome footage it is clear that the group of experienced anglers around me had ensured that it was only out of the water for a couple of minutes. My bad stomach problem was not helped by the excitement and I had to retire to my camper van and shut my eyes for a while, and even though I was in agony, I was still overcome with a warm, smug, glow of contentment which went some way to easing the pain.

From then on I expected to bag up with jigs at Blithfield, but that did not happen. It's not the sort of water that you just turn up at and bag up with any method, but jigs did produce some more pike for me, including some taken vertical fishing. There were no more of any great size, but other anglers using jigs did take personal bests. Blithfield has to be tackled with a variety of methods rather than sticking to one approach and I think it is wise to use them all as and when appropriate, and I later took 20 lb plus pike on other methods including spoons, crank baits and flies.

Shortly afterwards, Fox International, my major tackle sponsor, introduced the world to their Chubby Shad range of jigs, and I can honestly say that they have been one of my favourite and most productive lures ever since. I have lost track of the large numbers of predators I've caught on them, and in particular large zander. Having to test them and promote them through the media has been a 'labour of love'. I have caught hundreds of fish with the Chubby Shads, and on the drains and rivers I fish locally, the five inch version has been the most reliable. If I had to pick just one colour, it would be the green mackerel. I have used the Chubby Shads to take some mammoth hauls. They have been fantastic lures at night and work extremely well in the filthiest coloured water imaginable. Their vibration must be perfectly tuned to the predator's senses. They are so easy to fish

'I HAVE USED THE CHUBBY SHADS TO TAKE SOME MAMMOTH HAULS.'

too. A straight retrieve often works well, as does an erratic jigging motion. When straight retrieving, I like to keep in close contact with the bottom, by halting the jig's movement occasionally, then feeling it back until it touches down, before swiftly getting it moving again.

As with all lures, the way jigs are worked can be vital to their success and you must always be totally focused on what you are doing, needing to concentrate all of the time. It's a fact that some anglers can get it right, and others just can't. I've been out with anglers who just cannot catch on jigs, whereas others I have given the same set up to seem to get it right straight away. I often hear of anglers who don't rate jigs very highly and maybe this is the reason why. It really is a matter of 'feel' and you need to practice to get confidence, and believe me, I've had a lot of practice! Suddenly, whatever it is that you have to do to make them work is done by second nature.

Having a purpose designed jig rod helps keep contact with the jig and gives the sensitivity required to feel for the bites. Fortunately, Fox asked me at the same time to develop a range of jigging rods, and I was soon using rods which were built to suit my own requirements and which sold very well.

'...WHEN THE STINGER HOOK IS TAKEN INTO THE THROAT ENTRANCE...'

I've already mentioned that these lures don't have to be 'jigged' and can be straight retrieved by using the weight in the head to keep them down at the right working depth. This has worked very well for me for pike in big clear waters like Chew Valley, and when the reservoir water was very clear on one of my visits, the Red Head pattern of the seven inch Action Shad was a real winner. It does pay to have a good colour range to work through, as you will often find one particular colour that works better than another.

There are lots of little tricks with jigs which can give you an edge as with any style of lure fishing. One that stands out in my jig fishing is a technique I use on every retrieve, and the pike fall for it time and time again. It's difficult to describe, but in essence, at any point in the retrieve I will stop winding and simultaneously raise the rod tip, gently easing the jig higher in the water by a couple of feet or so. Then, on a tight line, 'feel' the jig back down, and then start retrieving again as soon as I contact the bottom. It is on the 'pause and drop back' that the pike makes its move and attacks the jig. I will also keep the jig in the water under the rod tip at the end of a retrieve for 20 seconds or so using a similar ,lift and drop back' technique in a vertical mode. It's been very rewarding!

Suspending jigs under a drifting boat at various mid water levels is a good way of systematically exploring deep water venues, a lesson I first really appreciated when summer fishing on the Baltic Sea where success at a particular time of year depends upon finding the depth in which pike are lying. A suspended jig can be fished on a 'dead' rod, laid across the boat, while you cast lures on another rod; a technique used widely by continental competition anglers. Jigs can also be fished vertically from bridges and jetties, and these places can be real hot areas for pike if they have not been hammered by other anglers. When I've got time on my hands, I'll often have a day 'bridging', moving from one bridge to another and fishing each one for about 20 minutes with vertically fished jigs. That's usually all the time you need as you usually get fish straight away if you are going to get them at all. Such techniques also work well for perch and have scored big successes for me at Grafham and Chew Reservoirs. The biggest perch I have ever seen in my life took my jig in extremely coloured water on a February day at Chew, but sadly it dropped off. You can't win them all!

Continental anglers often incorporate an extra hook on the tail of their jigs, which is usually a small treble, attached through a wire link which is clipped to the eye of the hook. Known as a 'stinger', it is useful for times when pike (and zander) are annoyingly 'coming short' and just 'nipping' the tail, as they would a live fish in order to disable it. It can be very frustrating when this behaviour results in the tail being completely nipped off. Adding a 'stinger' undoubtedly leads to a lot more fish being hooked, but I have found that this can sometimes lead to a damaged fish when the jig is taken well back into its throat. It's more of a problem with zander, and when the stinger hook is taken into the throat entrance it can often be difficult to remove, frequently causing bleeding and turning me against the general use of them. When pike and zander are feeding voraciously, I will usually refrain from using a stinger even though it might cost me a fish or two. On the other hand, in the colder winter months when predators are less likely to swallow jigs, I will consider using one. When using a stinger hook, you should also be aware that snagging on bottom debris can become a much bigger problem.

THE JIGS SCORED WELL ON ALL THE TROUT RESERVOIRS.

I once used vertical jig fishing to solve a very unusual and difficult fishing problem. I'd been planning to fish a section of the Sixteen Foot drain, only to find it totally covered in duckweed from bank to bank. Duckweed can be very annoying because it can completely cover the surface of a venue, making it almost impossible to fish if it gets too thick. Many of the fenland drains are like this in the summer months and often remain so well into the autumn. The section of drain I was interested in was completely covered in the stuff, and had been abandoned by other pike anglers. It then occurred to me to put one of my boats on the drain, position it over a known reliable area for predators and try lowering a jig through it. It was really hard going, pushing the boat through surface weed which continually accumulated around the hull and propeller. Once in position, there was no need to anchor as the duckweed was so dense it held the boat stationary. All I needed to do was clear a small hole in the weed next to the boat using my rod tip and lower the jig, a five inch Action Shad, into the nine foot deep water below. It was then a matter of vertically fishing the jig, which I did, and a bite was very quick to come and I caught a fish straight away. As I was fishing in a very limited area, I would wait ten minutes before jigging again, and it didn't take long for another bite to come. It was all over after about two hours, but the swim produced six quality pike and zander. The bites were extremely bold as the fish hadn't been fished for in several months due to the weed covering, and the shade of the surface weed must have given them extra confidence to feed more freely, even though the water was gin clear.

Jigging rates amongst my very favourite fishing methods, and I try to have a jig rod with me wherever I go where there may be a chance of catching predators. Nowadays I'm using the Storm range which I am slowly working through and finding them to be first class. I wish I'd used them long ago, but commercial loyalties have meant that I have had to exclusively use the jigs manufactured by Fox, my sponsors, but they have been great jigs too. Lure anglers are really spoilt for choice nowadays and jig anglers, due to the vast ranges of soft plastic lures available, must be spoilt more than any others!!

'...WE'D ALSO TAKEN NINE PIKE, WHICH INCLUDED SEVERAL UPPER 'DOUBLES'...'

CHAPTER 16

Kings Of The Coloured Water

Imagine that you are driving along on a cold winter's night. You approach the river, and as you cross the bridge through the town, from the warmth of the car you can see the water pushing through with a bit of pace compared to its normal sedate nature, and its colour is a dark uninviting shade of brown. Even to an angler it looks pretty grim, but to the general public it must look quite frightening and forbidding. Worse still, the air temperature has dropped, there's a sharp frost coming down, and the icy cold water is getting even colder. As it's nearly one o'clock in the morning and you are driving a police car, you would be quite right to suspect that anyone messing around on the river at that time of night, and in those conditions, is up to no good!

With your partner backing you up, you approach two shady looking characters that are well padded out against the cold. With their breath filling the cold air, they tell you they are taking a break from a bit of fishing and trying to keep warm, and that unlikely story further arouses your suspicions.

One perceptive officer glances at the red raw hands of one of the suspects, noticing a slight trace of blood from a cut, but his partner, realising that they are telling the truth quips that they do stink of fish, and adds that they would have great difficulty breaking and entering whilst wearing ten layers of clothing, and even more trouble making a fast getaway wearing moon boots!

They then notice the little rods and a net lying on the ground, and after a quick look into a small haversack, realise they really have been fishing. Hurrying to get back to the warmth of the car, one is overheard to say to the other, 'they must be f*****g mad'!

Maybe my mate and I might be a little mad, but not aware of it! The fact is though that we'd just had a blinding lure fishing session. We'd gone out for an 'after dark' session for zander with jigs in the early hours of the evening, planning to have a couple of hours or so as sport had been very reliable for some days previously, but we'd got rather carried away. We had no doubts we would catch a couple of fish, we usually did, but this was to be a night when the zander went crazy and we could not walk away from it. Before we knew it, it was well past midnight, and by the time the police came to question us we'd put 15 zander in our nets and dropped off a few more! What's more, we'd also taken nine pike which included several upper 'doubles', and once again had dropped a couple more off. The pike were a bonus as we were after zander at the time, but this was yet another session which confirmed to me that pike are perfectly at home in coloured water, and even if it is cold and flowing they will still feed if they want to – day or night!

Confident of this fact, I am quite happy searching for pike in coloured water if it's a venue I want to fish or are forced to fish for any reason through my work. If I am not catching them, I consider that I have not yet located any or those which I have covered are not feeding, and the search continues. Coloured water is not a reason for not going pike fishing, and on my local waters I have learnt to pick the right places and to fish at the right times. You do need to have your finger on the pulse though as location is paramount, and these are not the conditions to be exploring new venues. The fishing can sometimes become frustrating in rivers and drains if the coloured water is carrying sediment from the land, and this can be a nightmare to contend with when it builds up on your line, making bait fishing difficult and lure fishing not much fun either. I'm not suggesting it's always easy by any means!

Most pike anglers don't like fishing in coloured water. It easily puts them off, especially if it looks uninviting when it's associated with floodwater conditions. I'd rather not fish in these conditions myself, but when I'm booked to do a magazine feature and working to a printing deadline, I often have no choice and are expected to pull something out of the bag. This is a time when I really have to draw on my knowledge and experience and fish somewhere where I have a reasonable chance of a pike or two. My own pleasure fishing sessions are designed to get me ready to meet these types of demands from my paymasters. Even if the magazine feature involves fishing a venue that I've never fished before, I at

'SUDDEN INFLUXES OF COLOURED WATER ARE MUCH MORE OF A PROBLEM...'

least have the confidence to know that it is possible to catch in coloured water if I approach it correctly. In my business there are no excuses allowed, and you are expected to perform!

First of all I don't panic, even if it's raining 'cats and dogs', rivers are bank high and reservoirs are filling up with coloured water from incoming streams or from being pumped in. Of course I will always try to find an alternative venue with clear water, but circumstances often dictate that I have to fish in coloured water more times than I would like to if the feature is about a particular venue. The first thing I do is to consider whether the coloured water is normal or caused by a sudden influx of new water.

If the water is always coloured I am not concerned in the least, as pike adapt to this or any other water conditions that they find themselves in on a regular basis. This condition could range from a tinge of grey or green through to a chocolate brown soup. Many Irish waters have a permanent peaty hue which, although darkening the water, does not affect the pike fishing in the least, whilst many Scandinavian waters take on a black appearance but fish well all the same. Waters with lots of carp and well stocked commercial fisheries, where bottom feeding fish continually stir up the bottom, are usually the colour of tea most of the time, but pike can still thrive even in this extreme situation, although their lifestyle usually has to adapt. Pike often change in appearance in coloured water and become much paler to blend in with their environment. Such waters may look very uninspiring to pike anglers but can produce some very good pike fishing, especially when the prey fish are of a suitable size and plentiful. Prey fish often thrive in coloured water as they are a lot safer from other predators such as cormorants and grebes, which is naturally in the pike's favour. Quite recently a well coloured stock pond on a local fishery was netted, and a 32 pounder turned up which no one was even aware of. Wish I'd fished it now!

For pike in waters which are normally coloured, I tend to use my regular pike fishing methods. Pike will be feeding in a typical routine as dictated by water temperature and will have no problem detecting lures, livebaits or deadbaits. I don't prescribe to the theory that deadbaits are the best approach for pike in coloured water as some do. They will, of course, work very well, but so will lures and livebaits used in the same measure. You just need the confidence to persevere with them.

A slight seasonal colouring of the water can work wonders, often making pike feed more confidently, and I would rather fish water with a slight tinge of colour than one which is gin clear. When the water is extremely clear, it often limits prey fish activity to low light conditions when they feel safer from predators, and where this is the case, pike may also adapt their feeding to dawn and dusk or even in the dark. However, a dull, overcast or windy day will sometimes provide suitable conditions for both pike and their prey to feed throughout the day.

Sudden influxes of coloured water are much more of a problem, whether in rivers or still waters, and can deter pike from feeding for a while until they adapt. The pike may experience gill clogging through suspended sediment or be affected by deoxygenation if stale water is pumped from the land. I always take these things into account, but if they don't seem to be a likely problem I will fish confidently. Rivers tend to settle and fine down once the rain stops, but reservoirs can be affected for very lengthy periods. This is normally associated with flood water being pumped in from nearby rivers or entering naturally through incoming streams which can affect either part or the whole of the reservoir. Pike in waters that suddenly becomes coloured can be much harder to catch than those in waters which are always coloured until the pike adjust. Whether in rivers or stillwaters, location becomes even more important than usual and I always consider that the incoming water may have concentrated the pike and their prey into favourable areas where they can cope better. Finding them can lead to bumper catches!

In rivers it can be pretty obvious where they are as they will get out of the flow and enter backwaters, side ditches and any slacker areas. I have had some fantastic sport from river backwaters which can fish really well in coloured winter water. Slacks on the main river sometimes fish well, but problems with debris and snagging can make it frustrating. When I lived in the Midlands I enjoyed fabulous sport in

PIC: MATT HAYES

'...A FLYING RETURN VISIT A FEW YEARS AGO, ENDED WITH A BRACE OF 20 POUNDERS...' THIS 21 LB 11 OZ PIKE TOOK A DEAD DACE.

the flooded river Severn backwaters, but nowadays I live on the opposite side of the country and don't fish them so often. However, a flying return visit a few years ago ended with a brace of 20 pounders, one on a lure and the other on a deadbait, even though the river was very coloured.

The rivers in the area where I live today, in the Lincolnshire and Cambridgeshire region, rarely carry heavy floodwater like those in the west, and provided the current does not become too strong, the pike often stay where they are in the main river. Extensive knowledge of river beds gained through the use of an echo sounder, makes it very obvious to me how they can do this because even these uninteresting looking rivers have very variable bottom contours which can provide respite from heavy flow. The River Nene for example, has a run of several miles at a seemingly constant depth of six to eight feet, but the echo sounder has revealed three large localised holes which are 13 feet deep. The Great Ouse River has surprisingly contrasting depths from one side to the other due to uneven dredging and the lower Welland was found to have two huge snags where the river shallows from 11to12 feet to within five feet of the surface. They appear to be man made features to divert the flow, and in flood conditions pike and prey fish gather in slack water below them. This sort of knowledge helps me to understand why pike, and other species, can be comfortable in the main river during a flood as they can drop into areas of slacker water which are not always apparent from the surface. The angler's job is to find them!

Stillwaters which suddenly colour up can pose bigger problems, and you have to take each one on its merits and look for an opportunity to exploit. On one small West Country trout water for example, I arrived to find all of the trout gathered in the flow of the floodwater rushing in from an adjacent stream, giving themselves away by leaping and splashing everywhere. I had 20 livebaits with me, and the pike that were attracted to those trout had taken every one of them before the morning was out! It was great fun 'trotting' the livebaits in the flow of the incoming brown water and watching the red float slamming under time after time until I ran out of bait!

On Chew Valley reservoir during one of the February pike fishing open days, I found the water to be the colour of chocolate on my arrival, so I headed for the most likely place to expect them to be at that time of year. As it was getting close to spawning time, I felt that they would be in shallow water. Jan and I searched the shallower margins all morning, moving four or five times without a single run, but then we found them at around mid day! They were stacked into a very tight area and proved very easy to catch, and before it got dark we built up a catch of 14 pike to 25 lb 8 oz, all of which were very eager to pick up float fished smelts. Had we not found that swim, we might easily have concluded that the coloured water was a problem. No one else was catching much that day and, as usual, the hopefuls descended upon us and tried to muscle in on our action, but the 'hotspot' was so tight that nothing was caught either side of us. I could have shouted across that we had already fished the swims they were in, but these events are like a game of chess where you are competing as much with the other anglers as you are with the fish! These events can be good fun and reputations are made on easy big fish, but it's not my favourite way of catching pike.

'IN THE MUDDY WATER THAT IS TYPICAL OF CARP AND COMMERCIAL FISHERIES...'

Prolonged coloured water of any nature will see pike feeding as and when they want to. They will need to feed at some time and you should always consider how much they need to eat at the particular time of year you are fishing. In spring and early autumn, pike need to consume a lot of food whereas in mid winter they can survive for weeks without eating at all. Well fed pike will be a problem at any time, whether the water is

'...WE BUILT UP A CATCH OF 14 PIKE TO 25 LB 8 OZ...'

coloured or not. Such facts affect my judgement regarding how to fish, where to fish and how much effort I should be putting into searching the water.

It's true that the pike is primarily a sight feeder, but ongoing experiences of fishing in coloured water with all methods continually reinforces the fact that the pike's other senses for detecting its food are just as reliable. Have no doubt that pike feed in coloured water. They do so if they want to but whether they want to is another matter!

In the muddy water that is typical of carp and commercial fisheries, pike often adopt a lifestyle which sees the plentiful supplies of coarse angler's baits of halibut pellets and fish meal boilies included in their diet. After all, they are made from fish, but are presented in a different form. Pike will detect this very easily by using their sensitive snouts and will often browse on such bait though the summer. This is a time when pike often tend to browse feed anyway, saving themselves for the real feast to come in the autumn and winter and such snacks fit the bill perfectly.

I was fishing such a venue in Cambridgeshire for the first time a few seasons ago, and had an experience which typified this situation. I was actually fishing for catfish, and as there had only been three cats stocked into the lake I became quite excited when I actually had a run on a popped up live roach within minutes of casting it out. It was a catfish, but only a 'kitten' of three or four pounds; the first evidence that the stock fish had spawned. I was delighted to catch it, if nothing else from an interest point of view.

Then I was in trouble! The club secretary who was fishing not too far away, came down and gave me a right rollicking for using livebait. In all innocence (honestly) I'd not considered that I was inadvertently breaking a club rule which did not allow pike fishing in the summer months. I never stopped to think, as catfishing to me is about using livebaits as the first tactic I consider. I was wrong and apolo-

'...ANOTHER PIKE WITH THE PELLETS HANGING FROM ITS JAWS...'

gised, and off he went having given me a second chance.

I changed the rigs to multiple 21 mm halibut pellets on two rods and to luncheon meat on the third, and plastered the swim with about a kilo of pellets. I was 'away' on pellets in no time at all, and what I thought to be another cat turned out to be a pike! It was a decent one too of about 15 lb, hooked fairly and squarely in the scissors with the size 4/0 single hook! While returning it another rod went, and after a right old scrap I was unhooking a 12 lb pike which had taken the meat. Naturally this drew attention to me again and the club secretary was soon back in my swim. I showed him my rigs and they were clearly not pike rigs, but he gave me a look that left me in no doubt that he thought I was up to something (who me?)!

Throughout the day runs came steady, no more to the luncheon meat but seven or eight to the multiple halibut pellets. To cut a long story short, I landed another five double figure pike with the best at 17 lb. The club secretary finally came and watched me, and after seeing me reel in another pike with the pellets hanging from its jaws, walked away scratching his head as I was doing nothing wrong. (Really I wasn't). In actual fact, I didn't want to catch the pike. It's the last thing I ever want to do when the water temperature is high, but this is a problem I have had to come to terms with when catfishing in the summer months and are now very careful not to draw attention to any pike I accidentally catch. I am happy that I handle them with due care, but concerned that catching them might lead to catfishing being banned or methods restricted. I have minimised my pike captures by only fishing for the cats in the dark now, using the daytime period to fish for roach and bream. This has actually worked in my favour as piling in loads of groundbait, pellets and boilies for them has also drawn catfish into my swims. I still catch quite a few pike though, I will admit.

The proliferation of commercial type fisheries and heavily stocked coarse fisheries, with their associated coloured water, is something I think pike anglers will increasingly have to learn to contend with as some of them will also have very good pike fishing if you can get onto them. My advice would be to tackle them with the full range of pike fishing methods when the water cools down and pleasure anglers' numbers dwindle, making more swims available. This will also give more room to cast lures around, a method not to be neglected in coloured water.

I have fared very well using lures on many rivers when they have been carrying coloured water ranging from the faster rivers of the west like the Severn, to the more sedate rivers of the east like the Welland. Of course, I would much prefer to fish them in better conditions, but often find myself in unexpected situations where I have no choice. I still carry on with a degree of confidence, especially as most of the rivers I fish nowadays also contain zander. I am actually fishing for zander in the first instance, that's my current preference, but I know that I will be in with an excellent chance of catching pike too. The fact is that I've taken some very big catches of pike in coloured rivers in winter using lures. Jigs have probably been the most successful, but crankbaits, spinners and especially spinnerbaits have had their moments too.

Some of the best coloured water hauls of lure caught pike I have ever made were from the River Welland, but sadly nowadays the pike all seem to have gone, as they have also gone from many of my other favourite local venues. It didn't take very long for some of the most prolific pike fishing I have ever enjoyed to be wiped out by new 'pike anglers' to the area who have been taking them for eating. For more than 20 years we looked after, and enjoyed, fantastic winter pike fishing, but it's nearly all finished now. The days when we used to catch anything from 20 to 40 pike and sometimes more, are replaced with days when we struggle for a single fish. If nothing else this illustrates the point that pike stocks are not inexhaustible and that good pike fishing can easily be ruined by a few thoughtless anglers for whatever reason. If you are struggling to catch pike, bear in mind the fact that even the best pike angler in the world will struggle where pike numbers are low. Enough of that topic, it's too late now, but hopefully we shall see some recovery one day!

My confidence to fish for pike in coloured water is based upon an understanding of the pike's senses. Its vision might be restricted, but its keen sense of smell and its ability to detect vibration more than compensate when necessary. Each sense is, I am sure, more than enough to detect prey, and combinations of these senses must be a formidable hunting system.

The pike's sense of smell is very acute and I have watched pike easily locate pieces of deadbait which are lying on the bottom, sometimes hidden by weed. The pike's sense of smell is not only, in my opinion, a means for detecting dead prey though, I think it is also used for detecting live prey. We don't really tend to think in terms of live fish having a smell, but of course they must do, and a distinctive part of it must emanate from their excrement trail which is instrumental in giving away their presence. Just imagine a shoal of 500 bream and the excrement scent trail they would leave behind them! I'm certain that pike are just as efficient as cats and dogs at detecting scents with their noses.

The reverse must also be true as pike also leaving a scent trail, one to be avoided by prey fish. A recent research theory suggests that pike always return to the same area to digest their food and excrete their faeces, somewhere then avoided by prey fish because they can detect the presence of pike through this smell. I quite like that theory, and it might even be connected with other popular theories of 'hot spots', places where pike gather together. Like a lot of popular thinking, there is room for expansion and discussion, but over millions of years a natural pattern must have emerged which enables pike and prey to co exist in a reasonable and sustainable way. Whether its coloured or not, life under the water still goes on, and as anglers we just need to adapt our thinking and tactics.

Despite the coloured water I had two runs at the same time!

When the birds start roosting, the pike start stirring!

CHAPTER 17

Open All Hours

It's mid January, and three hours into darkness as I struggle to get into my sleeping bag with all my winter gear on except my boots. There's been a big moon but it's disappeared now, and the clear sky is slowly being replaced with approaching black clouds. A full moon and a weather change often signal the possibility of a feeding spell, but I'm more concerned at the moment with surviving for the next three or four hours. I'm not too cold just yet, but as I get tired I know I will start to feel uncomfortable, so I pull my sleeping bag over my head and listen out for my alarms. Three rods nearby are rigged with legered deadbaits and set up with electronic 'drop off' bite indicators, and even though struggling with the elements, I'm feeling very content!

I'm not bivvied out with the intention of sleeping. I just want to keep warm and dry as I fish through until midnight which, at this time of year, gives me nearly six hours in the dark. Jan's already asleep in the camper van parked nearby, ready to help me get some photos should I get lucky and land one of the big pike which we know live in the pit. It's an unusual time to fish for pike and the hours are anti social, but every now and again I like a session in the dark, especially when daytime fishing has been slow or when my work stops me from fishing in the hours of daylight.

My eyes are shut but I'm not sleeping, just planning what I'll do if, or when, a run comes. I'm mentally if not physically alert, and I'll be out of the bag as soon as the alarm screams out its single note continuous tone. I'll slip my boots on in seconds and be down the bank to bend into the fish very quickly. While I'm playing the fish I'll back up to my bivvy, turn on my big lamp and walk it back to the margin so I can see clearly where the hooks are before attempting to chin or net the pike. My landing net is positioned between the rods and my head torch is hanging from one of the rod butts so I can clip it on while playing the fish. It can't go wrong – can it?

The alarm suddenly screams out, sending my heart thumping. Things usually go to plan but not this time! I've turned over in the sleeping bag, and in the pitch blackness have become disorientated. I get out from the wrong side of the bed chair, come quickly into contact with the bivvy wall, and realising what I've done, turn around and tip the bed chair over. I can't find my boots so run to the waters edge in my socks, soaking up moisture from the damp ground and tripping over the landing net handle. I'm bent into the fish alright, but can't find the lamp as it's rolled down the bank in the confusion!

No problem, at least the pike is hooked, but seconds into playing what feels quite a 'lump', another alarm sounds out! I've not snagged the line so it must be another 'run'! The first fish is bundled into the net and is a really fat pike, thankfully putting up very little resistance due to the cold water. My feet are now feeling really cold! The second fish is hooked and feels just as big! Jan appears with the lamp and starts making up the spare landing net. She really has saved the day because, as I slip the net under a second big fish, my third alarm starts to sound out!

Jan alternates between the two landing nets to ensure that the pike don't spin round and tangle the trebles in the mesh, but in the cold conditions they lie very still. The third fish is one I recognise, a low 'twenty'. I have to chin it out as I have no net and decide to unhook it and let it go. My mind is racing, not only at the exhausting few minutes I've had, but from thinking about one of the other pike which looked very fat indeed.

I lift the first pike from the net while Jan drags the unhooking matt over and sets up the camera to take a few quick pics. A weight of 25 lb 7 oz really pleases me, and I recognise this one too as a fish caught the previous season. The second pike I've saved until last as it looked the biggest, and so it proved to be at 26 lb 10 oz, a new fish for the water and a magnificent looking specimen. The tape measure shows it to be only 38 inches long and it's a really stockily built fish with its bulk being in its width rather than its depth. A few pics are taken of that one too, and while Jan puts the kettle on, I sort out the absolute shambles of gear spread all over the place, feeling very pleased with myself!

The black sky starts to turn very clear again and is brightened by thousands of stars as the temperature really starts to plummet. The mesh of the spare net is already starting to freeze as I try to pack it way, and as the steam from our mugs of tea fills the night air, we realised we should leave or we will freeze to death. With my toes numbed inside my wet socks, I know enough is enough!

Pike live in a very different environment to us, and their feeding behaviour is not at all like ours. Whereas humans tend to fit in meals with their daily schedules, and we are very predictable in this way, pike have to feed where and when they can. This is a constantly changing scenario affected largely by seasonal conditions, although feeding can fall into patterns which last for a while until something changes. Pike could choose any period around the clock in which to feed, and they often choose to do so in the dark hours when most pike anglers are at home or in bed. We do tend to largely restrict our fishing to the hours of daylight, but this can be a big disadvantage when pike prefer to feed at night. Considering that we typically tend to fish sessions of about eight to ten hours long, it is no wonder that we don't always catch what we would wish for when we are only fishing for about a third of the pike's potential feeding time, and most pike anglers rarely, if ever, fish in the dark.

I have not found a consistent pattern with night feeding. It does vary from water to water and at different times of the year. It is an undisputable fact though that night feeding is quite normal and we can miss the full potential of any water if we choose to neglect or ignore this. Some waters fish especially well after dark and in particular those with very clear water. Waters which endure heavy daytime fishing pressure can also produce better after dark. It would be very neat and tidy to claim that these are firm rules, but in actual practice I have had fantastic results after dark in totally unexpected situations.

Night fishing for pike can be extremely viable and is sometimes better than daytime fishing. There is enough evidence to suggest that you should not rule out fishing after dark if you are not getting the daytime results you expect from your chosen water. There are many other benefits to fishing in the dark, and to find that I can catch pike at any time 'around the clock' is very beneficial in my business and allows me a great degree of flexibility. If I am urgently in need of pictures of pike or catch

'...AT 26 LB 10 OZ, A NEW FISH FOR THE WATER AND A MAGNIFICENT LOOKING SPECIMEN.'

stories, and time is against me, I will often go out in the dark and get the material I am after. Knowing that pike can be caught in any of the 24 hours of the day, I know that my work is not limited to the hours of daylight, especially useful in the short days of winter. I usually have plenty of work which can be carried out in the dark if I'm up against a tight schedule such as testing new tackle products for my sponsors which could be anything from wire traces to rods. It doesn't matter what time of the day I test them as long as I put them through their paces and get my reports in on time. If I have to work an evening or night shift, then so be it!

I have always known that pike feed in the dark and quickly learnt that lesson in my younger days whilst fishing for eels when pike frequently took my baits. For quite a while I never night fished for pike very extensively, simply because I fished enough hours in the daytime to satisfy myself. Even on longer trips I preferred to sleep in my van after a long hard day rather than bivvy out. I have always needed a period of deep sleep at some time during each day and try to get at least six hours. Sometimes I am so knackered I go out like a light, but if there is the promise of a later predictable feeding time in prospect, sleep never comes easy. There are a few waters where I will bivvy out and fish day and night for several days, but on most long sessions I will reel my rods in occasionally and get some proper sleep after having identified the likely quiet spells.

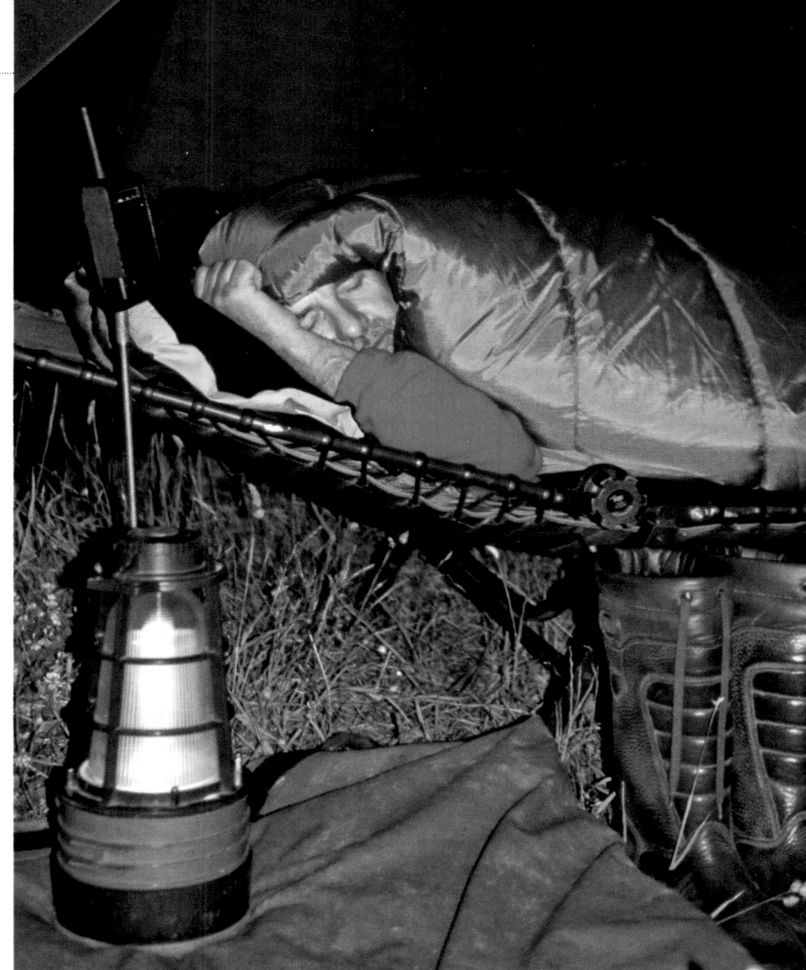

'I'LL BE OUT OF THE BAG AS SOON AS THE ALARM SCREAMS OUT...'

As darkness approaches, dusk can be a very productive time for pike and it is sometimes difficult to pack up because I know that this is often the start of a feeding period that could go on for much longer. If I am fishing a water that has seen quite a bit of pressure and the day has been uneventful, I am even more tempted to stay on for a while. About ten years ago I attended a charity day where I looked after a group of anglers at Patsull Park Fishery in Staffordshire. The day was very slow and hardly anything was caught. I mentioned to one of the younger anglers that it was worth staying for an hour or two in the dark when everyone else had left after throwing their deadbaits into the margins; a good place to fish a bait as the pike can get used to mopping them up in the dark. I was half way down the M6 when my mobile rang and he excitedly told me about the 29 pounder he had just caught in the dark – from the margin!

Night fishing for pike is not for the ill prepared though, and even if you are prepared it's not at all easy when you are cold and tired. Organisation is vital, and such sessions are much better carried out with a friend to help deal with the problems you will undoubtedly encounter. Most sessions should run smoothly if you prepare, but you have to be ready for the worst case scenario. If you are not, be sure something will happen! Bite indication must be well up to scratch, as it should be at any time, and you will need to think ahead about how you will deal with any pike caught, having everything to hand for unhooking and photographing. It all sounds pretty obvious, but in the pitch black these simple things will seem to be three times as difficult as they are normally because it is hard to see what you're doing. I always wear a powerful head torch and have a large lamp ready in case it's needed at any stage. You will often need some light when trying to net the fish and you will always need extra light when unhooking in the dark. You can't have too many head torches or lamps!

When boat fishing at night, you should ideally have navigation lights fitted to your boat, especially on rivers and larger waters. You might think that your boat would be easy to see and that other boats are unlikely to be moving in the dark, but I have had many a large boat come belting along at high speed, often without lights. You have to allow for the idiots! Lifejackets obviously need to worn in boats at all times and at night it's even more important. Even if I'm bank fishing on a fast river at night I'll wear a self inflating life jacket, especially if the banks are slippery and dangerous. A mobile phone is always a good idea at any time, especially at night, and it's wise to tell someone where you are fishing so that you can be found more easily if you do get into any trouble.

I really enjoy pike fishing in the dark if the weather is kind and I can get comfortable somewhere, whether on the bank or in a boat. You do need to know what you are doing though, especially if you are on your own. The lone pike angler can feel very isolated at any time, but at night this feeling is accentuated. It's often tempting to pack up and go home, but it's tiredness that makes you think this way. If there's anything I don't like about night fishing, it's that I never get a really good look at the fish I catch and photos taken at night rarely look very good. If you are on your own, 'self takes' in the dark are a nightmare, and unless it's a really special fish I just don't bother with the struggle. Sacking up is always a possibility, but I avoid this if I can. Nowadays, on the very rare occasions that I hold onto a fish for a short period at night, I use my catfish tubes which, although cumbersome to carry around, hold pike very safely. If I am not too far from home I have the luxury of phoning Jan and asking her to drive out, and I know I can trust her to do the job properly and she has photographed several 30 pounders in the dark for me. The following story illustrates many of the points I am trying to convey.

'Bite indication must be well upto scratch...'

Pic: Ralph Brown

I EXPECT TO CATCH ZANDER AS WELL AT NIGHT.

We were going through one of the coldest winters for a long time, when water temperatures had stayed low for most of the 'back end' of the season. A lake I had my mind set upon fishing was frozen for many weeks, and even when not frozen the water temperature remained as low as it could be without freezing again. North winds battered us unmercifully and it was just no pleasure to go pike fishing. When a window of opportunity appeared, despite the harsh conditions I just had to get some fishing in before the season ended. After quickly ruling out lures and deadbaits, which rarely work in these cold conditions, I concluded that the only way I was going to get a run was to slowly troll a decent sized livebait, fishing it very close to the bottom and literally dragging it over the pike's noses. This would be the only way to get them to react in these extreme conditions.

The fishing wasn't easy at all, but I managed to get a 'take' every now and again, and such successes were limited to one or two in a day. Persevering for a few more days and realising that a result from this water was never easy anyway, I managed to winkle out a few jacks and a mid double. On an afternoon trip where I really only intended to fish for three hours, the wind died completely, the sky blackened and snow started to flurry in from the north. We were obviously in for another bout of bad weather, but in a strange way it was really pleasant trolling 'on the oars', watching the snow gradually cover everything in the boat in a white shroud. I was warm enough though and happy that I was at least in with a chance of a pike on a water that potentially held a few big ones. The session became interesting when, in the three hours leading up to darkness, I had two 'takes' and landed two low doubles which was a good result for the conditions. I felt that I'd at least proven that I wasn't wasting my time and that pike were catchable with a little perseverance.

The recent weather had been so cold that I wouldn't have expected the pike to have been feeding much, but they obviously had. They were in top condition too, and judging by their fat bellies it looked like the cold spell had not stopped them from feeding at all. I wondered what one of the bigger pike might look like and now really wanted one!

Dusk drifted into darkness but I carried on trolling, my mind wandering to other boat sessions I have had in the dark with livebaits, ranging from trolling the River Bure in Norfolk to my night fishing adventures on the River Severn. In the blackness all around me I could hear the roar of the rush hour traffic in the far distance on the main road, and I felt a world apart from it all, isolated and feeling very vulnerable, but I wanted to do it. Lifejacket or not, if I ended up in the icy cold water beneath me I would probably only last a few minutes.

All thoughts of danger were soon forgotten when my 'baitrunner' clicked as a pike grabbed the live-bait aggressively and pulled the line tight. As I struck into the run, I instinctively switched on my head torch as I felt very uneasy as the boat wobbled beneath me as the pike surged away. The weak beam from the torch lit up the snow shrouded boat, revealing nothing more than blackness and cold deep water all around me.

Everything else in the world was forgotten for a few minutes while I eased the pike to the surface, anxious to get a look at it. It was not a monster, I had caught much bigger pike from the lake, but it was a beautifully coloured specimen, and just like the others caught that afternoon it was as fat as a pig. I would think under normal conditions it would have weighed around 18 lbs for its length, but it tipped the scales at an ounce over 20 lb!

While I still had any feeling left in my hands, I slid her freezing cold, snow covered body into a wet sack, lowered it carefully into the water and tied the cord to a rowlock. I can't find the words to relate how excited and satisfied I felt about catching that pike and the circumstances under which it had been caught. It made me realise that as much as I love to catch monster pike, they don't have to fall into that category to be special. I phoned Jan and asked her to come across and take some photos for me, and as it would take an hour or so I gently paddled my way back to the mooring, taking my time so as not to stress the pike in any way. It does seem illogical, after all I had caught so many much bigger pike, but the moment was so special that I wanted to be able to remember it forever. Photographs do this for us more than we realise. In more difficult circumstances, I have had to return specimen fish without photographs and I simply cannot remember what they looked like even though I can remember catching them.

'...HER FREEZING COLD, SNOW COVERED BODY...'

A lot of my night fishing takes place in prebaited swims. In the chapter about pre baiting, I mentioned how pike can become conditioned to feed in darkness if pre bait is regularly introduced late in the day. When fishing these swims I don't tend to arrive too early to avoid very long sessions, knowing that I will almost certainly stay in the dark for a few hours. I'd rather spend the morning at

'...IT TIPPED THE SCALES AT AN OUNCE OVER 20 LB!'

home getting some paperwork done, and there's loads of that in my job! If I'm fishing baited swims with clients though, they naturally want to fish a full day, from dawn till dusk, to give them value for money. If they have travelled long distances, they usually like to pack up when it gets dark so that they get home at a reasonable time, especially if the weather is bad. If the day has been unproductive though, I offer them the option of staying in the dark for an hour or two knowing that they still have a very good chance of catching. On so many occasions this has been when the biggest pike have been caught, not always from pre baited areas either.

I always give at least ten hours or more of my time to clients, but don't mind staying on a bit longer if required. Most prefer to get on their way as it gets dark, and if they do I will often spend an hour or two in the swim on my own, mainly because tackle ends up strewn everywhere and needs careful sorting out and packing away. Of course, whilst doing so, I will put out a couple of rods on alarms and I usually put the kettle on and relax with a well earned cup of tea! There have been so many times when my customer has been gone for less than half an hour or so and I have found myself alone and unhooking a good pike. If it's a 20 pounder, as it has been many times, I just don't have the heart to contact them to let them know. They would probably take it in good spirit I'm sure, but I wouldn't do anything to put a damper on their day.

My night time venues include rivers and stillwaters. Stillwaters tend to be very predictable because water conditions do not change too quickly, but rivers can be up and down during rainy periods. The pike in some of the rivers I fish really 'turn on' when the water starts to colour up, especially after a prolonged spell of clear water and I expect to catch zander as well in these conditions where they are present. The fishing can be just as good in the dark as it is in daylight, even if the water is running quite hard and is cold. Many of these river pike and zander are caught with lures and they frequently hit them with a lot of aggression, suggesting to me that they are very alert and in feeding mode.

I especially enjoy fishing at night with lures because the tackle required is so minimal compared with the paraphernalia of bait fishing, especially on short sessions, and in the dark there's less to go wrong with a lure approach. Trolling lures at night is also very viable and I do so quite a lot, but its not a good idea if you are inexperienced or ill prepared for it. Bait fishing can be enjoyable if you are well organised, and I fish all bait methods at night, sometimes from the bank and at other times from my boat. Bank fishing with baits is not a lot different to fishing in daylight with regards to methods. I tend to mostly ledger deadbaits and paternoster livebaits and the rods are always set up with alarms. Both methods are pretty straight forward but I would not suggest using them at night unless you are competent at fishing them in the daylight. It might be worth discussing paternostering in more detail as this seems to be a method which many anglers struggle with at any time.

'If its a 20-pounder, as it has been many times...'

Many anglers, whether fishing in the day or at night, seem to worry about bite indication when paternostering and pay special attention to detecting ''slack line' bites which occur if the pike moves towards the rod after taking the bait. I think it's only right that they should be concerned and I take this matter seriously too, but over a lifetime of fishing this method I have found that if rigged up in a particular way I rarely get a problem from deep hooked fish. If I use a small livebait, say four to five inches maximum, and a heavy lead of more than two ounces, almost every pike I catch is hooked in the scissors, even if I have been delayed from striking for any reason. This combination of a small bait and a heavy weight is, in my opinion, acting as a type of 'self hooking' rig. After the pike grabs the bait it feels the resistance of the float and weight relative to the small bait, and when it releases it to let it go or even if it should slacken off to attempt to swallow it, it is dragged to the corner of its mouth and the hooks catch in the scissors. It doesn't always work with a bigger bait though and dropped runs become more frequent. In the pitch black its vital to get this right. That's my theory, and whether I am right or wrong doesn't matter, the fact is that it works for me. You must find a way that works for you!

I can, if I wish, float fish my deadbaits at night using my home made 'night floats' which incorporate small 'glow in the dark' isotopes which I picked up at a car boot sale. I have no idea what they were originally made for but they have been Araldited to the top of Fox loaded pencil floats, the old type made from expanded polystyrene. I originally made them for close range fishing from difficult banks at night where I couldn't get rod rests in, but they have also proved to be invaluable for boat fishing with deadbaits at night and are clearly visible up to about 20 yards. They have a permanent glow and I no longer bother with fitting 'Starlights' to the tips of floats as they only last a short time. I have also used the recently introduced Greys night floats which are battery operated, and they can be seen at much greater distances. Even though they are bulky they are quite effective and dropped runs don't seem to be a problem. I prefer my own floats though.

ALL LURES WORK IN THE DARK.

If you have never tried fishing for pike at night, I don't want to encourage you to do so unless you are ready for it. For some anglers it might be a better option to fish at night if their time is limited and it can be a way of getting in a few extra hours. If you're one of those crafty anglers who don't want others to know where you are fishing, it's a good way of going about it. If you are not sure, just try it for a few hours first of all and see how you get on, you have nothing to lose. You don't have to fish in the ways I have described, but you do need to recognise your limitations until you become proficient.

Most of my night fishing for pike takes place during the winter months, but there are times when summer fishing can be productive and exciting too. Pike welfare becomes an issue in warmer water and it's up to you to decide whether pike in your water will suffer from being caught at that time of year. If you feel confident that they will not, and you have strong nerves, you could try fishing with surface lures in the dark. You might experience some heart stopping action, but make sure it's not the pikes heart that is stopped! My favourite surface lure in the dark is the large Arbogast Jitterbug. Its concave front vane creates a loud 'plip plop' sound when you get it working correctly, and you can clearly hear it coming through the darkness on a calm night. When it's engulfed with an almighty crash and the rod is nearly ripped from your hands, you will have experienced one of the most exciting moments in pike fishing!

Night fishing is becoming more popular with modern pike anglers, and although it can be productive and exciting, it can be detrimental to any water to fish it around the clock and overpressure it. It can also be a bad thing if you cannot handle pike properly in the dark. It's here to stay though, and it's up to us all to fish as responsibly as we can.

The baltic sea - the biggest pike water in the world!

Pic: thomas Søbir

CHAPTER 18

All At Sea

Twenty years ago, the Baltic Sea in Scandinavia was a far away place that most British pike anglers like me had only read about in catalogues from Swedish tackle companies like Abu. I became fascinated with the region when I read that pike actually lived in this sea, and I often dreamt about going to catch one. Little did I know that it was a pike angler's paradise just waiting to be 'discovered' by outsiders. Further research revealed that the pike didn't actually live in salt water but in the brackish water of many of the coastal areas, notably around the coast of Sweden, Finland and Germany. Pike also exist in the middle of the Baltic Sea, around a collection of Islands belonging to Finland called Aland. Through the nineties, my business activities enabled me to get across to Scandinavia by various means and spend many happy days exploring the area, fishing inland lakes as well as in the sea. Initially this was at my own expense, and later to promote the fishing there through my business by way of various angling related companies I worked with. I still make the occasional visit nowadays, but there is so much more to do. Had life nothing else to offer, I would gladly spend the rest of my days travelling and fishing for pike in these countries, but as fantastic as it is, I feel I have to keep moving on and fishing in new places and experiencing different fishing methods. You can't do it all, but the years I spent exploring Scandinavia have brought me so many good memories, not only of the fishing and the wonderful environment, but also of the warm and friendly people I met, many of whom are still good friends.

Nowadays we know a great deal more about pike fishing in this part of the world, and through holiday packages and better access to information, many other anglers have since sampled the pike fishing available. Twenty years ago it was very different and opportunities to go across to fish for pike were very limited unless you had contacts. Few British anglers had ventured there, and if they had it was usually with the help of a Scandinavian friend or on a business trip. Feedback was sparse, but foreign magazines and tackle brochures convinced me beyond all doubt that pike did exist in the Baltic Sea in good numbers, and some huge ones too. It became firmly planted in my thoughts that I would have to find a way of getting across there to catch a 'sea pike'! When and how, was another matter!

My first Scandinavian contact came in 1993 after reading an article in *Coarse Fishing Today* (Emap Publishing) magazine by a young Danish angler, Thomas Søbirk from Copenhagen. The article was a mouth watering account of his success with zander in lakes in the Danish Jutland peninsula, and as a result of reading it, Steve Younger from Kings Lynn and I made contact and arranged a trip to fish with him during the following spring.

Thomas proved to be a very friendly and intelligent young man and introduced us to our first Scandinavian predator fishing experience, and on that first trip, in May 1994 I caught a lot of predators, including two zander weighing over 14 lb from a large lake that we fished from a boat. Very unlike fishing in England, our permit for the lake also gave us permission to set long lines, nets and traps! We stuck to rod and line!

Scandinavia had already opened our eyes, even on a short visit. It was certainly the first time I'd caught pike, zander and sea trout from the same swim for example, and from a still water too; one which runs out into the sea a few miles away. We returned to Denmark in the autumn of 1994 and I caught my first Scandinavian 'twenty' from a large lake in Zeeland. Caught on a popped up herring, the 22 lb 6 oz pike was a new record for the pike club at the lake, and by showing the Danes the potential of deadbaiting, I hoped we had at least given something back. It was a big Scandinavian pike, but not the sea pike I had dreamt about catching one day!

I returned to Denmark many times and some of the names of the big lakes I fished are still in my memory, Ulse, Lyngby, Bagsvaerd, Kimmerslev, Fussing and Skandeborg. We were asked to keep quiet about some of the more productive lakes we fished to avoid a rush of anglers when we wrote about our trips. *Coarse Fisherman* magazine, in which I wrote of my travels, was also available in Denmark at the

This Danish pike of 22lb 6oz was a new record for the Pike Club.

time, and anglers over there are no different to those in the UK, descending upon any water which is publicised. To put them off the scent, I gave the lakes fictitious 'Danish sounding' names, put together with the help of a few Danish friends. I cannot repeat them, as I now realise that we had gone too far, so I'll try to describe them for you as inoffensively as I can! To name one lake, which we fished with very good results, we used Danish words which, politely put, means making a loud noise with your bottom! For another lake, we used words which described something that you are most likely to find happening in a bedroom between consenting couples!

We thought it no more than a bit of fun at the time, and of no consequence in the UK as no one would understand Danish. This proved to be the case, but we were reprimanded by the Danish Tourist Board who got to read the articles, and Thomas's mother was horrified when she saw a copy of the article in a magazine which Thomas had left lying around at home. Oh dear, it's no wonder Thomas's mother never invited us back for tea!

We came into contact with many Danish anglers on our trips, which made us aware of a growing interest in specimen angling amongst the younger Danes and also young Swedish anglers, and I was surprised to hear that they were following British specimen angling with great interest. It was an even greater surprise when top carp angler Kevin Maddocks and I were asked to speak at the inaugural Swedish Angling Conference, to be held at Stromsnabruck in Sweden in March 1995. Of course it was a great honour to do so, and suddenly the door to the Baltic Sea started to creak open!

I had been contacted through Fredrik Stjarnkvist from Malmo in the south of Sweden, a very successful pike angler and good friend of the conference organiser Rikard Bengtsson. He had kindly arranged to pick me up from Copenhagen Airport, take me to the conference and then to stay at his house for a few days. He also offered to take me fishing on the Lodde River which runs into the Baltic Sea in the South of Sweden and which had a reputation across Europe for its monster pike, even though most UK anglers had never even heard of it.

At the conference I delivered a talk about British deadbaiting tactics, which was a totally alien way of pike fishing to the Swedish anglers. It went down quite well, apart from when the slide projector was tipped over and all my precious slides were scattered around the feet of the audience! A useful tip is to number your slides when making a presentation, and having done so, I quickly had the show back on the road. Thank goodness for the advent of digital technology!

Before going fishing with the Swedish lads, I was privileged to visit the clubroom of the Malmo Specimen Group. Never before, or since, have I been in the same room with so many anglers who have caught pike of over 40 lb. The walls were adorned with pictures of numerous specimen pike, not to mention monster cod and salmon and many other species. Later, I was shown a cast of a perch which had weighed 7lb 15oz. This really was like a trip to Wonderland!

The fishing on the lower Lodde River, where it enters the sea, was as hard as I had been told it would be, and on the first day we couldn't get a 'take' on our float trolled livebaits. The next day, I quite fancied the look of a section further upstream where the river narrowed and became nicely tree lined. Most local anglers did not bother with this section as the 'monsters' usually only ventured into the lower part of the river when coming in from the sea for a few weeks at spawning time. It did, however, prove to be more productive for us, even though every fish was hard won in the bitter cold weather. In two days fishing, I managed nine pike which included seven 'doubles' and two 'twenties' at 25lb 8oz and 24lb 8oz, and they all took large roach livebaits. My friends put two more 'twenties' in our boat and fishing this area proved to be a very good move as no other big pike were reported from the lower river during that time. The anglers sticking it out on the lower river obviously knew a thing or two though, not wasting time with 'mid twenties', but I was to find out more about this on a later trip!

On the way home, I first took the ferry back to Copenhagen where I would pick up my return flight to London. Thomas Søbirk was there to meet me as we had arranged a night's zander fishing before I went back. 'Lady luck' was certainly on my side on that trip, as we both caught zander to over 12 lb on the coldest, darkest night you could possibly imagine. Wearing neoprene chest waders, we waded a hundred yards out into a large lake, precariously feeling around with our landing net handles to locate the drop off into deep water. Once in position, we drifted bream livebaits rigged under starlight floats into the blackness of the moonless night. The facing wind had set up an undercurrent in the murky brown water, assisted by flow from an incoming stream, and the baits drifted away from us perfectly. As our eyes strained to see the tiny yellow float tips, bobbing in the distance in the dark waves, they would disappear in a flash, and the line would zip through our fingers at high speed. These zander were not messing about, and in total blackness it was an eerie feeling. We could have caught more, but were sat-

Jorgen Larsson helps me cradle a Swedish 24 lb 8 oz river pike.

isfied with a 12 pounder apiece as we were getting really cold. We took the water temperature, it was one degree Centigrade, and although wearing thermal under suits inside our waders, we were just too cold to continue. In the early hours of the morning we retired to a nearby McDonald's to get warm, celebrate, and make plans for the future!

Before I went home, Thomas and I spent a lot of time talking about the Baltic pike. Even most Danish pike anglers had not yet taken advantage of the potential across the narrow strip of water which divided the two countries. It had only been very recently that pike had become of interest as a sport fish to the Danes rather than food or vermin, an attitude which was starting to change there just as it had back home in the latter part of the last century. Thomas then revealed that he had a contact who had been on an exploratory trip to the South Baltic near Karlshamn, on the south eastern tip of Sweden. The previous year he had caught a few pike and offered us some useful information to get us started. I'd also whetted Thomas's appetite with my account of catching the pike in the Lodde River, and he fancied having a crack at them too. The seeds for another Baltic adventure were sown!

The planning soon turned into action. Sea charts were bought, survival suits acquired and Thomas planned to get himself a boat that would be seaworthy. We were all fired up and well prepared, but it would have to wait until the following spring.

The spring of 1996 arrived and Thomas towed his boat across from Copenhagen. Tackling the Lodde River first, the fishing was predictably slow but Thomas took his first Swedish 'twenty pounder' from one of the productive areas I had located in the upper river during my first trip. As we were into April, we suspected that the bigger pike might have spawned and had returned to the sea, but it was hard to get any clear facts. The fishing there is always so hard, it's difficult to know if the pike are in the river or not. We decided they probably weren't in the river, and then a perch angler foul hooked a 33 pounder on a jig, which totally confounded us!

We had an ambitious agenda though and did not want to spend all of our time on the river, so having put a few pike under our belts, we decided to be more adventurous and head out of the river and into the sea where these pike normally live outside of the spawning period. Fredrik Stjarnkvist had already inspired us by taking a monster pike of 38lb on a lure in the previous summer from the shallow water shelf adjacent to the 'drop off' to the deep water. We were reliably informed that the pike would not be in this shallow water until the summer, so we planned to troll the 'drop off' where they might be waiting. The depth averages about six feet for half a mile out from the river mouth and is strewn with rocks which have to be very carefully negotiated to avoid damaging the propeller of the engine. When through the rocks, the water plummets to 30 feet deep, and you are out on the open sea!

PIC: THOMAS SØBIRK

'...COD! THE SEA WAS ALIVE WITH THEM...'

Such a large expanse of water can only be fished effectively by trolling with lures. We had brought a wide selection with us, but in hindsight probably not the right ones for such deep water if the pike were lying tight to the bottom. It wasn't very long before we realised that we were up against a serious and unexpected problem – cod! The sea was alive with them, and no matter which lure we trolled and at what depth

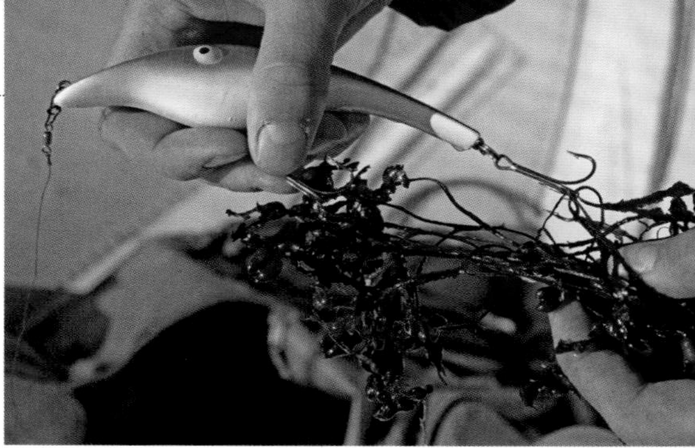

THE SEAWEED PROVED WE WERE FISHING IN THE SEA!

we trolled it, it would soon be rammed by cod from four to eight pounds, which is great fun but not what we were after. From Spinnerbaits to Super Shads they savaged them all, and we even had a four pound sea trout hit a Bomber Long 'A'. Three days spent trolling the drop off produced so many cod, I think we would have been in danger of sinking the boat had we decided to take them all. Extensive gill nets did little to inspire us either.

Returning from one of our 'cod bashing' trips, we bumped into Neville Fickling who was on an exploratory trip to the Lodde River with Martin Founds from Angler's World Holidays who had obviously picked up on the potential of Sweden as a pike fishing holiday destination. Along with Gord Burton who was also with them, they struggled on the river, as would anyone as the fishing is notoriously difficult. It was, however, useful to meet Martin and open up a working relationship which was to take me back to Sweden with him many times, and also to many other parts of the world to promote Angler's World Holidays including Ireland, America and Canada.

Driven mad by cod, we decided we had had enough and would put the next part of our plan into operation. We would now drive across to the south eastern tip of Sweden, launch at Karlsham and get out onto the sea and try the area where Thomas's friend had caught a couple of pike. Fredrik and his friend Niclas Nilsson would come with us for the first day as it would be a new adventure for them too.

This part of the Baltic is incredibly beautiful with a coastline dotted with rocks and islands of all sizes, many of which were still covered with snow when we arrived. The water is so clear that you can see a very long way into its depths, picking out boulders as big as Transit vans and deep, dark and mysterious looking crevasses amongst which you could imagine monster pike lurking. It's dangerous though, very dangerous! Picking your way through the unpredictable tips of rocks and reefs is quite worrying even when it's flat calm, but when the wind picks up it can be quite alarming. You can forget about relying on your echo sounder here other than as a rough guide, as a reef can emerge to within six inches of the surface at any time and from nowhere. Perfect terrain for predators!

We started quite close to the shore in the area adjacent to the inlet to the famous Blekinge Nature Reserve, a huge shallow spawning bay where Danish angler Johnny Jensen's famous 46 pound pike was caught the previous year. A steel gate prevented us from entering the reserve from the sea, so all we could do was to dream, sigh, and move on. Although we were excited by the prospect of further exploration, we started to become very concerned about the weather as it was so unsettled, and in the space of a few hours we went through fog, sunshine, rain and a freak snow blizzard. It was probably not a good time to head out to sea, but we decided to take a chance!

The two boats split up to fish different areas out of sight of each other. Although the wind picked up, the waves weren't too bad and we started to tackle the windward side of reefs and islands with Zalt lures, weighted down with spiral leads on the traces. Our combined experience told us this side of the reef would more likely produce pike than the calmer lee side. In very deep boulder strewn water, it was pointless putting the anchor down. Fredrick tried it with his boat and lost his anchor straight away, having to cut the rope when it became stuck solid. The only thing we could do was to keep the engine ticking over and in reverse gear, and this just about held our position steady while we cast.

We counted the Zalts down to the bottom of the reefs, retrieving them when we felt them contact rocks. Most of the time they seemed to be going down a good 30 feet, and we then retrieved them very slowly as the water was icy cold, not expecting the pike to be in a chasing mood. Snagging was a frequent occurrence but it was easy to get the lure back, usually dragging a huge chunk of seaweed with it, proof enough that this really was the sea. It was hard to keep our footing at times, but comforting to know that our survival suits would save us if we were flipped over the side provided we were pulled back into the boat before we froze to death. Out on the open sea it was very cold indeed!

As we cast, I wondered whether Thomas could remember the way back. I certainly couldn't, we

'THROUGH ITS REMARKABLE BEAUTY, IT WAS AN AWESOME LOOKING PIKE...'

had gone so far. We had no GPS on the boat and had come a very long way from the launch ramp, navigating around many islands and negotiating miles of dangerous rock strewn bays. It was a great adventure though, and as we cast we chatted endlessly, comparing our experiences of fishing for predators in our own local waters, mine over seven hundred miles away in England and Thomas's around the Danish capital city of Copenhagen. Thomas was fascinated with the English style of fishing with deadbaits and I was equally interested in his experiences of night trolling with lures for zander. In the early nineties, many things that we nowadays take for granted were yet to happen, and I think we were both at the dawn of realising just how blinkered it was to consider that fishing revolved around ones own local area.

Hours passed and we covered reef after reef, fishing amongst snow capped protruding rocks and small islands, sparsely covered with tiny trees and mosses that had survived the harshest of environments. Just when I thought it would never happen, something pulled back, and almost in disbelief I started to crank up a fish. Half expecting to see another bloody cod, I was overjoyed to see the familiar green flank of a pike, a most beautifully coloured and marked fish which, due to the cold water, gave up without much of a struggle. Chinning it into the boat was no simple matter and fraught with danger as the boat rolled and pitched in the waves. While Thomas struggled to keep the boat from the rocks, intermittently snapping away with his camera, I wedged a leg under the boat seat to ensure I wasn't flipped into the sea whilst reaching for the pike.

As I swung it over the side, trying not to let it slip from my frozen fingers, Thomas shouted 'Mick, you have just caught your first sea pike!' and then steered us to calmer water behind an island. We photographed the fish as best we could in a boat that was rocking and rolling all over the place and in danger of hitting the rocks all around us. Through its remarkable beauty, it was an awesome looking pike, not spectacular in size but as colourful as any pike I had ever seen. It looked as perfect as I could ever imagine a pike could be, with perfect fins and an unblemished body which looked as though it had been varnished to produce a high gloss finish.

After returning the pike I looked around me, and was left in no doubt that this was something really special. The sparsely vegetated, weather beaten, islands were still covered with traces of the snow from the winter, and this was as remote and as wild a place to catch a pike as it could possibly be. In disbelief I had to taste the water, not believing it really was salt water. It is said to be brackish water, water with a salt content below that of saline, but believe me, even the small sip I took was as salty as anything I have ever tasted and I was nearly sick. There was now no doubt in my mind that this really was the sea, and that pike can and do live in very salty water.

At last I'd caught a sea pike! It wasn't a monster but a 'mid double' which we didn't weigh, but it's a fish which stands out as one of my most memorable pike captures. It had all the elements of adventure, camaraderie and drama, set against a wonderful backdrop that makes a moment so special and unforgettable. This was just the start of a three day adventure, and on the following two days when the wind eased, we caught another two dozen sea pike to over 24 lb. Once we had cracked the method, it was just a matter of finding similar swims and persevering. They all came on Zalt lures, which are well known in Sweden where they are manufactured. Nowadays they are also available in the UK and I have since had great success with them on many home waters such as Rutland and Pitsford.

Just as time was running out on our last day, we were greeted with a change in the weather which almost proved to be our downfall. The wind suddenly picked up, this time though coming from the open sea to the east, and before long the waves became enormous, bigger than any I have ever been in before or since. There was absolutely no chance of heading to the shore through the wave pounded rocks. We had to go back the way we came! For the return journey we had to negotiate several miles of rocks and reefs to get back to the harbour! I'm not afraid to admit I was frightened, very frightened, at the prospect. More frightened than when I had to row three miles across Lough Mask on my own in a big wind after my engine failed. I never thought anything could be scarier than that nightmare!

Thomas was well aware of our predicament and the serious danger we were in, and I had to put my faith in his judgement about what we should do. He decided to head out to the open sea where there would probably (?) be no rocks and reefs, but it would add several miles to an already long journey. In essence, we would go the long way round. In fact it would be a very long way round, but at least it would minimise the risk of hitting a rock which would be fatal. Looking out into the vast rolling ocean filled us both with fear, but if we stayed where we were, we would soon be battered into the rocks of an uninhabited shoreline.

With the seals of our survival suits tightened down we headed out to sea, one second being below the enormous waves then, seconds later, teetering on a foaming crest with the expectation of the boat tipping sideways and flipping us over.

Thomas kept calm as we battled against wave after wave and I tried to use my weight to balance the boat at each precarious moment. For more than two hours, we hardly said a word. Thomas had a great responsibility and I would not have liked to have been in his position. Had the engine cut out or ran out of fuel, we would have lost control and been tipped over within seconds. I won't drag out the story except to say that it was a horrific journey which I'd rather forget. We got back in one piece, but were so totally exhausted that we booked into a nearby hotel to recover, even though it took us well outside of our budget. We were just glad to be alive!

No sooner had I unpacked in England, I was packing again for a trip to Finland to visit the Rapala factory. I had recently edited a book for them titled *'How to Fish a Rapala by the Book'* as previously mentioned in chapter 1. I was well paid for doing so and then invited, along with some of the ten contributors who I had engaged for the project, to see

PIC: THOMAS SØBIRK

'...THE WIND EASED AND WE CAUGHT ANOTHER TWO DOZEN SEA PIKE TO OVER 24 LB...'

'THERE WAS ABSOLUTELY NO CHANCE OF HEADING TO THE SHORE THROUGH THE WAVE POUNDED ROCKS.'

how Rapala lures are manufactured and then to have a few days fishing. Readers may not be aware of this publication as it does not bear my name. Just as it was ready for printing I was taken on as a consultant by Shimano, a competitor of Normark who were the UK distributors for Rapala lures at that time. They simply took my name out of the book and attributed the editing to Bob James their new consultant! Business is business!

I landed in Helsinki in May of 1996 with contributors Gord Burton, Steve Burke and Vic Sampson, and we were swiftly taken to the nearby town of Vaasky where the Rapala factory is located and offered the finest hospitality. After being wined and dined, we were taken the next day to see the factory to get a chance to take a closer look at the processes used in the manufacture of the world famous Rapala lures. As a trained production engineer myself, I could see without doubt that their lures are made to a very high technical specification. The wood used in their lures is of a very high grade and is seasoned over many years before it is used, and every finished lure is 'tank tested' exactly as it says on the packet! While we were there they were putting the final touches to new colours of the world famous Super Shad, and we were asked to give our opinions regarding the finish for the roach pattern. As we had to choose from about 30 finished samples, each varying slightly in colour and appearance, it was clear that they take every aspect of lure design and production very seriously. Little did I realise that I would use such lures to take pike to 34 lb in the years that followed!

The factory visit alone would have been enough to have made it a great trip, but there was more to come as they had arranged to take us for three days fishing in the Aland Islands, a province of Finland in the middle of the Baltic Sea. Before the trip we were allowed to help ourselves to a few suitable lures from their large warehouse. After half an hour of 'temptation', I caught up with Gordy, telling him how guilty I felt as I'd filled my carrier bags with over 70 lures! Seeing that Gordy was laden down with enough lures to stock a major retail outlet, I didn't feel quite so bad!

A light plane whisked us to Mariehamn in Aland the next day where we met up with Jan Eggars from Holland and some of the Rapala staff. Jan needs no introduction to most serious pike anglers, being well known for his vast research and knowledge of big pike caught around the world and from which he had gained the nickname of 'The Pike Ferret'. At the time, Jan was a consultant for Rapala, and I had already had the pleasure of meeting him a couple of times previously, once in Holland on a Rapala organised fishing trip and then, along with Perti Rautio from Rapala, when he came to visit me in England to discuss the production of the Rapala Book. The discussions during that visit were instrumental in setting me on my course to fish the Baltic when Perti related many great stories of catching pike in amongst the melting ice which forms along the inshore sections of the Baltic. And now I was actually there!

It was now spring though, and although the ice was gone it was still very cold so we needed full winter gear to go out in the boats arranged for us with local guides. Trolling was to be the main method, but we were to do some casting too in areas where it was more appropriate. The trolling proved quite demanding, requiring very close lure contact with the bottom contours to get 'hits'. With depths from ten to sixteen feet, it was perfect for trolling the Rebel Windcheaters we had brought with us and the Rapala 18 cm Magnums we had picked up from the warehouse we had 'raided'.

We fished several large bays, and success was very much dependant on local water temperature. Where the surface water temperature was only one or two degrees Centigrade we caught pike, but it was unclear whether they had spawned or not. They certainly didn't look spawn laden, but they didn't look thin like post spawned pike either. In the bays where the water was several degrees warmer, we didn't catch anything at all and were told that the pike had probably spawned and left them, as they would eventually leave all the relatively shallow areas once the spawning was over and head out to deep water to feed on herrings.

The fishing required a lot of concentration, and if you didn't keep regular contact with the bottom, which seemed to be mainly composed of sand, you didn't catch anything. Working to this principle we caught a procession of 'doubles' up to about 16 lb, then I suddenly snagged up – or so I thought! The boatman told me that snagging was impossible on the sand bottom, and although he knew the water intimately, I was sure he was wrong. I was convinced it was a snag and we had to stop the boat and back up.

As my line shortened, I was convinced I would be bringing up an old rope or a tree branch as I was hauling up a very solid dead weight. When it surfaced, it was a very long pike which appeared to be totally unaware of its predicament – that was until it saw our ugly faces staring at it! Off she went and plunged to the bottom, refusing to come up again for a while, but steady pressure kept her coming our way. Just one point of the Magnums rear treble was all that was keeping her from me, and I had that sickly feeling that she would come adrift at any second. With the boat sides being so high, I couldn't easily reach for her, so Gordy did the honours and chinned her perfectly without any rush or panic. She was a very long pike and I suspected that she had spawned, but she still weighed a very pleasing 26 lb, much to my delight. 'Good old Gordy' had certainly saved me from losing her, and the next day I was able to repay him by chinning a 'twenty' for him in return.

'...WE WERE ALLOWED TO HELP OURSELVES TO A FEW SUITABLE LURES FROM THEIR LARGE WAREHOUSE.'

Our base for the trip was a wooden cabin on a secluded small island, and nearby, a small eating place had been primed for feeding us. Local regulations encourage self sufficiency for the islanders and the importation of certain food stuffs is restricted. As a result, the menu mainly consisted of locally caught fish. Breakfast would be a plate of deep fried perch, lunch was smoked salmon and for dinner an ample helping of cod was served up. The menu didn't vary from day to day, but as I love eating fish I was more than happy to live with that. Even our flasks were filled with a chunky fish soup which I think was sea trout. Along with the roaring log fires back at the cabin and plenty of alcohol, not to mention the pike fishing, I think that I could have happily spent a lot more time there. It would be expensive to do so though, and I was very fortunate that my work had taken me there for a while.

We caught dozens of quality pike and some nice perch and sea trout too. Many useful lessons were also learnt which I still find valuable today. It was when trolling these waters that I first realised that when a pike takes a lure, it is often one of several pike that are chasing it. It became apparent that when someone hooked a pike, someone else would often get a hit as he retrieved his lure alongside the pike that was being played to the boat. This was an accidental discovery, but when I put this theory into practice, I had many bonus 'hook ups' by keeping my lure as close as possible to the pike that was being played by another angler. This is a little dodge that I still use today when trolling with other anglers. Of course I don't broadcast this fact, but that's another cat out of the bag!

Although the purpose of the trip to Finland was to visit the Rapala factory and help to promote Rapala lures by writing about it later, it had been a very memorable experience. The islands in the middle of the Baltic Sea are very remote, and the local inhabitants fiercely protect their way of life. Although they are not aggressive or unfriendly, they make their feelings clear by keeping themselves to themselves. As the fishing on our last day was really starting to hot up towards dusk, a bullet from a high powered hunting rifle whistled through the air and buried in the water, just six feet from our boat. We were assured that this was a local 'friendly' warning signal from the hunters hidden on a nearby island to let us know that we were in the way of incoming geese. We quickly departed, pondering upon what we might have caught if we had stayed, and what we had learnt!

'...SHE STILL WEIGHED A VERY PLEASING 26 LB, MUCH TO MY DELIGHT.'

Driving back home from Heathrow amidst the madness of the M25 motorway traffic, I felt I had returned from a very unspoilt world, very different to our own, where the inhabitants had made maximum use of modern technology to enhance their traditional way of life and make it much less gruelling than it must have been in previous times.

I hope that relating just a couple of stories of my adventures in Scandinavia is enough to give the reader a feel for the atmosphere and nature of this pike angler's paradise. There is so much more to tell, but I have suddenly realised it would take up a whole book on its own. In the years that have followed, I have made many more trips to Sweden, working with the Swedish Tourist Board and Angler's World Holidays in order to promote the fishing both inland and on the Baltic Sea itself. Some of it is now opened up through holiday packages, and should you be thinking of making a visit yourself, this is probably the best option to take at first unless you have plenty of time and money on your hands to explore. For me, the exploration and discovery has been the best part of it all. I didn't have amazing fishing on every venue I fished, but the experience of simply tackling them was satisfying enough. In all honesty I can't remember all of the venues I fished as there were so many, but they include the Byalven and Klaralven Rivers near Karlstad where Jan and I also ventured onto the mighty Lake Vanern, the largest lake in Sweden and the third largest lake in Europe. I realised I needed a bigger boat on Vanern when the propeller of the engine on my 16ft Orkney spent more time out of the water than in it! In the end I gave up and trolled the Byalven River from its mouth to the weir at Saffle, many miles up river, catching plenty of pike and zander along the way. Unfortunately, I left it too late to return safely, and we had to sleep in the boat overnight. Of course, I put a zander deadbait rod out!

'...WITH LOCAL FISHING GUIDE ANDERS FORSBERG. WE CAUGHT HUNDREDS OF PIKE FROM HIS BOAT...'

There were many more waters including Store Treen Lake to the north of Karlstad which I fished with Gord Burton, and Foxen Lake on the Norwegian border which Jan and I trolled and caught loads of pike up to seventeen pounds. These waters are so enormous that you know immediately that you will get no more than a taste of what they have to offer, and it's refreshing to know that such places exist which will never be overfished by anglers.

Although anglers could never deplete these massive waters, the visiting angler should be aware that a few of them have been commercially fished in the past, and some on a very large scale using trawling tactics. One such water is the 60 sq mile Lake Asnen in Smaland in the south of Sweden, which we fished for several days only to find that the trawlers had taken the pike and zander, along with the silver fish, and left it relatively barren. Visiting anglers must do their homework, and research the venues they are planning to fish. They all look fantastic, but a small number of them aren't what they appear to be.

Undoubtedly, the most well known Swedish pike fishing venue for visiting anglers is the coastal fishing on the Baltic Sea in the Stockholm region, and in particular around the town of Vastervik. For a couple of miles offshore along this coast there are thousands of reefs and islands, and some amazing pike fishing if you can put yourself in the right places. Along with Martin Founds from Angler's World Holidays, I had the chance to open up this fishing to British anglers, working in conjunction with local fishing guide Anders Forsberg. We caught hundreds of pike from his boat when doing promotional work. They were feeding on massive herring shoals, and initially it seemed strange to chin a pike which was belching out huge quantities of herring oil, flattening the water's surface and smelling pretty evil. Over several years, I learnt a great deal about deep water reef fishing for pike on the biggest pike water in the world, where swims are typically several miles apart! On waters of this magnitude, the use of a GPS was instrumental in pinpointing swims, allowing us to quickly move between them.

With other projects on the horizon I left the Baltic fishing after a few years, but not before returning with Matt Hayes to make a film about its pike fishing for the Wet Nets series on the Discovery Home and Leisure channel. For the next few years, making films with Matt was to become a big part of my life and I had to forego a lot of my pike fishing plans as it was clear that television would be a lot more lucrative in the long term. Had television work not become a viable option for me, I think I would have further developed my pike fishing interests in Scandinavia and Europe. There is so much potential, and modern technology is opening up fishing on waters which were once considered to be too difficult to tackle. Much of it is now being exploited as 'sport fishing' for pike spreads like wildfire amongst the new generation of European anglers, most of whom are approaching it with a 'catch and release' attitude.

I can't leave this chapter without briefly mentioning one of the most memorable events of my pike fishing career, which happened in Sweden in the spring of 1997. This was the third year of the Swedish Angling Conference, and I had arrived with top specialist angler Graham Marsden, who was to be the British guest speaker for that year. Graham and I were promised two days pike fishing on the Lodde River after the conference, and a phone call while we were there informed us that the river was in top condition.

The day after the conference we were heading across to the river which was over an hour's car journey away, when one of my travelling companion's mobile phone rang. Smiling, he told me that his friends, who were already fishing that morning, had a large pike in a sack which they had kept for us to see. It had been caught by Dick Persson and weighed 16.5 kilograms. I quickly translated this to over 36 lb! As we got closer to the venue, another phone call told us that Mikael Paulsson, fishing from the same boat, had taken a fish of 15.9 kilograms, which would make it approx 35 lb!! They had kept that one to show us too, and as the water was icy cold, keeping the fish in this way would pose no risk to them whatsoever.

On arrival at the river, we quickly jumped into our extreme weather clothing and set off to the meeting place by the river, excited to see a brace of monster pike. A crowd had already gathered, but the looks of disbelief on their faces gave away the fact that there was more to this than was apparent. They had decided to keep the biggest news until we arrived! THREE sacks were carefully lifted from the river and placed on unhooking mats, and first of all the two monster pike they had told us about were slowly removed to show us. As if that was not impressive enough, they carefully peeled the sack from around the biggest pike I have ever seen in my life, and probably ever likely to see. It was enormous and had been very honestly weighed at 19.9 kilograms, just short of the magical 20 kilogram mark which most Scandinavian anglers only ever dream about. In imperial weight that is 43 lb 12 oz!

The capture was reported all over Europe and I felt proud and privileged to have seen the fish. We fished ourselves for a few hours on that day, and not surprisingly we didn't get a single run between us, but that is the nature of this fishing. You do need local knowledge, and Dick Persson proved this beyond all doubt by getting back into his boat and catching another huge pike of 15.5 kilograms! Peter Grahn, a journalist from Gothenburg who had travelled with us, also took a superb pike of just over 30 lb, now taking this amazing day into the realms of fantasy. The following day there were many boats out on the river, including ours, and only one angler had a run – it was meeeeeeeeee! Sadly, my name cannot be added to the roll of honour, as the one pound plus live roach I was trolling was taken by a 13 pounder! This caused great amusement to the Swedish pike anglers who rubbed it in by saying that they rarely catch such tiny pike, and that it would be considered to be a 'jack pike' in their circles!

Oh well, I can't always be lucky, in fact I was extremely unlucky on that trip to the point where I almost had my nose broken and nearly drowned into the bargain. Here is a lesson for newcomers to boat fishing - never look over the shoulder of a sixteen stone Scandinavian who is struggling to start the outboard motor. As Charlie Nielson's large fist came sharply backwards as he pulled the starter cord, it introduced itself to my jaw, sending me into a spin and heading over the side. Half in and half out of the water, all I can remember is being manhandled back on board and checking where the blood was coming from! Luckily, although my teeth were bleeding, none were dislodged and my nose bruised but intact. That'll teach me to keep my sticky beak out of matters that don't concern me!

Scandinavia has been a mind opening experience for me, and in particular going in search of the pike which live in the sea. There is so much more about the Baltic region which I would never have room to relate, but may I suggest that you check out internet web sites for some very interesting reading and information about the region, and also about the science behind the brackish water phenomena. Better still, why not get over there and find out for yourself!

The three monster sea pike which came into the river to spawn.

PIC: MATT HAYES

'...I FONDLY RECALL DAYS PAST WHEN THE FISHING WAS GOOD AND THE WEATHER BETTER.'

CHAPTER 19

Fly In The Ointment

Wiping away the condensation from the side window of my ageing camper van, I survey the gloomy dawn scene before me at the reservoir's edge. It doesn't look welcoming, but I'm drawn to its challenge with a confident feeling that I'm on to something! Yesterday defeated me, but the warmth of the van is a safe place to lick my wounds and prepare for another day. Sitting contentedly and eating my toast, I get a simple pleasure from studying the water, and in my mind it's not the blank featureless scene that it might at first appear as I fondly recall days past when the fishing was good and the weather better. Cars race past on the nearby road in the madness of the rush hour, but I am already at work. Well, it's a sort of work! I need some pictures for a forthcoming tackle catalogue and have a new pike fly rod blank to put through its paces. Somebody has to do these things so it might as well be me I keep reminding myself, but the distinction between work and sheer self indulgence became rather blurred quite a long time ago!

Tea and toast finished, I leave the comfort of the van, and struggle outside in the drizzle to pull on my cold damp chest waders, not even slightly dried out from the day before. The wind picks up and the rain starts lashing down and I quickly get myself cocooned into my jacket, hood pulled tight, neck strap buckled and my scarf across my mouth and nose. It's cold, very cold, but after all it is well into autumn. 'What absolute madness' I think to myself as I cut into the wind, and then the waves hit my legs as I venture into the water and wade out as far as I dare to get a bit more casting distance. 'It's not really madness is it?' I ask myself. 'I know what I'm doing and why I'm doing it' I inwardly reply. When you spend a lot of time alone, you often have these inner conversations and ask yourself questions. It's only natural to talk to yourself in this way – isn't it?

Now in waist deep water it's getting harder to move my legs, and through the muffling of my headgear I can hear the water behind me lapping against bankside stones. In front of me the bottom slopes away, littered with bigger stones and scattered patches of sand upon which, on a bright calm day, you can often make out the shape of a large pike or even two, laying quietly in wait. Further out, hidden beneath the surface in deeper water is a clump of sunken stumps from large trees, cut down when the reservoir was formed many decades ago. How many other anglers know this? Any experienced pike angler will tell you that such a feature is a potential 'pike lair' and I imagine them lying close to the woodwork, waiting for passing prey. That's where I'm aiming to place my fly!

After biding my time, I propel my fly forward during a slight easing of the winds strength, and allow it to sink to a carefully judged depth. I get it 'spot on', after all I've done it so many times, and at the very start of the retrieve, a pike hits the fly so suddenly that I almost loose my footing. It's 'on' for a second, the line pulls tight – but then it's gone! After another frustrating hour with no more hits, I retire to the van once more as the storm picks up even more violently.

For a few moments I question my sanity yet again. Just what am I doing? A married man, very happily so, and with a comfortable home and loving family 100 miles away, yet I choose to be sleeping in the back of an old camper van, fully clothed and sandwiched between two old king sized duvets, covered by a waterproof overthrow!

I put the kettle on as I wipe the window, and while waiting for it to boil I watch the storm intensify and lash the reservoir. I'm trying not to get my bedding wet from my dripping clothes, but it would take too much time and too much effort to take them off so I sit on a plastic sheet. I'm feeling like a half drowned rat, but warm and happy, thinking about the pike that hit my fly. Having already taken two 30 pounders from the swim on lures in previous seasons, my imagination is working overtime. The weather is getting worse, I don't fancy fishing in it and get my wet gear

PIC: MATT HAYES

'...IT'S A GREAT WAY OF CATCHING PIKE, POSSIBLY THE BEST IN MY VIEW.'

off, wondering whether I will be able to cast again today.

'We'll be Ok Bob, we've been through worse than this' I say aloud as I sup the hot tea. I've even given the van a name, and worse still I'm now talking to it! Loneliness and separation from civilisation can do that!'

I hope this little extract from my memory might give you some insight into the world I have lived in for best part of my adult life, and also into the workings of a pike fly fisherman's mind. It's not all been about catching loads of pike on perfect days. There's been many a miserable day and many a fruitless one too, but I seem to find a way of enjoying it all. I hope I would have the sense to stop if I didn't! The main thing I've learnt from these moments when I have time to reflect, is not to take it too seriously. Health and family come first and are far more important, even though there have been many times when I have ignored my own advice. It pays to stop occasionally, relax for a while and put the kettle on and enjoy just being there. I do it often!

Fly fishing for pike is a topic that has generated extensive comment from the ignorant and the ill informed who seek to find fault with the method. Having practiced it extensively, I can tell you quite confidently that it's a great way of catching pike, possibly the best in my view. Its critics often suggest that it's a method which employs inadequate tackle and is practiced in water conditions which will exhaust pike. In my experience there is perfectly adequate tackle available, and warm water conditions are rarely conducive to good pike fishing with any method.

To be fair to those who would chose to knock this wonderful way of fishing for pike, the early attempts of some devotees did generate quite a bad press. There's a right way and a wrong way of doing anything of course, and fly fishing for pike did seem to involve a very long learning curve in the UK. There were a few anglers who were ahead of their time, but there were also those who used vastly underrated tackle which would lead to unnecessarily long fights. Mono leaders were often too low in breaking strain, not permitting the angler to 'fight' the pike with any conviction. I don't point the finger at anyone as most of us got it wrong initially in one way or another, but fortunately those mistakes, and the discussions that followed, have eventually led to a much healthier state of affairs whereby nowadays, appropriate tackle is not only advised but is readily available.

I suppose the term 'fly fishing' is not strictly accurate when applied to catching pike. It is a term that stems from the game fishing world where an artificial bait did actually attempt to represent a fly or other winged creature in the many stages of its development. The use of a special rod and line evolved as a means of delivering a relatively small bait in a delicate and natural presentation, using the weight of the line to do so as opposed to the alternative of using cumbersome paraphernalia on a normal rod and line. Presenting baits in this way is often considered to be more skilful and more sporting, and to use an old fashioned term it is simply a more delightful way of fooling and capturing the quarry, rather than catching it at any cost.

As fly fishing for game fish progressed, the artificial bait became more than a representation of an insect and it developed into using imitations of other food items of trout and salmon such as small fish. To do so for other predators was a natural progression. Whether applied to freshwater or saltwater species, at home or abroad, it is now quite common to use 'fly' tackle, and it is not in the least surprising that fly fishing for pike should evolve as a popular method.

Fly fishing has an edge in the delicacy of presentation it provides, and there are places where it will be superior to all other methods. Shallow water and water of great clarity are just two obvious examples. Most pike fly anglers I know though use the method for one simple and less logical reason – it is great fun to catch pike in this way!

This way of catching pike conjures up pictures of sunny days and bold aggressive pike, jumping out of the water and making long powerful runs. It can be this way if you choose it to be, but for the pike fly fanatic it is a year round sport and can be successful in all but the most extremes of weather conditions. Like any other form of pike fishing it can fire your imagination and take you away from home in all weather conditions to feel the bite once more and the line tightening and powering away!

My earliest attempts at fly fishing for pike were a struggle to say the very least. In fact I look back with a little embarrassment, but I will shame the devil and tell the tale! With no one to advise me, and I am talking about almost 20 years ago, long before fly tactics received much attention from pike anglers, I decided to have a go. First of all I needed a rod. Fly rods surely need to be long and whippy I decided, and all I had that was suitable, to my mind anyway, was a 12 foot 6 inch Bruce and Walker Hexagraph carp rod! I am sure that modern day pike fly fishing specialists are already doubled up with laughter! I teamed the rod up with one of my father's old trout reels and decided to see if this unlikely

'FLY FISHING HAS AN EDGE IN THE DELICACY OF PRESENTATION IT PROVIDES...'

combination could cast a pike fly. I knew it wasn't right, but I had to start from somewhere. I could actually cast the six weight line despite the ungainliness of the rod and reel combination, and I was soon laying my first pike fly on the water on a warm still May morning.

I couldn't cast very far onto the calm surface of the large Lincolnshire gravel pit, but this was not a problem as pike in the pit were plentiful and on that morning were patrolling for the abundance of turquoise blue damsel flies which littered the margins. They were easily within my limited casting range and the inquisitive nature of the smaller pike soon had them snaffling my small floating mouse imitation, the only 'fly' I possessed. It was difficult but it was fun, but not that much fun to persuade me to persevere with the method.

Even catching a 20 pounder on a fly a few days later didn't spur me on, but perhaps the way it happened provided more fun than inspiration. Walking the bank in the early morning sun, looking for carp actually, I noticed a very large pike lying near a coot's nest which straddled the brown stems of last year's reed bed. That explained why the young coots ran away from the lake rather than back into it as I approached them as they grazed on the bank.

This pike was an old timer and knew its business well, lying very still, waiting and watching for the young birds to return to the nest. I rushed home, just a mile away, and feverishly fashioned a large fly from white chicken feathers which I had picked up quite recently with that very intention. I strapped a couple of feathers to a long shank 6/0 single hook and weighted it slightly with a wrap of lead wire. There was no time for varnishing; it had to go as it was. That pike would not wait!

A quick 'test run' back at the lake, followed by a slight adjustment to the weighting, saw me heading back to the swim to see if the pike was still there. She was! There she lay, motionless but clearly calculating and her fins rippling gently in her gin clear domain. I recognised her. From her distinctive markings I could tell she was a 23 pounder that I had caught on a deadbait on a bitterly cold day just a few months previously.

I landed the fly a couple of yards behind her, let it sink to the bottom and kept very still. She didn't budge, I hadn't spooked her. I waited another full minute before starting the retrieve. The way I had whipped on the feathers allowed them to pulsate, and I swear my hurried attempt looked like a bird swimming under the water - and towards the nest!

She turned. The water rocked the nest as she did so and the fly was engulfed. As she furrowed the calm surface it was a new feeling, unknown to me before when playing a pike. There was no reel handle to turn nor bending into her or using side strain. I had to quickly 'invent' a new way of playing a pike. In the ungraceful confusion that followed, I used the stretch of the line to slow her down, pulling it with my left hand and keeping the rod tip pointing at her as it bent far too much when I attempted to lift it. The line was old and the thinner 'running section' burnt my fingers as she took it from me in a power burst which sent her cart wheeling in front of the reed bed to my left.

Finally she ran out of steam and I inched her over the submerged straw coloured reed stems. She was tangled in a mat of decaying reeds and it was too awkward to slip the net under her, so gripping the fly line with my right hand, I chinned her out with my left, holding her aloft but having to drop her back in quickly when she thrashed like fury as I didn't want to risk damaging her jaw. As she darted through the sharp reed stems, the old fly line was cut cleanly and she was gone! She'd missed her breakfast, the coots were happy and I had just become a pike fly fisherman. I just needed to learn how to do it properly now!

In the years that followed I dabbled further at pike fly fishing, but had so many other things to do that I neglected it. Consequently neither my tackle nor my technique moved on very much until about seven or eight years later when I decided to pick up from where I had left off. I progressed to a 'proper' fly rod, a Bruce and Walker nine weight reservoir trout rod, but it was still not really up to the job. My local fen drains were ideal for practicing, and especially from a boat I used to keep on the Old River Nene where pike were very prolific at the time. You can't do it all though, and there was plenty of other fishing in that era which distracted me, and although my technique never improved much I certainly had some great fun. Even though I had tempted a 20 pounder on the fly I still hadn't seen the full potential, but

'In the years that followed I dabbled further at pike fly fishing...'

then again neither had most other pike anglers either!

I finally got to grips with the technique when Fox International, my tackle sponsors, decided that they should include a pike fly rod in their new predator range, and this was a great opportunity for me to get the rod I'd always wanted. Rods were becoming increasingly available from other manufacturers at the same time, but they didn't seem up to the job for the flies I was now using. I had 'progressed' to making my own flies, and coming from a pike angler's perspective rather than that of a fly fisherman I will admit that they were rather outlandish and outrageous, and some were rather large too! Consequently the rod I developed for Fox was much stiffer than I would use today after another ten years of experience.

Making your own flies is great fun, and initially I made them from anything and everything around me. One of my earliest favourites was 'knocked together' in a most unlikely way, but this must have been how it all started many centuries ago. The bulky body section was produced from the straw coloured under fur from my golden retriever, and the light brown coloured flexible tail was made from locks of my wife's hair after she gave in to my nagging. I remember the first fly taking shape and everyone at home thought it was hilarious and challenged me to catch a pike with it. An hour later I caught a six pounder with it from a local gravel pit! There is really no need to spend a fortune making pike flies if you are on a tight budget as there are so many materials around us that can be used.

Initially I used anything that looked useful such as Christmas tinsel, wool, feathers, animal fur and many other things which I came across. Combined with polystyrene foam to make them more buoyant or weights to make them sink faster, I soon had a great arsenal of flies to choose from. I look at them now and smile when I think of how things have moved on. When finally tempted to work with the increasingly available synthetic materials, like EP fibres, which do not retain water in the way that natural materials do, my flies became much lighter in weight and consequently so much easier to cast.

SOME OF MY EARLIER FLIES WERE REAL MONSTERS OF UP TO 13 INCHES LONG!

Some of my earlier flies were real monsters of up to 13 inches long! Approaching fly fishing as a pike angler, I felt that bigger flies would be better and thought they would give me an edge. They were certainly very effective and I caught pike from my local waters up to 28 lb 10 oz with them, but they were so difficult to cast that they eventually only came out on special occasions. When over deep water in a drifting boat for example, I would cast them as far as I could, and use a technique which involved letting out line and retrieving it against the drift, pulsing the fly with a series of short tugs to give it movement which resembled a swimming water bird like a coot or grebe. It wasn't fly fishing of course, but I did catch several gravel pit twenty pounders when doing so. They have also been used as trolling lures on a standard lure rod, and on some days, especially in the spring months when pike are really aggressive and will readily attack large baits, they are hard to beat. They present a large profile but crumple easily into the pikes mouth, and 'hook ups' have been very good.

In my early pike fly casting days, I endured a long and painful bout of tennis elbow. This was entirely my own fault and due to using unbalanced tackle, poorly designed flies and a casting technique which left a lot of room for improvement! I recall those days of experimenting with great fondness, but the time had to come though when I conformed to more acceptable standards and I started to make flies from lightweight modern materials and much smaller in size too. The man made fibres proved very easy to work with and it didn't take long to learn how to make some cracking looking flies. Making ones that worked though was another matter, and it was soon very apparent to me that some worked much better than others. I went to great lengths to 'fine tune' each fly on the bank by carefully shaping its profile and thinning out the material to reduce weight yet retain the appearance of bulk. It became clear though that what looked right to me, didn't necessarily appeal to the pike. I have come across this phenomenon with lures, also finding that some worked better than others and yet they look the same in the water. It was no different with flies, and I had some which caught consistently and others which never seemed to catch much at all. As with my lures, each fly has to prove itself before going into my box of 'catchers'! The others I get rid off!

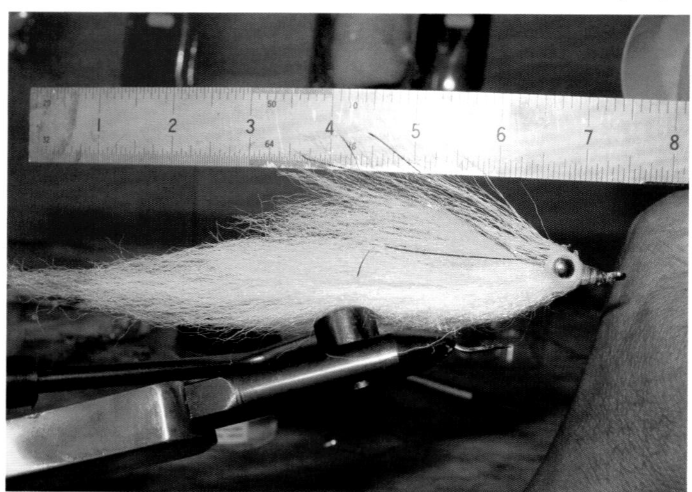

'...IT DIDN'T TAKE LONG TO LEARN HOW TO MAKE SOME CRACKING LOOKING FLIES.'

If I had to choose one favourite pike fly, it would be a simple buck tail pattern, sparsely dressed on a size 4/0 hook, and the ones I currently tie are only four and a half inches long. If I had to pick one colour which stands out

'They were certainly very effective and I caught pike from my local waters up to 28 lb 10 oz with them…'

above all others, it would be yellow. Nowadays I use this pattern in drains, gravel pits, rivers and reservoirs and catch enough pike to please me. It's too easy to fall into the trap of making hundreds of flies of all shapes and sizes and not using most of them. I've seen the same thing with trout fly fisherman. I'm sure I can hold my own nowadays with just half a dozen pike fly patterns, using them on different lines to fish them at the depth necessary.

Pike fly fishing lends itself to both bank and boat fishing. I enjoy both, but boat fishing has the edge for me as a lot more water can be covered in a day, quickly motoring between good areas. There are times when anchoring up is the better option and other times when casting from a drifting boat is better, using a drogue to slow the boat down if it's windy. It all depends upon the nature of the section of water you are fishing. When boat fishing, an echo sounder is put to good use to determine depths and prey location just as with any other form of pike fishing from a boat. Most of my 'fly' days are dedicated to fly fishing only, but I often carry a fly rod with me on more regular pike sessions, only bringing it into play when I want to. It's often purely for the fun of it rather than it being a superior method.

The opening story was all about NOT catching pike, but it's not always like that and you have to accept the bad times along with the good ones. Luck plays its part, but I always try and accept

'The spring fishing had been quite successful...'

that blank sessions are also learning or information gathering exercises. I need to make the distinction between whether it has been my fault or simply a lack of knowledge. If I feel I've made mistakes then I'll make sure I don't make them again. There's nothing worse to me than blanking and then afterwards realising that I had rushed into the session without being properly prepared. At other times though, I know it has been out of my control to a greater or lesser extent. This could be, for example, that I just didn't know enough about the venue in terms of where pike were located or what tactics were required, and I need to put in more time. Even on follow up visits I still might not get it right, but if I can see it's heading somewhere positive, I will keep going. The following story illustrates these points.

The trout reservoir where I blanked in the rain in the opening story was not a new water for me as I had fished it previously on pike 'open days' with lures. I'd had a few trout fly fishing sessions there too, and I'd also done a little pike fly fishing in the spring months with Matt Hayes. The spring fishing had been quite successful, producing quite a few fish including several 20 pounders to over 26 lb for both of us. Fly fishing for reservoir pike in the autumn, however, was a new venture for me, and although the spring experience was a useful starting point, I only had my intuition to guide me. With Matt being abroad for this period, I had no one now to bounce ideas off which had been so useful in the past.

A 26 lb 2 oz fly caught pike for Matt.

I quickly found that the productive spring pike swims did not hold them in the autumn. I suspected they had dropped into deep water for the summer and it was now a matter of finding where they would start their autumn feeding as the water temperature started to fall, tempting them to enter into shallower water again to feed. Naturally it would be a good idea to fish the swims where I had caught them on lures in previous autumns.

I'd finished my spring pike fly fishing on the reservoir at the end of May when the water temperature started to reach a point where I didn't think it to be a good idea to fish for them any longer. I know that pike are fished for with the fly on other reservoirs in the summer months, but I didn't fancy doing so here. Whether summer fishing for trout water pike with a fly rod is a good or a bad thing, I can't really comment as I have never done much of it, except for a couple of days when Matt Hayes and I filmed on Chew Valley lake. In the few hours that we actually got to fish when making this film, we didn't really catch enough fish to draw any conclusions. My gut feeling though is that one should proceed with caution and be prepared to stop if any fish caught appear to be stressed or exhausted.

Starting again on the reservoir in late September, I found the water very low and the pike quite difficult to catch, but eventually I found a very tight area which quite a few pike had packed into. This produced ten fish in two sessions, a week apart, with eight of them being 'doubles' and the biggest of 15 lb. In between these sessions I had a couple of days on a local gravel pit with the fly rod and fared somewhat better, taking 12 pike which included an 18 pounder and one of 20 lb 8 oz.

A local gravel pit produced this 20 lb 8 oz pike to a home tied fly.

Three more day sessions back at the reservoir produced two or three fish each time. Not a lot of pike for the effort put in, but at least most of them were 'high doubles' with the biggest topping out at 19 lb. I was becoming very frustrated though as, apart from the productive area I had located, I couldn't catch anywhere else on the reservoir. At least the weather had been very pleasant and it was a pleasure just casting in dry and sunny conditions. The weather then changed for the worst, which now brings us to the session outlined in the opening story which ended in a miserable blank. That could easily have been my last session of the season if the autumn rains had continued and coloured up the water. It's hard enough catching pike there in good conditions, and although I love fly fishing my life doesn't revolve around it. There is other pike fishing to do too and I could have easily decided to bring things to a close. As it happened, the rainfall that followed over the next few days wasn't too bad after all and the weather actually improved. Not being able to get it out of my system I decided that, even though it was nearly November, I would have one more go, my head buzzing with ideas and an even stronger urge to get back. I guess that's what being obsessive is all about, never knowing when to give up, always searching for the seemingly impossible.

The 100 mile journey to the reservoir passed very quickly as my mind was full of unfinished business. There were a few new swims to try out, new flies to test and thoughts about different retrieve styles, and naturally the prospect of a big pike! Two more days at the water would give me plenty of time to experiment. I couldn't get my waders on quick enough when I arrived, and was soon into the water and casting. I spent the first day in familiar swims and by perseverance ended with three doubles to 16 lb. The second day was to be reserved for trying out a new area.

All was quiet at first, but whilst wading along a section of bank where the water was very coloured due to the effects of the wave action on the clay bottom, I missed a couple of bites. Then, as I waded a few paces further along, I had quite a shock when I felt myself stumbling over a pike which seemed to be using the coloured water for cover. Then I trod on another one, and then another nearly knocked me off my feet as it powered away from where I was about to step! Then another one! The swim was alive with them!

THE PIKE WERE AMBUSHING FORM THE COLOURED WATER.

The coloured water went out to the extent of my safe wading range, about two rod lengths out from the margin, and at that point there was a very distinct colour change from the very brown marginal water to the gin clear water of the main body of the reservoir. With no marginal features to hide in, I felt sure that the pike had very cleverly decided to lie in the murky water and use it to ambush passing prey from. There were plenty of prey to attract the pike to the area, and the margin was alive with small roach which dimpled the surface, and they were regularly being scattered by rainbows, giving themselves away with scrappy splashes as they waded through the shoals. With roach and trout in the area the pike had ample food to dine upon, but there was no telling what their preference would be, if they had one at all. They probably grabbed anything that offered itself easily as I'm convinced that pike anywhere do. By the time the day had ended I'd eventually had eight, maybe nine, pike bump into my waders as I slowly and methodically inched my way along the coloured water section, so goodness knows how many must have been in the area. To my disbelief, I ended the day fishless and kicked myself that I couldn't catch them. I was determined to get it right the next time! True anglers will always go home with that strong urge to get back, and if I ever don't feel that way, I'll know its time to pack it in.

Before my next visit I was expecting some useful feedback from other anglers as, over the following weekend, there was to be a pike fishing event on the reservoir with more than 40 top anglers fishing with lures. I looked forward to feedback from friends who would be fishing the event to give me more idea of the current form of the reservoir, and especially of any areas where pike were caught.

The weekend fishing by the syndicate produced more than 100 pike, many were 'doubles' but there were only four or five 20 pounders reported. I was not surprised to hear where a couple of them had come from as it was quite close to where I had stumbled upon them during my last visit. I really had to get back there now!

Armed with a bit more information about where pike had been caught, and another boxful of newly made flies, I started in my 'reliable' swim which had produced more pike for me than any others, even though none of any large size. Later on in the morning, I planned to fish where the pike had bumped into my waders. As I made my first cast of the day, I wondered why I hadn't caught any of the bigger pike in the last few weeks. It seemed that the bigger pike had not moved back into the margins just yet, but as I have mentioned elsewhere in the book, you can be fishing swims that are full of pike which, if not in the mood, can be very difficult, if not impossible, to catch.

I didn't have to work hard to hook the first pike of the morning, but went straight into panic mode as it took line like no other pike I'd ever hooked before on the fly. The 'running' line was soon all out and the 'backing' line started to disappear rapidly as the pike surged and boiled out in the dark blue waves. This was a swim where I'd caught mid thirties on lures, and my mind started racing. I followed it along the bank, trying to get line back, but it kept going and going. Thanks goodness I'd put over 100 yards of backing line on the reel rather than listen to those who told me that 30 yards was enough for pike!

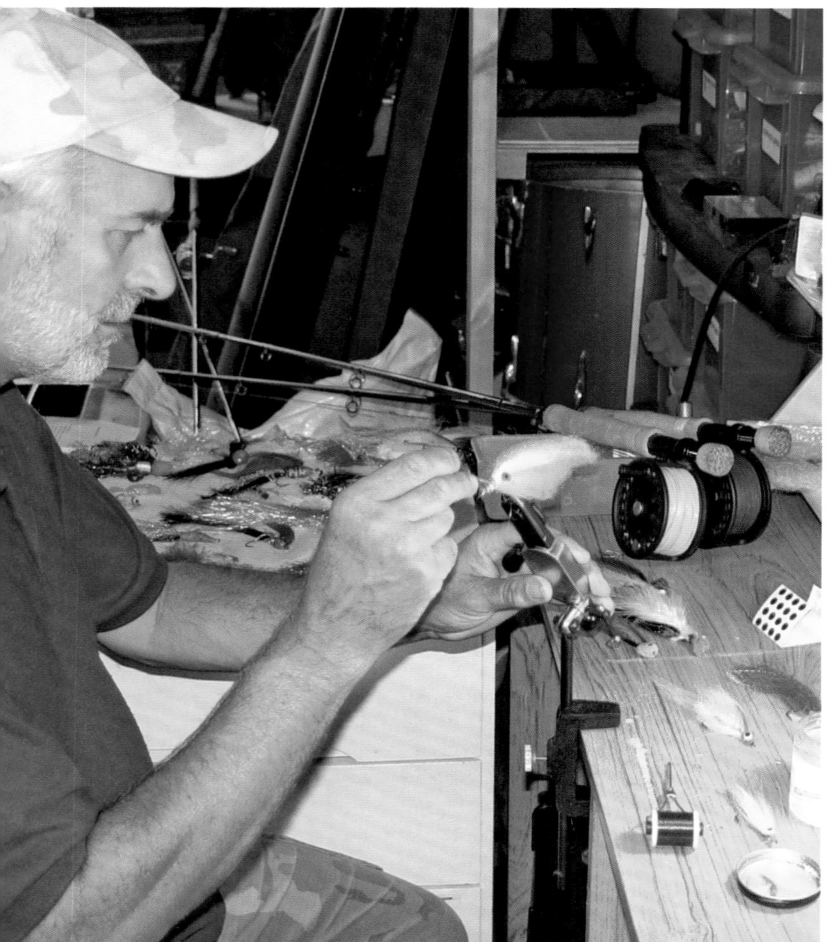

'...And another boxful of newly made flies...'

When it jumped, a good 60 yards out, figures like '40 lb' kept echoing in my mind. I'd never hooked a pike on the fly before which I wondered if I would ever land; it normally seemed like a formality. At this stage I knew something had to be wrong, pike don't fight this hard and for this long - unless they are mis hooked!

The pike calmed down, but it took another five minutes to drag it in, now feeling no more than a heavy weight. It was mis hooked and right in the wrist of the tail! Suddenly my '40 pounder' looked more like a 16 pounder, and my heart sank. As I released her, something else made sense. During the last few sessions I'd had loads of 'knocks' which I'd put down to trout. This, and other similar tail hooking experiences on other waters, may be due to pike hitting its prey with its tail to disable or disorientate it before grabbing it. I think it happens.

The morning session wasn't over yet though, and half an hour later I landed a pike of 20 lb 4 oz. It was a great fish to catch on the fly and yet I had a tinge of disappointment after being robbed of my 'monster'. Of course, I was getting things out of perspective. It was a great anti climax, but you

'She pulled the scales to 24 lb 1 oz and I couldn't believe my luck!'

cannot loose something you never had – if that makes sense!

After a quick snack, I drove to the part of the reservoir where I'd been 'treading' on the pike, and by now the wind had picked up and the colour line was very distinctive. This time I had a new plan to put into operation. Instead of casting and drawing the fly back to the coloured water, I would cast along the colour change line, running the fly parallel to the bank. This should give the pike more time to inspect it I thought.

I waded to the edge of the colour line into water which was above waist deep, and kept as quiet as possible. Were the pike still there I asked myself, as I made the first cast. Whack! My bucktail fly was hit really hard on a short line, nearly pulling me off balance. The pike surged out into the reservoir, but was not too difficult to stop even though it felt heavy. When properly hooked, pike are rarely much trouble on a fly rod as you use the stretch in the line to play and tire them and not the rod. After a series of ever shortening runs she was guided over the drawstring of the net. A really fat pike at last! I was very happy with a weight of exactly 26 lb and a passing trout angler obliged with my camera, but not before telling me he'd caught bigger pike on trout lures! Knowing the reputation this water has, he probably had! The next two hours in the swim produced a 15 pounder and then a move to an area I had never fished before saw pike of 13 lb and 18 lb landed, making it a very productive and enjoyable day. I had been thinking about going home that night as I had been neglecting other commitments, but couldn't resist camping out and having a morning session!

'SHE WENT 25 LB 15 OZ AND WAS RETURNED AFTER A COUPLE OF QUICK SNAPS, USING MY CAMERA ON ITS TIMER.'

Sleep didn't come easy that night. I was up at daybreak, but started as always with a good breakfast. I love my fishing but will never miss my breakfast!! Maybe I should have started a bit earlier as the pike were 'mad on' from the start and I had an eight pounder on the first cast in a new swim I was trying, quickly followed by another of similar size and then a 17 pounder. I'd really got the technique down to a fine art now, cutting my polycarbonate leader to the optimum length, judging the sink rate of the fly and using a retrieve technique which provoked the pike. Stopping the fly occasionally and allowing it to sink for a few seconds, often produced a hit as it fell towards the bottom.

It was now time to revisit the coloured water area. It had been given a good rest, allowing time for other pike to come into it after the disturbance from the previous day. Methodically working along its length, I eventually made contact with a pike which fought very doggedly. She was easily worn down by my strong tackle though and pulled the scales to 24 lb 1 oz. I couldn't believe my luck! This was more like it and was what I'd been working towards. Spending time on my technique and tactics was starting to pay off and I was now casting with expectation rather than hope. I finally latched onto another pike on the colour change line about an hour later and it was another very good looking fish of 22 lb 8 oz. 'At last', I thought to myself, 'it's finally all come together!'

By now my back and my casting arm were starting to ache, but I had one more swim to get out of my system which involved wading out along a shallow bar with deep water to either side. I spent longer than I wanted to in the swim and the time passed very quickly, but I added two more pike of 8 lb and 14 lb. Even though there was still some daylight left, I decided to go while I still had enough energy for the long drive ahead of me. To catch nearly 200 pounds of pike in a weekend with four 'twenties' amongst them is a bit special, but to take them on home tied flies is very special in my book, and a trip I won't forget!

The fishing on the reservoir finishes at the end of November, but despite a rapid fall in temperature, I couldn't resist going back for a final fling. My expenses for this project were mounting up, but the business could afford it as I had plenty of work coming in to pay for it. The marginal area was covered in ice on my arrival at daybreak so I had to sit in the van and wait until mid morning before it had melted enough to cast in. I waded out about five yards to get past the ice line and started to cast along it. I figured that the pike might use the cover of the marginal ice in the same way that they had used the colour line on the previous trip.

I knew my chances were very slim, but I was drawn to the water. The fishing in the cold water was predictably hard, and despite wearing my thermal under suit my legs felt very uncomfortable and I could hardly feel my hands, but I had to get just one more bite before the season ended. After an hour of casting, a gentle pluck gave me the bite I wanted and a 16 pounder came begrudgingly to the net, the ripples cracking the icy surface of the margin. Feeling too cold to carry on, I found refuge in the camper to get some feeling back into my arms and legs.

In between hot drinks in the van I'd nip out for a cast or two, but had to decide just how much I wanted to suffer to try for another bite. In the middle of the afternoon when all seemed lost it came! That bite made the long drive and the cold limbs worthwhile as a 'mid twenty' hit the bucktail hard, and on the way to the net smashed the marginal ice into thousands of pieces. I weighed her and then 'sacked' her up while I set up my tripod. She went 25 lb 15 oz and was returned after a couple of quick snaps using my camera on its timer. Totally elated, I carried on fishing straight away and had another bite within half an hour from a 15 pounder.

Now I was really fired up, but although I tried to carry on I had to concede that I'd had enough as I just felt too uncomfortable. My hands were numb and my back and neck were killing me from getting cold and damp over so many recent sessions. I drove home slowly with the heater full on and a big smile on my face, and my mind overflowing with pike fishing. Like the fanatic I had become, I planned to fish a local pre baited swim with deadbaits the next day and couldn't wait for morning to come! I know that this must seem like a tale of an expensive self indulgence, but I have no problem with it as it is all tax deductable and very useful in my work!

Since that season, I have got the 'fly fishing obsession' under more control and now only fish with a fly rod when I want to. It's easy to get carried away and become a 'one method' man, but there are so many other ways of catching pike. As with all other pike catching methods, I have pursued fly fishing to an extent where I am confident and comfortable with it. It involved pushing myself hard to get there, and now I can carry on building on my pike fly fishing skills as I go along. You never know what opportunities will arise where a fly rod is a good option, but I'm now confident that I can identify them and take advantage!

'...CLAMPED ACROSS THE BACK OF A VERY BIG CHUB, CERTAINLY OVER 5 LB WHICH WOULD MAKE IT OVER 20 INCHES LONG.'

CHAPTER 20

Close Encounters

Seeing pike in their natural environment gives me as much pleasure as actually catching them, and the month of May is a great time of year for observing them. Mid spring is a time when they are very active, feeding voraciously to get themselves back into condition after the effort of spawning has followed on from a long hard winter. This is a time when I'm at my most observant, especially when fishing clear water venues. A local gravel pit I fish regularly is always reliable for spotting pike at this time, but you do need to have your wits about you and be looking for them. A warm May morning a few seasons ago didn't let me down and it all started with a pleasure fishing session from my boat.

The lake is well endowed with chub, the descendants from a few which were stocked over 50 years ago from a nearby river while the pit was being excavated. Some of them are very large now and I've taken many 'six pounders' and even one over 'seven', but they are very difficult to approach. On this particular morning, I'd crept up on the shoal in my small aluminium boat, using an electric motor to approach with stealth. I anchored in six feet of water, adjacent to the shallow bay where the chub were shoaled up. In just two feet of water, where the bottom was composed of clean gravel and silt, they were responding well to sprayed maggots, and my waggler float had gone under twice and I'd put two five pounders in the landing net. It was one of those days when you realise why you go fishing, away from it all and the hot sun on your back. It couldn't get any better – could it?

The enjoyment of catching these chub was enhanced because of the clear water. I could see them very clearly as they fought around the boat and came to the landing net. When releasing them, they looked amazing as they swam down into the thick weed and hid away. Sometimes a pike would follow them to the landing net and that really was a sight to see as the lake holds some very big pike, and these were usually the ones that followed.

I was just about to recast, when I noticed a pike's tail was sticking out of the thick weed just beneath the boat. It was motionless, and I was feeling a little concerned as I thought it could be a spawning casualty in the last moments of its life. My thoughts changed when the pike backed out of the weed, adjusted its position, and then buried its head into the weed again, and it was clearly in perfect condition. What strange behaviour I thought, I had never seen anything quite like it before. It didn't disturb my chub fishing though so I just carried on, but kept an eye on its progress.

Time and time again, it ventured in and out of the weed, with more than half of its bodied being buried at times. This went on for twenty minutes or so, and in that time I never had another chub bite, even though I had got them feeding on the maggots. The fishing needed concentration but the pike was distracting me, and I eventually stopped fishing to watch it. All of a sudden, it powered forward and disappeared totally into the weed. This unusual behaviour was now going from strange to bizarre, but all was revealed when it emerged from under the weed, two or three yards away, with its jaws tightly clamped across the back of a very big chub, certainly over 5 lb which would make it over 20 inches long. It lay there for a minute or so, just four or five feet beneath the boat, giving me time to recognise it as a 24 pounder I had caught in the winter, its distinctive tail markings clearly giving it away.

I quickly set up my camera in the hope of recording the incident, as the pike swam up onto the shallow gravel margin and lay there with its prize. I quietly pulled up the anchor and inched towards the pike with a short burst from the electric motor. She soon swam away across the shallow water, but I managed to fire off half a dozen shots before she disappeared over the shelf with her dinner, into one of the deepest parts of the lake.

The pictures were as good as I could have hoped for in the hurried circumstances, and that to me felt as exciting as catching her. I've caught plenty of twenty pounders, but not captured many 'on film' in this way. Apart from the satisfaction I get from looking back at such pictures, they are very useful in my work for illustrating articles and using in talks and tackle catalogues. Newcomers to the sport might find this attitude to be rather strange, but it's one I have arrived at over time. There are no ground rules in pike fishing and you can take from it whatever you wish to, as the pleasure you derive from it is a personal thing and we are all different in our outlook. Many continental lure anglers, for example, count the number of attacks made on their lures, rather than the number of fish caught. It's nice to catch the pike but they also get pleasure from seeing them attack or feeling them strike. Until I realised this, I wondered how they reported so many more pike than was feasible! British anglers might struggle to see their point, but I am now starting to appreciate their philosophy. You can't change what happens, but you can change how you value and interpret it!

As much as I'd like a record on film of all of the amazing sights I've seen of pike in action, they happen so infrequently, and usually so quickly, that there isn't usually time to get the camera out. Keeping my eyes constantly scanning the water for the chance of an interesting photo has led to many observations that may not have produced a photo, but have resulted in a pike capture which would not have happened had I not been alert in this way. I'm not only using my eyes when seeking pike, but also my ears too! I'm listening for the giveaway sound made by an attacking pike. When a pike chases its prey to the surface, it's often accompanied by an unmistakeable swirl, and if you don't see it, you can often hear it. Many times I've heard the water 'churn' behind me when boat fishing, and turned round to see the distinctive surface disturbance from a pike attack. Covering it quickly with a lure or livebait, or even retrieving a float fished deadbait across the swirl, has often resulted in a bonus pike in the net.

A pike usually makes an unmistakeable sound as it wades through a shoal of prey fish, sending them scattering and scurrying everywhere. If it happens in front of you it's obvious, but when it happens out of sight, behind a bush maybe, you can easily miss it if you are not in tune with your surroundings and using all of your senses.

Pike are not always obvious when they feed, they can be very crafty and cunning too! They often loom into view in a calculated and menacing fashion as I found to my shock one morning on a large Irish Lough. The morning was so foggy, I couldn't even see to the end of my boat. I'd just landed a pike though on a trolled roach deadbait, listening for the ratchet on the reel to sound rather than struggling to see the float. The bait had come off and was now floating right next to the boat, but I wanted it back to use again. As I reached for it, just a few inches from the hull, a very large pike's head appeared and snatched it from my grip! It left me shaking and feeling very vulnerable for a few seconds. In a 'pea soup' fog and with just a few millimetres of fibreglass keeping me from thirty fleet of water beneath the boat, I sensed the reality of how small I was in the midst of a harsh, cold and dangerous environment, and that I couldn't just walk away from it too easily if I wanted to. It was time to stop and have a cup of cold flask tea and compose myself! I knew I was in no danger, but for a few minutes panic set in and I wondered what the hell I was doing, so far away from home and on my own. I often wonder nowadays whether a pike, or several pike, are skulking around under my boat without me even knowing about it. Dropping a livebait next to the boat now and again occasionally proves they are!

'...SCULKING UNDER MY BOAT WITH OUT ME EVEN KNOWING ABOUT IT...

Pike do not attack human beings, but they can make silly mistakes and there are many instances of pike grabbing hands and fingers while anglers have been washing them in the margin. The fact is that a pike will attack anything it thinks it can eat, and anything that looks or sounds like a meal is fair game. Once in a while they get it wrong! I was reminded of this fact when fishing an estate lake in the spring, when my arm became trapped under the water for a few minutes!

I'd hooked a small pike and it promptly swam under a very large sunken tree trunk lying under the surface of the lake. It was only a few inches beneath the water and stretched out perpendicularly from the bank. The pike became stuck beneath it and it seemed as though the wire trace had caught on the underside. It was possible to walk out onto it, keeping balance by holding onto smaller overhanging branches from a bankside bush, so I decided to remove some top clothing in case I fell in and attempt to free it. I kept my balance and got my arm under the large piece of timber, and managed to feel the pike and the trace. It seemed that the plan was working fine – that is until one of the trebles became nicked between my thumb and first finger and I couldn't pull it back without it digging it in past the barb. The pike was stuck and so was I, precariously hanging on and wondering what to do next!!

I'm not one to panic normally, but my legs were starting to ache and I had to quickly consider my options. I was just about to drop into the water, which was only about five feet deep, so that I could use my other hand to release the hook, when the pike shot away and my hand came free. I'd been very lucky as it could have been quite nasty if the hook had pulled into my hand, but thankfully 'Sods Law' can sometimes work in reverse!

The 'jack' was landed, and as I stood on the bank drying myself, a good sized tench shot from under the tree trunk where my arm had been stuck. Seconds later, it was followed by a very big pike which I'd guess to be about 20 – 22 lb. In front of my very eyes, and only three feet from the bank, it's flared jaws clamped across the back of the tench. It had to work hard to prevent the tench from writhing and wriggling and breaking free, and was so focused that it was totally oblivious to me standing there. I even had time to go to the car and get my camera, and had further time to take a few pictures before she returned to her lair under the tree trunk with the now lifeless victim. One of those shots was sold to Blinker magazine, a German publication which I have written for quite a lot, and this is exactly the sort of pictures they like to use, so I made a tidy profit from this little skirmish!

On the way home, I did wonder whether the pike had eyed up my forearm while it was trapped down there. It occurred to me that it's about the same size and colour as a five pound tench! Probably not, but the thought still sent a shiver down my spine!

When seeing a pike in the water in front of you, or the giveaway disturbance it makes, there's always a danger of reacting hastily, scaring it away before you have given yourself a chance of catching it. Rarely are they going very far and it's best to take your time, thinking carefully about how to proceed rather than just casting blindly. You have to quickly assess the best tactics you should try, but you will always be limited by the tackle and bait you have with you.

Jan and I had been lure fishing on a cold day in late winter and it had been very productive. I had taken a 20 lb 11 oz pike from a really hard water and was feeling very pleased with myself. I'd seen this pike follow many times in recent visits, but it always held back and wasn't very obvious unless you were really looking carefully for anything following the lure. This careful observation had encouraged me to persevere at trying to catch it and I finally had. I thought my days work was done when the unexpected happened!

As the day drew to a close, the secretary from a club that leased a nearby water came over for a chat. After I'd told him about my big pike, he said he'd heard of a big one being seen in his lake. Not being slow at coming forward, I steered the conversation around until I obtained permission to try for it for the rest of the day, and also the following day too if I wanted to. I'd always longed to fish the lake, and although it had no recent reputation for big pike, it had produced an occasional 'twenty' in the past - so I jumped at the chance!

While I sorted out the van, Jan went on ahead with a lure rod and net as we only had an hour before dark. Five minutes later, she returned in a panic. A huge pike had swirled at her lure, which she was working just beneath the surface as the swim she had started in proved to be very weedy. I dropped everything and was across there like a shot!

After determining where the pike had attacked her lure, I ran a Micro Demon just beneath the sur-

'...ITS FLARED JAWS CLAMPED ACROSS THE BACK OF THE TENCH.'

face of the clear water. I tried three times, but felt that that was enough. To my left it looked as if the water deepened under a large overhanging bush, and I said to Jan that it's where I would lie in this swim if I was a pike. I flicked the lure in front of the bush, felt it down, and started to retrieve as soon as I contacted weed. As I slowly brought the lure towards me, a matter of a few metres, I turned to Jan to suggest that we should come back in the morning with livebaits. As I was about to lift the lure from the water, it carried on moving past me and to my right. A pike had grabbed it and quickly surged forward, giving a 'slack line' bite. I had a fraction of a second to catch up with the slack line and strike, instinctively flicking across the anti reverse lever on the reel and sending the bale arm spinning madly and rapping my knuckles.

The pike never ran very far and it was one of those fights that take place 'on the spot' in a great flurry of foaming and churning water. It was clearly a very big pike and Jan wasted no time in getting the net under it whilst I shouted instructions. They were totally irrelevant as she knew exactly what to do, having done it so many times before. Being married to a 'good old fen girl' does have its advantages, and Jan has many times been the 'unsung hero' behind many of my catches.

There would have been no need to panic as the hookhold was good. In fact I had to cut the treble with my mini bolt croppers so that it could be removed from the pike's teeth without damaging them. The reading on the scales then completed a remarkable story. I had fished a new water for about ten minutes and caught a 'thirty'!! She pulled the digital scales to 30 lb 3 oz, and as we looked more closely

'I had fished a new water for about 10 minutes and caught a '30'!!'

'...A MEMORABLE 25LB RIVER PIKE WHICH GRABBED A LIVEBAIT RIGHT UNDER THE ROD TIP...'

at her, she was a very unusual looking pike with a two-tone coloured head. One side was the normal green colour and the other was a shade of gold, and there was a distinctive dividing line down the middle of her skull. Unfortunately, the flash photos never did this feature justice. As I lowered her back into the lake, my fingers never even noticed the icy cold water. The adrenaline running through my body was temporarily making me oblivious to how cold it was getting as darkness fell over the still fenland landscape. We slowly gathered up the slimy wet weigh sling, unhooking mat and net, and bundled them into the van to be sorted out in the morning at home. The journey home went in a flash as we relived every second of the day's events, over and over again, looking forward to the stew in the fridge waiting to be heated in the microwave. Moving from the city hadn't been a bad idea at all!

Seeing and catching pike at close quarters is very exciting, and I've been very privileged to have seen some fantastic sights. Many pike anglers, even those with many years of experience, tell me that they just don't see these things. If you cast out and listen to the radio or read a book, you will probably miss a lot, but if that's what gives you pleasure, who am I to try and change your view. I'll only settle down comfortably myself in this way if I have good reason to do so; otherwise I like to be active and looking for opportunities. At the very start of every session, the very least I do is check out the margin before casting further afield and have had many big pike from right under my feet in this way, including a memorable 25lb river pike which grabbed a livebait right under the rod tip as I checked out the reed bed next to the boat where I'd anchored.

Being quiet at these times is a big advantage, and many anglers I've fished with ruin their chances (and mine) right from the start, as they are just too NOISY! Pike are as timid as any other species and will move away from any disturbance. If you disturb prey fish and they move away, any pike watching them might move away with them. Stealth will definitely lead to putting more pike in your net.

I hope by now, the reader might realise that my relationship with pike goes way beyond just catching them. Reeling them in and adding up the tally is no longer enough for me. I like to feel that I have forged an understanding of pike which enables me to catch them when I want to, but the actual capture itself is not the 'end result', if that makes any sense. Nowadays my sessions are less rushed as the pleasure comes from the interest that the fishing generates rather than from what I catch. If I just wanted to rack up a large number of big pike, my approach would be very different. I've worked out how to do it but it would involve fishing waters I don't like and using tactics that bore me, so I don't! That's how it has evolved for me, for others it is bound to be different!

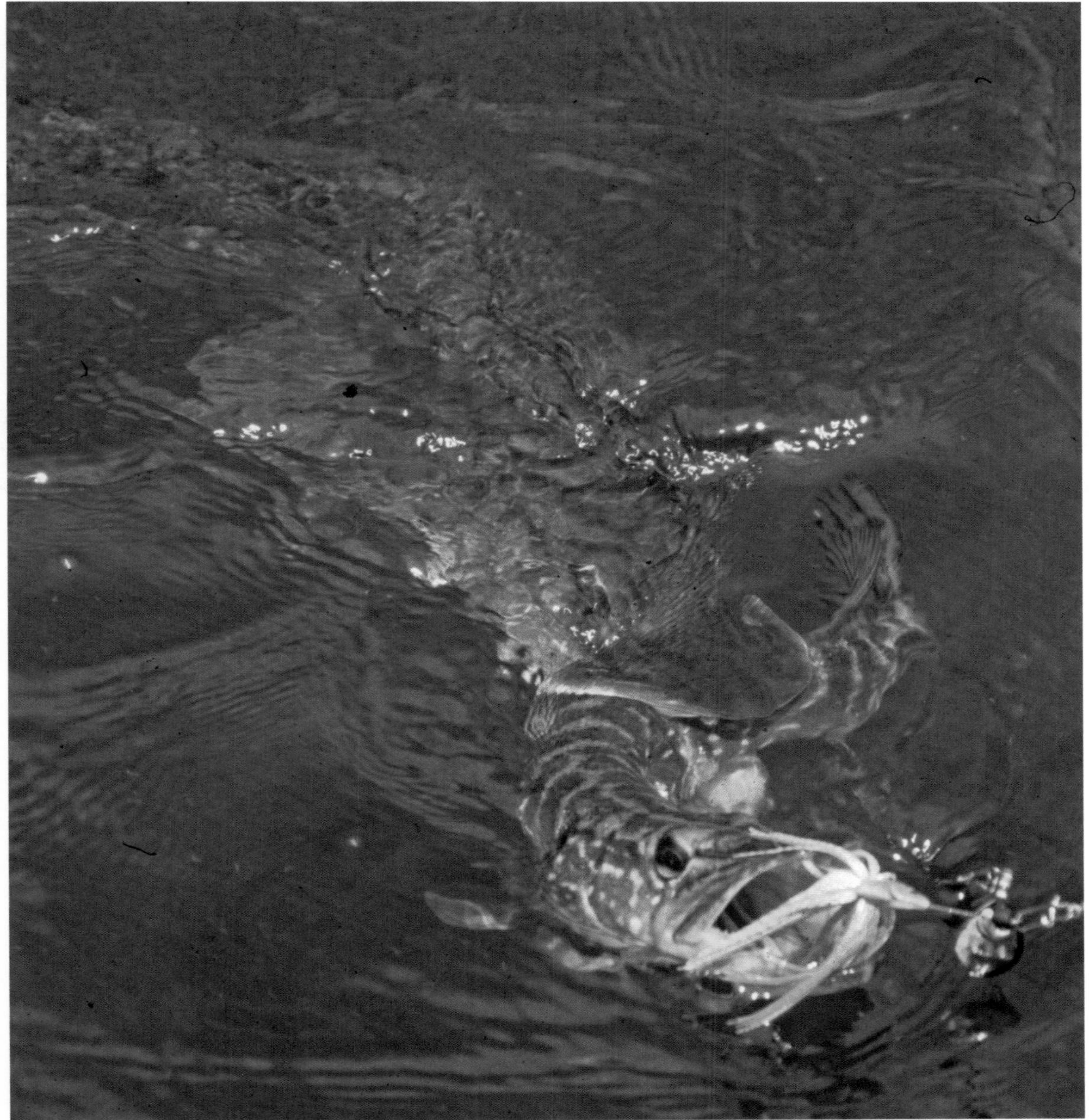

'...I'VE BEEN VERY PRIVILEGED TO HAVE SEEN SOME FANTASTIC SIGHTS.'

'It's a water which makes you work for its pike.'

CHAPTER 21

Go For It!

Driving to the lake on a cold December morning, I kept telling myself I'm going to get it right today! I'd realised where I'd gone wrong on my last session and this time I was going for it. I'm tackling a lake that I've chosen for a winter project and this will be my third visit of the season to the lake, and so far I haven't cracked it. It's a strange water where, if you don't make it happen, it usually won't. It's not the sort of water where you can cast out a couple of baits, sit there in one swim all day and get a few runs. It's a water which makes you work for its pike.

On my first visit, a week previously, I must admit I didn't fish well. I was feeling quite worn out after fishing for Zander in the dark the evening before, and had not got to bed until well after midnight. Furthermore, I was totally out of touch with the lake, having not fished it since the previous winter. I hadn't really got into the swing of things yet, and in retrospect I knew I'd treated the fishing with a far too relaxed and casual attitude. I'd only moved the boat once and only fished with deadbaits, and I didn't get a single run. That's the trouble when you get over tired, you can easily waste a day by not putting in enough effort. I did have the sense though to chop up my left over deadbaits and scatter them around in a deeper area where the bottom contours are more irregular than the surrounding area. At least I was planning ahead!

My second visit saw me in a better mood and prepared to make a lot more effort. I repositioned my deadbaits in the deeper water several times, and consequently covered a lot more area. Whilst doing so, I also thrashed the 13 foot deep swims with a variety of lures including spoons, jigs, Jerkbaits and rubber tailed baits, all of which had caught fish there in previous seasons. It didn't make any difference though and it was as if the lake was devoid of fish, yet December should be a prime pike fishing time.

My next thought was to fish shallower water. More than two thirds of this lake is less than six feet deep, and much of it is only half this depth. In previous winters I had ruled out this very shallow water, but the mid depth water of six to nine feet had produced pike in cold weather. I headed across to a point where the deep water shelved up to the mid depth water and anchored up.

I cast around the swim with two of my favourite tail baits, a Rooter and a Micro Demon, and I must say that I have supreme confidence in them having taken many 'twenties' and a 'thirty' on them in winters past. Nothing even followed them so I decided that it was time to drop down to another area. At last I'd got my 'fishing head' back on and was working at it! A little voice in my head, suddenly told me to try a jerk bait. Such a lure can often wind up lethargic pike, and that little trick had almost slipped my mind. A well battered Loz Harrop Darter, yellow with black stripes, was quickly clipped on and sent flying to the horizon. I tried to keep its gliding motion as slow and gentle as possible and had it coming back nicely without picking up any weed. As it came into sight after the third cast, it became one of those moments that pike anglers live for when a dark sinister shape loomed up behind it, only to turn away sharply when it saw me. It was a good fish and well worth catching! Next cast, a smaller pike followed, but again refused the jerk bait. I worked the swim for another hour, occasionally going back to the tail baits, but it was only the jerk bait that interested them. The smaller pike showed interest several times as did a different fish, a 'mid double'.

'A well battered Loz Harrop Darter...'

Finally the jerk bait was nailed by the 'mid double' and I watched it clamp onto the lure

'...I SPENT AN HOUR IN THE FREEZING COLD IN MY WORKSHOP...'

right next to the boat. After a lot of splashing and a flurry of foam, I was able to chin her and easily remove the lure with my pliers. It was a fabulous looking pike which I didn't weigh, but she was clearly over 15 lb. I didn't want to waste any time, because the first fish I'd seen was far bigger!

I carried on until last light, and although I wasn't entirely sure, I thought I'd seen the bigger pike follow the Rooter several times, but the failing light was working against me and playing tricks on my eyes. I just had to get back the next day and have another go for her! As I rowed across the deeper water in the dark, I stopped off where I had thrown in my chopped deadbait leftovers on the first visit, and piled in the chopped up contents of my deadbait cool bag, about ten fish in all. My mind was now working overtime, hatching a grand plan that would involve a little work at home that evening, and I knew I'd have trouble sleeping that night! It was time to go for it!

Back at home I thought about how the Rooter had interested the big pike, but how it had refused it. Because of the possibility of it catching up on weed, I knew I had been working it just a little too fast. It's a floating lure which dives down to about four feet on the retrieve, but due to its buoyancy you have to keep retrieving quite quickly to make it stay at that depth. As soon as I slowed the retrieve down, it would rise in the water and the pike would lose interest. I needed to modify it so that it had much less buoyancy, which would enable me to work it extremely slowly, keeping it at its working depth for longer and giving the pike more time to consider whether to take it.

After dinner that evening, I spent an hour in the freezing cold in my workshop, drilling a hole in the underside of the Rooter and forcing into it an SSG shot, then checking it in the kitchen sink to see the effect. The additional weight had converted the floating diver to a very slow sinking lure. It could have done with a little bit more weight to make it sink a bit faster, but I knew that by the time I had Araldited the weight into position and sealed it, the glue would add the little extra weight required. In the warmth of the house, the Araldite would set very quickly and the lure would be ready for the next morning! I went to bed early, but before doing so persuaded Jan to drive across to fish with me later the next morning after she had been shopping, and if all went well to help me photograph that pike if I caught it. Getting decent photos is an important part of my work and snapshots are just not good enough. In fact it's a waste of time in this business if photos are not of a high professional standard, so I do need someone with me who knows what they are doing. Photography is a part of this job that I hate, and because I tend to fish a lot on my own, so many beautiful looking pike have to be slipped back unrecorded.

The weather remained settled for the next day, being very cold but with only a light breeze coming in from the North West. I was really firing on all cylinders now, prepared to attack the fishing with my entire armoury. If you are not careful, bringing a lot of tackle can work against you, so it's important to be tidy. Piling it all into the boat at the mooring tends to be a hectic affair, so I like to use the first swim I stop in as somewhere I can get the boat better organised and have a cup of coffee. The first swim was to be the pre baited area, as it was deep and would be less affected by the clattering of tackle as I got sorted out.

The morning started quite chilly but pleasant. It was one of those days where the cold, damp air smells really good, bringing reminders of past glories. Two deadbait rods were set up and cast to the pre baited area, and now feeling a little bit more relaxed, I poured a cup of coffee whilst tidying up the boat. Keeping one eye on the floats, I made the central area of the boat free of any clutter, ready for a big pike to come on board, and then sorted out my lures.

Coffee finished, I went through my lure fishing routine, whilst every now and again picking up a deadbait rod and twitching the bait back to me by a couple of metres or so. I was itching to get across to the mid depth area where I had seen the big pike, and was eager to try out my modified Rooter. I was just thinking about lifting the anchor when one of the red bungs just melted away into the still grey water. A big pike was hooked and slowly brought to the net, not giving me much trouble, the very cold water slowing her down considerably.

It wasn't long before she was on the unhooking mat with a well ragged herring tail protruding from her jaw. The size four trebles were easily removed as she struggled very little in the cold air, and at 21 lb 7 oz it was a great start to the day. What is more, I hadn't even fished the swim where I had seen the big pike yet! Almost as if working to a script, Jan arrived and photographed the fish and then joined me in the boat.

We were soon anchored in the swim where I had seen the big pike. For the first twenty minutes or so, I cast my special Rooter around the area, but nothing followed it this time. Being much better prepared, I had six lively roach in the bait bucket, and one was cast out mounted on two size four trebles

'...AT 21 LB 7 OZ IT WAS A GREAT START TO THE DAY.'

'...IT'S SOLITARY TREBLE WAS IMPOSSIBLE TO TURN WITH MY FORCEPS...'

on a free roaming float rig. The floating main line and the gentle breeze ensured that the livebait moved briskly through the swim, and knowing there was a big pike in the area, it was a very viable alternative.

The unpredictable weed in the swim started to cause problems and I frequently needed to reel the livebait back to the boat to remove it. I was just about to put my lure rod down towards the end of a retrieve so I could check the livebait, when the Rooter was stopped in its tracks with a violent snatch. Line was easily gained though and I soon had an obviously big pike under control. When she came into sight in the clear water, I had no doubts that it was the fish I had seen the day before.

Jan netted her, and as the very fat fish lay quietly on the unhooking mat, I became concerned because the lure had been taken well into the back of its mouth and its solitary treble was impossible to turn with my forceps or pliers. Being well prepared, it took just a couple of seconds to snip the offending point of the treble with my long handled bolt croppers and the lure came free with no damage occurring. At 23 lb, it was a great pike to catch on a lure at any time, but to catch her in December made it feel a much greater achievement. We drifted against the bank, photographed her and released her in superb condition, as Jan's pictures clearly testify.

That would have been enough for me, but there was still some daylight left and I knew I was 'on a roll'. Sometimes I just know it's going to happen and within two minutes of dropping into a new swim, my red livebait float plopped under with a real vengeance, the line snatching from the line clip and running rapidly through the rod rings. This one did give a reasonable fight, throwing the livebait from its jaw in a furious display of anger at being hooked. At 20 lb 2 oz, it was not as pretty looking as the other two 'twenties', having a badly deformed jaw and dorsal fin. She didn't make a particularly good picture either, but that's not the end of her story. Four years later she turned up again, and despite the fact that her jaw deformity must have impeded her feeding ability to some extent, she had piled on the pounds and had reached an impressive weight of 29 lb 1 oz!

Basking in our glory, against the backdrop of a spectacular sunset which reddened the whole sky, we continued fishing until we could no longer see the floats. The rapidly falling temperature then told us it was unwise to stay any longer and the prospect of a hot meal finally drew us away. I slept much better that night!

On the session described, I really had pulled all the stops out, and making an effort can make a big difference to your results. There's a well worn saying that 'effort equals results', but that's only true up to a point I find. The effort needs to be channelled intelligently and wisely. Anyone can be a 'busy fool', putting in the hours or casting all over the place with all the latest gear. Getting results demands something more. A good angler usually doesn't look any different to a poor one, until you examine what they are both doing in more detail. You can sometimes try too hard as well as not hard enough and it's important to know when to wait and when to do something. Such decisions make all the difference, but no one will get it right all the time. You just try to get it right as often as you can!

This starts with fishing the right water. Many anglers do not do enough research and are targeting waters which, in reality, have been flogged to death by other anglers or do not have the quality of pike fishing they are seeking. I have known anglers base their venue choice on the most ridiculous conclusions. 'It looks very pikey', 'no one else is fishing there' or even that 'a man they had met said there were big pike in there'!

Finding a good water is vital, and there's no point advancing to the next stages of location and technique until you are working on a water that has the pike you are after. Finding waters with bigger pike poses a bigger problem than finding 'bagging up' waters, and in my business I'm continually seeking

The 23 pounder which took my modified Rooter.

DESPITE THE HANDICAP OF A DEFORMED JAW, SHE REACHED THE STAGGERING WEIGHT OF 29 LB 1 OZ. FOR THE STATISTICIANS, THIS WAS MY 300TH PIKE WEIGHING OVER 20 LB.

both types of water. The 'bag up' waters are ideal for doing instructional magazine features when fishing time is limited, but for more in-depth articles I need to find waters with bigger pike to better illustrate a point.

As an angling writer, it would be a lot easier to do the circuit of well known waters, but frankly I get bored with following on from other anglers and try to find my own venues. From my articles, you would never know where they are as I have learnt to only give away those that are of no consequence, and I've always kept back anything I value. It's a matter of mixing and matching to come up with what publishers want, still remaining truthful and factual but protecting my own interests. Readers of my work might be surprised at this, but doing otherwise would have soon ruined waters by attracting too much attention to them, spoiling my own fishing and that off others.

A lot of success has simply come from taking chances rather than following other anglers around. It's been about continually keeping my eyes and ears open for potential waters and biding my time, or going out of my way to make it happen. One very special pike came in this way. In fact it was the last pike I caught from a winter campaign on a water that had produced plenty of pike up to 19 lb, but where I suspected there should be a bigger fish judging by the exceptionally good head of large prey fish.

It had been stocked with trout in the past, although there weren't any in there at the time, but it had large numbers of tench, big roach and eels. It just had to have a big pike or two I thought. At the time of getting permission to fish there, I was informed that the trout had all died in the previous season and that the trout fishing had been abandoned. They didn't think there were many pike left as they had been taking them out for the last ten years. I wouldn't be put off by this and still thought it worth spending some time there, especially when one of the trout men told me of a 'monster pike' he had seen following his lure during the last winter. You do tend to hear lots of exaggerated stories, but I didn't think this project was worth writing off until I'd had a session or two.

'...Against the backdrop of a spectacular sunset...'

The fishing wasn't prolific but enjoyable all the same, and each session usually produced up to three pike or an occasional blank. The pike didn't look particularly well fed, but they were in good condition and had clearly not been caught before, otherwise they would have been taken out. Towards the end of the season, I'd taken about two dozen pike with the biggest at 19 lb, and as part of the deal I'd moved them to a coarse fishing lake nearby.

I was rather disappointed that I hadn't had a twenty pounder, and I think that several of the 'upper doubles' would have been 'twenties' if they'd had the benefit of the bonus trout to feed on. With the winter rapidly disappearing, I was told that my time on the lake had almost run out and they were planning to stock with trout again very soon. With just a week to go, I decided to see the project through to the bitter end and fit in a final session.

Many of the pike I'd caught had taken sea deadbaits, which is not a common occurrence on many trout waters, but they were hungry and eating whatever came easy to them. To offer them encouragement, I had an area where I dumped all of my unwanted deadbaits into, not so much pre baiting but more of an irregular introduction of bait. With my last day rapidly coming to an end, I had a run on a herring tail in this swim and boated an 18 pounder. It seemed a nice end to the winter project, but as it came to the net, my Polaroid's revealed a much larger pike swimming beneath it and I was convinced it was a twenty pounder. Nothing else happened for a while so I moved and quickly tried two other spots. With darkness almost upon me, thoughts of the potential 'twenty' drew me back to the swim where I'd seen it, and I decided to spend the last half hour of daylight there. I knew that my time on the water was all but gone, but kept up my ritual of inch retrieving my deadbaits every now and again. A firm pluck on a lamprey bait, seconds after picking up the rod, indicated that it had been grabbed, and as the bait was quite small I didn't waste any time in striking.

It felt heavy, and I would have been very disappointed if this wasn't the 'twenty' I'd been hoping for. I didn't panic at all, not even when she surfaced and completely left the water as she powered away, as I could see she was well hooked. I now had no doubt in my mind that it was a 'twenty' and I estimated about 24 lb when I calmly netted her. The first attempt to lift the net was halted while I repositioned my footing to steady the little aluminium boat, which seemed in danger of tipping over under the weight. I got a better grip and in she came, and in an instant I could see she was much bigger than I had first thought. On the unhooking mat, her fat belly spread out and revealed her full size. The scales then told me that I still hadn't got a 'twenty' from the lake – it was a THIRTY! Weighing 31 lb 1 oz, it was another milestone on my journey and had been well worth the effort and perseverance. As I sat by the sack for over an hour in the freezing cold, waiting for Jan to drive down and photograph the pike, I knew it had been well worth 'going for it'.

Of course, I like to relate tales of success, but these results have to be seen in context. I don't go around catching big pike all the time and have many disappointing sessions too. I also fish waters which rarely turn up big pike, but I still put in the same effort, even if the end result may not be so impressive. Whenever I go piking, I like to get the best result I can from the day and won't settle for whatever comes along. On my local river venues for example, where catching a 'twenty' is a Red Letter Day, I still keep on the move, vary tactics and use all the little tricks I've learnt. I'm always looking for anything out of the ordinary or the unusual. There's so much going on around us when we fish, most of it hidden beneath the waters surface, and there are clues if you look for them which can result in catching more pike. I'll finish this chapter with a catch that came in a very unusual way through being observant.

On a mid winter afternoon, it seemed like the pike in the heavily overgrown lake I was tackling were not feeding, but I kept searching swims, hoping to eventually drop onto one or two. My efforts were not rewarded on this occasion, and I had to decide what to do for the last few hours. About 30 yards to my left, I'd been watching mink scurrying over a flattened reed bed, slipping into the water and occasionally coming back out gripping onto a quality roach. Then it registered to me that the mink had found the prey fish for me, and surely the pike wouldn't be far away either!

I crept into the swim and lowered a smelt into the clear water in front of the matted reeds, and a long snout came straight out and nailed it. A 12 pounder was returned, and as I hadn't caused much distur-

'I STILL HADN'T GOT A 'TWENTY' – IT WAS A THIRTY!'

bance when landing it, I waited ten minutes and lowered another bait over the rushes. It was grabbed instantly by another 'double', but this one went berserk and tore up the reed bed, making catching another one doubtful. I tried of course, but sport was over apart from another good pike which looked at my bait, but turned away from it.

In any pike fishing situation, there will be a number of different ways of catching them. When the options are many, you should have one of them within your ability range, even if that means no more than slinging out a deadbait and watching a float. As the options reduce, as will happen on hard waters or in difficult water conditions, they might be outside of your repertoire. You might not even recognize what they are. This is where a wide range of skills and a knowledge of pike behaviour becomes important.

To catch a lot of pike, it's important to try to make things happen, looking for opportunities rather than waiting for them to show themselves. When they do come along, don't waste them – 'go for it'!

CHAPTER 22

Catching the Impossible

'...THERE IS ONE WATER WHICH HAS TOTALLY CONFOUNDED ME...'

I have fished hundreds of waters for pike, and taken 20 lb plus fish from more than fifty of them. Some have been easy and some quite difficult, but in my search for bigger pike there is one water which has totally confounded me. It's less than ten acres in area and is a stocked rainbow trout water, and I have fished it for 22 winters. In that time, I have only caught about 20 pike, nine of which weighed more than 20 lbs, with the biggest going over 28 lb. Some seasons I have put in 15 – 20 sessions, but because it is such a hard water to crack, I have sometimes had to walk away from a new campaign after half a dozen blanks.

You might ask why the hell do I keep going back? To average one 20 pounder every two winters is hardly great pike fishing. That might be so, but this water has been my greatest challenge because I believe that during most seasons, there has been a pike present that would make me very happy indeed. In the first season I fished there, a pike of enormous proportions roared in after my wobbled deadbait.

In the crystal clear water, I saw every inch of its bulky body and massive head. I saw it just once and never again. This was only a few months after I'd caught the Gailey Reservoir monster pike detailed in my first book, and with it fresh in my memory I was well aware of what a huge pike looked like.

Two seasons later, a club member reported to me how he had dragged a big dead pike out with the help of a friend. It was never photographed, but they said it was almost the width of the tailgate of their four wheel drive truck! It was cut in half to see if there were any trout inside it and then taken away in two bin liners for dumping. Other big dead pike were reported in the years that followed, and yet all I was catching was the occasional jack or low double, or once in a blue moon, a low 20 pounder.

Then I found a big dead one for myself, 45 inches long and weighing 35 lb 10oz! It was fresh and clean, probably only dead for a few hours, having just dropped its spawn with just a few remaining eggs showing at its vent. The livebaits I'd fished there a few weeks previously were probably within the territory of a pike of close to, if not in excess of, 40 lbs! The following season I found yet another dead pike of the same length, too smelly to weigh but clearly of similar proportions.

The fishing was always hard for season after season, and I always approached it with mixed feelings. It seemed as though as soon as I tackled this water, all my knowledge, experience and ability, counted for nothing and it drained my confidence. In the winter of 2006/7 I decided to concentrate on the wa-

I FISHED IN ALL WEATHER CONDITIONS.

'...MY FINAL KICK IN THE TEETH...'

ter almost exclusively, sacrificing most of my other pike fishing in an all out attempt to try to get the big pike I was becoming desperate for. Throughout December I hammered away with lures and wobbled deadbaits, and drifted livebaits across the lake. Conditions were good, being mild and windy, but all I had to show for it was a 12 pounder which took a 40 gm Gladiator spoon.

I was starting to enjoy the challenge, I don't know why, but despite my lack of results, thoughts of those dead monster pike kept driving me on and on and I felt that eventually something had to crack. Crack it did, and in a short burst over a few days I landed four pike, all over 20 lb and all different fish! One took the 40 gm Gladiator spoon, one took a Fox Micro Demon, one took a livebait and another took a lamprey section. Hardly a pattern developing though! It was now just a matter of time I thought, but through the final six weeks of the season, I only got one more pike, another new 'twenty' which took a Micro Demon, despite the weather conditions being 'spot on'.

Surely, if I had taken five different 'twenties' without a recapture, the odds were in favour of several more big pike being present. Of course I was happy to have caught what I did, but I was now as confused and frustrated as ever as they were still so hard to catch. Since then, despite fishing as hard as I can, I have only caught one more 20 pounder from the lake and have not spotted any big fish during that time.

At one stage I convinced myself that I just needed to pinpoint where they lay when digesting their food for long periods of time. One winter, the water level became very low and I was surprised at just how many hiding places were revealed. There were undercut banks I was unaware of and the tangles of tree branches and roots that they could get into were much more extensive than I had realised. I fished near them all, but it made no difference! It always feels like it's all against me when I fish there, and I wonder if I will ever get the pike I want. This situation epitomises a love/hate relationship, but like a fool I know I shall go back!

LOW WATER REVEALED MANY HIDING PLACES LIKE TREE ROOTS...

For the last three seasons I have trout fished on the lake, and very enjoyable it has been too. As well as enjoying this sport, I do of course have a hidden agenda! Whilst playing every trout, and there have been a lot of them, rather than get them quickly into the net I have allowed them plenty of time to swim and splash around in the hope that they might attract a big pike. Just to glimpse a big pike in this way would be enough to carry me through another winter's heartache. Not one single pike of any size did I see! Surely there were none left to be caught.

Convinced that this was the case, I received my final kick in the teeth in the spring of 2010 when I found three large dead pike. They weighed 24, 30 and 36 lbs! The smaller one had been killed by a trout angler (idiot) and the biggest one was spawn bound. At the time of writing, my heart isn't in it any more. With those three big pike gone there can't be much, if anything, left to fish for can there?!! So frustrating, such a small water and so many big pike I haven't caught that have come and gone.

...AND UNDERCUT BANKS.

Trying to analyse the situation, I have had to console myself with some sort of an answer. For the pike to have grown so big there needs to be an adequate and easily obtainable food supply – and there is. A good stocking with rainbows supplements a very healthy eel population. The eels average well over two pounds in weight and they are frequently found dead in the winter with their heads partly digested, indicating that they may have been disgorged by pike. Apart from a few perch, no other fish exist there. From these facts, I can only presume that the pike are totally pre occupied with larger food

THIS EASILY IDENTIFIABLE 21 LB 10 OZ PIKE WAS ONLY EVER CAUGHT ONCE, DESPITE EXTENSIVE TIME SPENT FISHING THE WATER.

items, which enables them to spend a lot more time digesting than feeding. With such an abundance of food, the feeding spells must be short, sharp and quite rare. In the gin clear water, this might also take place at night. Night fishing has only ever produced one run for me, a very large brown trout which took a live roach. This was a rare fish for the water and from a stocking many years previously, and these 'browns' are never caught by the trout syndicate members.

On other waters in similar situations, I have had a degree of success by trolling with livebaits. In the depths of winter this normally requires trolling the bait very close to the bottom, and I have often had to literally drag bottom with the livebait and inch it along painfully slowly. Although this approach has cracked other 'hard' waters, it has not been able to work on this one because of a major problem – weed.

The weed just never goes away on this pit, and to make any progress at all you have to troll with the bait well off bottom. Even then, you have to wind in every 20 yards or so to remove weed, and you frequently snag on rogue fronds which rise to mid water. There are two very weedy corners where it's impossible to troll, lure fish or in fact use any method with a good presentation. Is this where they live?

Of the big pike I have found dead at this lake, none have been fish I have ever caught which make things even more frustrating. I can be sure of this as it is easy to identify them. Bigger pike can easily be identified through their unique markings, very much in the way that humans can be individually identified by their finger prints. In particular, patterns around the wrist of the tail and the areas where the body spots blend into the white underside of the pike are usually giveaways. More obvious features can be damage in the form of split fins or scars, whilst other pike might have physical abnormalities such as protruding teeth or eye problems. With good quality photographs, it normally takes just a few minutes for the trained eye to assess whether a pike is recognised as a recapture or a new fish. Indeed, anglers who are interested in this topic frequently recognise recaptures, even as they slide into the landing net or are laid on the unhooking mat.

Being able to identify pike is the key to discovering that certain pike can live their lives without ever being caught. We only know of such fish when they turn up dead. When fishing regularly on other small enclosed waters, and even some much bigger waters, I can usually build up a picture of the big pike population through recaptures of those I catch. I have never had a recapture here though!

Of course such pike may have been previously caught at much lower weights, at which time they could have gone unnoticed or unrecorded. We do have to set criteria though, and for me this is to recognise pike weighing over twenty pounds. On some waters pike may never reach this weight, so this inspection must apply to the biggest pike in the water, and in such instances it is nonetheless interesting.

There are a couple of other waters which I have yet to come to terms with. They are kept on the 'back burner' while I wait for the inspiration to tackle them any further. Some have beaten me so far and I've had to walk away from them for a while as I know that there are limits to how much time I can afford to spend on 'impossible' waters. On my latest new water, I endured six blanks in ideal conditions, feeling I had fished very thoroughly. Then I found a dead 28 pounder! I still have to make a living, and stories about 'blanking' don't sell magazines! I hope to be lucky on some of these waters at some stage before I totally give up, but even I can only have so much luck!

So where is this leading me to? There are said to be three phases that an angler goes through in his fishing life. First of all, he wants to catch as many fish as possible and then he moves on and attempts to catch the biggest. I've probably got both of these phases out of my system now and I think I must have moved on to phase three.

This is said to come at the end of a long career, and it's at this stage that success is measured on its merits or value. It's at this point that the angler wants to catch the most difficult fish, and I can now relate to this and see myself heading that way in my final years. I can't walk away from these challenging waters now. As I approach retirement age, with my business winding down and more time for myself, I hope to spend more time fishing and will spend my time chasing, and maybe even catching, once in a while - the impossible!

A kebab rig is made from freshly cut chunks of fish and should be dripping with blood and body fluids.

CHAPTER 23

New Ideas

Alex Bones looked at me in total amazement as I opened a pre production sample of the new Dynamite Bait's kebab baits. I rigged one up, cast it to my right, and then put traditional herring and mackerel baits on my other two rigs. Being primarily a match angler, Alex looked at the kebab bait, scratched his head, and admitted that he just didn't get it!

He was out with me while he was working as Media Manager for Dynamite Baits, in the hope of getting photos to promote the new range of pike products which they were about to launch, and which I had developed for them. It proved to be quite a slow day with the first two runs eventually coming to herring baits, both pike being less than six pounds in weight. Towards the end of the day, the float went zooming away on the kebab rig and Alex finally had the chance to do his job and get some great pics of a superbly athletic 20 lb 8 oz pike which jumped all over the place before coming to the net. There were no dramas with tangling in the mesh as the rig has just one treble which was easy to remove from the pikes jaws. Even as a match angler, Alex could see the sense in using one treble, it just made life so easy for me and for the pike. Job done! Moments like this when my work comes together, take my fishing to new levels of satisfaction. Making a catch which is both interesting and exciting gives me a good feeling which I am unable to describe or explain. I won't even try!

The 'kebab' comes good again with a 20 lb 8 oz pike!

I'd been using unconventional deadbaits for several decades in the form of sections, chunks and fillets, and I had even used backbones with success. To keep my bait bill down, I once bought several boxes of heads and backbones from filleted coley from Grimsby Docks to try out. After pre baiting with them, I found that the pike soon mopped them up, so to try one as a hook bait was a natural progression in the experiments. If it's fishy, they will eat almost anything in waters where deadbaits are normally accepted.

The 'kebab' is really the culmination of all my thoughts, brought together in a simple to rig method. Long ago I worked out that pike, even very big pike, will pick up all sorts of scraps of fish, and for much of the time we simply do not need to be using pristine and perfect looking baits. On the fens and broads back in the seventies and eighties, when bait supplies were dwindling I proved this to myself many times by using anything I had left, no matter how small or damaged it looked. It became my normal practice to put on small pieces of previously used baits that had been chewed up by pike and get further use from them. This was partly a matter of economics as money was much tighter in those days, but it didn't take me long to realise that doing so rarely provided any disadvantage. In fact, on hard fished waters, where 'normal' baits were often treated with suspicion by the pike, I would frequently winkle one out by using just a head, a tail or a middle section, usually mounted on just one treble hook or sometimes a single.

This was a tactic I used regularly on a heavily fished section of the River Welland near my home. I would often fish such a bait quite close to the bank, replicating what would happen when I discarded a piece of useless looking bait into the margin. On tatty bits of bait I caught lots of pike, often bigger ones, and events of this nature reinforced my long held belief that discarded baits are often quickly mopped up right under our feet while we are casting much further out! Where lots of pike anglers are fishing on a regular basis, the action of them throwing in bait at the end of, or during, their session is a form of pre baiting. Pike get used to picking up scraps of bait of all shapes and sizes, and where bank fishing is prevalent this is usually in the margins. It's easy to see how this discovery contributed to me considering an organised pre baiting campaign.

Knowing how effective it is to use left over scraps of bait, I later progressed to cutting whole fish into chunks and using them in this way from the outset. I was really inspired into viewing 'chunking', as I call it, as a viable predator method after using it to catch Stripers and Blue Fish in the USA when fishing with Jan's brother Mike and their good friend Captain Ed Mc Laughlin, off the Rhode Island coast. I just loved the simplicity of inserting a big single hook into a freshly cut chunk of fish, dripping with blood and body fluids, and dropping it behind the boat to be drifted down tide. It only needed a few simple modifications to make this an equally effective pike or zander tactic. Used in conjunction with pre baiting, where the feed is cut into similar sized chunks, it doesn't take much imagination to realise how acceptable such an offering can be as a hook bait, and what a simple rig it can be used on.

In 2006 I made a trip to the River Ebro in Spain to sample the incredible catfishing there. That trip was responsible for starting a chain of events which led me to fine tune my tactics and develop the 'kebab'. To say the catfishing was incredible would be an understatement – it was absolutely phenomenal. In my weeks fishing I landed 66 catfish, 22 of them weighing over 100 lbs and for a total weight of over 5000 lbs! I fished very casually from breakfast until teatime and didn't push myself hard at all, and I know for sure that I could have caught considerably more had I wanted to. It was not difficult fishing by any stretch of the imagination, and there would be no merit in catching any more. There seemed to be no point in knackering myself, it was just fantastic 'fun fishing' and it's the fishing guides who do most of the hard physical work! Catfish in Spain are tackled nowadays with multiple large halibut pellets on a hair rig, which is the method I used to take my mammoth haul, and being convinced that it would work on my English catfish waters, I applied it on my return.

As expected, it proved to be just as effective at home as it was in Spain. It was certainly a lot easier than trying to catch livebaits and taking them out with a bait boat or 'winch rigging' them out, hoping they would stay alive all night. There was a flaw to this little plan though because the catfish quickly 'wised up' to being caught on the pellets. Fortunately the livebaits remained as effective as ever!

On one of my catfish waters where fish baits are not allowed in the summer months to protect the pike stocks, pellets seemed to be the natural way to go. It was a very hard catfish water with just a couple of big ones, and even though I tried pellets I didn't catch any of the cats on them. I did though, to my surprise, catch large numbers of pike as mentioned in the chapter about coloured water. Having thought about it since, it's not really surprising as halibut pellets are made from fish and are a pike's natural food presented in a different form.

The use of pellets for pike hasn't yet caught on, but I suspect that there will be more developments in the future. It's currently a very viable method on waters where plenty of pellets are thrown in for other

'...IT PROVED TO BE JUST AS EFFECTIVE AT HOME AS IT WAS IN SPAIN.

species and the pike have learned to take advantage, particularly in the summer months when they tend to feed less aggressively and seem content to 'graze' on pellets as an easy supplementary food form to get them through the summer. I have since heard from correspondents about pike being caught by design on pellets in rivers and natural lakes too, so it seems that there are others prepared to give it a try.

I have picked up a few zander when using pellets in my trials, and I am convinced that they also would take advantage of such an easy food supply if they needed to and if it was readily available, as would be the case in rivers where pellets are used in vast amounts for barbel. When I first mentioned this, I could tell I was not being taken seriously. A new record zander, weighing 21 lb 7 oz was then caught in 2008 from the River Severn by a barbel angler - who was fishing with halibut pellets!

I am not suggesting for one minute that we should all start using halibut pellets for pike or zander. The reason I have mentioned my experiences with pellets is to explain the chain of events that led me to take things further, and replace the pellets on my rigs with similar sized chunks of fish. It seemed a natural progression, the right thing to do. While experimenting, I also tried multiple baits on the rig consisting of a mixture of pellets, boilies and luncheon meat alongside fish chunks. They all caught pike! It did resemble something you would drop onto a barbeque though, and purely for fun I decided to call it a 'kebab' rig. I prefer the simplicity of a fish kebab though. It's a lot more practical and cheaper too. The kebab was found to work well virtually everywhere I tried it where pike normally take deadbaits. The 'fish kebab' has been very successful on gravel pits, drains and particularly on rivers where it has caught plenty of zander too. It has also proved devastating for catfish and helped me crack a particularly hard water where it accounted for three different cats over 60 lb.

I think it is so effective because of the amount of fluids that it leaks out from the many cut surfaces. Many deadbait anglers pierce their deadbaits to let out these attractive body fluids, and I see the kebab as taking this concept a step further. It is important to use fresh bait and it must be absolutely dripping with blood and juices when cast out to get the best results, and if it starts to look stale, I'll replace it with fresher pieces. I also use a 'pop up' version by adding a polyball to lift it above bottom debris. I liken the kebab to adding a swim feeder packed with chopped fish to my rig to draw pike to my hook bait, another method I used a lot for pike before the kebab came along. The kebab is bait and feeder all in one!

Dynamite Baits have now discontinued their frozen Kebab baits. Unfortunately they were not economically viable to produce. To meet my specification, which required them to be dripping with blood and fish oils and packed on the plastic rig pin in a tight and compact way, made the process too labour intensive and consequently expensive. Rather than have an inferior product in the range, it was decided to drop it. I hope those who bought them were sensible enough to have kept the rig pins they came on and used them to make up their own kebabs!

Other important benefits to 'chunk' and 'kebab' fishing became apparent as I used it more. The kebab system is perfect for the use of just one hook, which may be a large single, typically size 2/0, or a solitary treble which is usually a size four. Using one hook is something that I always try to do nowadays to get away from some of the frustrations caused by 'two treble' rigs. Such rigs are a liability when netting and handling pike and a prime cause of potential damage to fish and angler alike due to the problems they present when catching in the mesh of the landing net or when trying to extract them from very lively pike. If you use one hook, you will quickly see the benefits.

The kebab has certainly been taken up by quite a few anglers and I frequently get feedback of a very positive nature, including the capture of a pike weighing over 30 lb on the method. I do receive a little negative comment from some anglers, most of whom I know have never even tried a kebab rig, and from a few others who are just biased or ill informed. The kebab rig is not a universal method for all pike fishing applications and neither is 'chunking'. These methods are at their most useful in baited swims and where smaller baits are effective, but can never be ruled out elsewhere and provide another approach to any fishing situation. I still use two trebles on rigs where a larger bait is essential, but for anglers who are locked into a certain way of thinking, the benefits of using the kebab may never be realised.

Clients, who have fished with me on my tuition days, have sampled its benefits at first hand on gravel pits and on rivers. I always start the day by setting them up with traditional rigs, and they experience everything that is frustrating about pike fishing such as tangled trebles in nets, fish damage and danger to themselves. I do my best to ensure that no one or any pike comes to any harm, but I did have one unfortunate customer go home with a treble in his thumb. I can tell you from first hand experience (several times) that it really hurts, and getting it removed in hospital is even worse. I wouldn't wish such an experience on anyone which is, in itself, a good enough reason to find ways of avoiding it.

'THE USE OF PELLETS FOR PIKE HASN'T YET CAUGHT ON...'

Towards the end of the session, I always change a couple of rigs over to kebabs. We rarely get a slow down in sport, and frequently this alternative presentation brings a fresh burst of activity in swims we've already fished with conventional baits, and on occasions we have had incredible numbers of runs on kebabs. Perhaps it's due to the 'end of the day' bait disposal scenario I've already talked about.

'The kebab was found to work well virtually everywhere I tried it...'

One thing that all my clients invariably remark about is how much easier life is with the kebab rig, and they often ask why I didn't start them off with it in the first place! I tell them that they have to do it the hard way first, or they will never appreciate the easy way. Correspondence that follows later, often shows I've made many happy converts who now use the method where and when it's appropriate, as I'd suggested to them.

Another useful practice I've used a lot in recent years is groundbaiting for pike. I'd already used cereal groundbait to attract prey fish into the swim in the past, which in turn attracts pike, but I decided to take this a little further by making the groundbait attractive to both pike and prey fish. It was all about the ingredients. The base mix is a halibut pellet groundbait enhanced with mixed particles like crushed hemp, crushed maize and various seeds. It is flavoured with fishy liquids and laced with small chunks of chopped fish. When made up in the correct proportions, it binds very well into balls which can be catapulted further than you can cast. My early trials were carried out in areas known to have pike and prey fish present, and simply involved balling the bait into an area and fishing my baits over it. These could be conventional baits but were often kebabs or chunks. It worked well!

My next leap forward was inspired during a bream session when using a method feeder and self

'I DECIDED TO TAKE THIS A LITTLE FURTHER BY MAKING THE GROUNDBAIT ATTRACTIVE TO BOTH PIKE AND PREY FISH.'

hooking rig. It seemed logical that if I developed a beefed up version of the bream rig and combined it with an appropriate hook bait, 'self hooking' could work for pike. A few days later I returned with my new rig; my pike groundbait packed onto a large carp method feeder and a chunk of herring impaled on a size 2/0 single as bait.

After a little fine tuning, I got it to work very well and found it quite viable to rig for 'self hooking' on waters where pike were keen to pick up small chunks of deadbait. The rig features a short wire hook trace about eight inches long, and a 'non tether' style of wire 'up trace' on which the large method feeder slides. If the main line should break for any reason when playing a pike, the feeder will slide over the up trace and the pike will not drag it and risk it catching on something which tethers it.

The essence of how it works is pretty straight forward. When the rig is on the bottom, the ball of groundbait on the feeder starts to break up, sending lighter particles into suspension and spreading heavier ingredients around the area. When prey fish tackle it, the effect is quicker and more dramatic. The oils in the groundbait spread with any current or undercurrent, and help to draw pike into the area. When pike approach, the sight of feeding prey fish draws them to investigate closer. The prey fish scarper leaving a fishy pong, chunks of fish from the groundbait ball – and the hook bait! The pike now has a feast to mop up! A full blooded run becomes quite likely if a pike picks up the hook bait and the resistance of the heavy feeder causes the hook to catch in its jaw. The short hook link also limits the bait from going too far into its mouth! It doesn't always run off immediately like a carp run, but the erratic signals from the bobbin and alarm leave you in no doubt about what's happening. Pike tend to bumble about when the hook has nicked the jaw, often not aware of what is happening, unlike carp which normally bolt away instantly upon feeling the hook. I often strike at this point rather than wait for a proper run. Quite often the run is just like that from a carp as a pike bolts away.

Admittedly, it's all starting to sound a bit like carp fishing as it is a self hooking bolt rig on which the pike hooks itself, eventually swimming away and sending the front alarm screaming out. What if it is, lots of anglers like to fish in this way, and if the pike are usually hooked in the jaw with just one hook, I can see this style of pike fishing eventually becoming popular. It's not a casual approach though and requires dedication and application. To get the best results requires skill in rigging, accurately baiting the swim and good bite indication, and carp anglers would most likely be more in tune with this way of fishing than pike anglers, at least from my observations.

One of the things I like about this way of fishing is that it keeps me busy and thinking about how I can outwit the pike. I am now, for example, putting layers of mashed fish and fish groundbait in Fox Arma Mesh solid mesh stocking to form a fish 'sausage' which is oozing with juices and oils. This insoluble product really holds the soft ingredients together and is almost invisible when packed tightly with bait. A size 2/0 single or size four treble is nicked lightly into the end of the sausage and it is fished in a groundbaited swim. I started using it for catfish and all I caught was pike after pike after pike! You have to sit up and take notice of this.

Where these experiments will lead to is uncertain, but I can see myself increasingly using and developing such tactics on venues where I can set up for longer sessions, in areas known to have plenty of pike and prey fish. These venues are very different to the wild and natural waters that I have mentioned in other parts of the book which need a searching approach, but such fishing is not easily available for everyone. This is an alternative way of fishing for pike, and one which I enjoy occasionally on certain venues. I believe that we have yet to see pike fishing in this way taken to its full potential, where pike are treated like any other fish with proper attention to safe hooking with single hooks. I look forward to seeing how the next generation of pike anglers develop this theme!

One thing I have noticed is that anglers who fish almost exclusively for pike tend to get very set in their ways, and are very unresponsive to new ideas. That's their prerogative of course, but I think that there are valid reasons for making changes to current pike fishing practices which we should be taking seriously. To be quite blunt, treble hooks cause harm to pike when taking into account the many rigs and lures which use them. I am not on an 'anti treble hook' campaign; rather I wish I didn't have to use them in any of my pike fishing. In experienced hands they can be used reasonably safely, but in inexperienced hands they can lead to considerable damage. I would consider half of the pike anglers I come across to be incompetent at bite indication and in fish handling. They are a danger to the pike and also to themselves. This might sound harsh or unfair comment, but even though there has been great progress in the last thirty years, I still don't see pike getting the same considerate treatment as other species. Deep hooking and poor handling are commonplace and no amount of education seems to be reducing this to an acceptable level. For this reason, despite what others might think about experimentation with alternative methods, I think we need to be working towards a better way.

As I may never write another book about pike fishing, and I'm approaching the end of my pike fish-

A 21lb 5 oz pike caught on a self hooking rig.

ing days, I think I should be honest and speak my mind. Pike anglers are trying to catch a fish which has sharp teeth, can bolt down baits rapidly and can thrash about violently when out of the water. Combine these facts with treble hooks and something can and WILL go badly wrong! If we really care about pike, then I think we will eventually have to do something about it! Alternatively, we can accept that this is what the sport involves, put these things to the back of our minds, and live with the consequences. We have gone a long way down the road of 'sport fishing' for pike now and have enough collective experience to decide where pike fishing goes in the future.

To think that I can come up with a system that will be safe for pike everywhere is a pipe dream I know, but I believe that it's possible to approach some pike fishing situations in a safer manner and that would be a start. This could include replacing treble hooks with singles where we can or finding safer ways of using trebles. It might even mean restraining ourselves from using very large singles or trebles, accepting that some alternative methods might not be as efficient at hooking. Due to ever increasing problems caused by both animal and human pike killers, I am seeing more and more pike waters becoming managed to protect them. With restrictions often applied on such waters to 'normal' pike fishing methods, alternative approaches like those outlined in this chapter are well worth considering, and could become a basis for developing future methods.

It would be a great pity to think that the freedom to search for pike in wild waters with exciting methods has to be compromised in this way. It would also be a pity to see competent pike anglers restricted by the incompetence or indifference of the majority. There's no way we can change the attitude of all anglers and certainly no way it could be policed anyway, but slow progress through new ideas is better than no progress at all!

'...TRYING TO CATCH A FISH WHICH HAS SHARP TEETH...'

PIC: MICK ROUSE

'...THE RESISTANCE OF THE HEAVY FEEDER CAUSES THE HOOK TO CATCH IN ITS JAW.'

Pic: Mick Rouse

'...Mick was struggling to keep hi footing, but he was determined to captui the moment...'

CHAPTER 24

Catching For The Camera

The printed media are very quick to latch onto anything new, and are always in need of something interesting to fill their pages. It must be a nightmare having to produce fresh looking publications, month after month, and even worse, week after week! Providing material for them is not a very well paid part of my business, but plays an important part in fulfilling my contracts with sponsors who expect to see me appear in angling publications using their products on a regular basis. When developing my 'self hooking rig' for pike, as mentioned in the chapter on 'New Ideas', Angling Times asked me whether I could demonstrate it and catch a fish for their cameraman.

I was up for the challenge, as always, and arranged to meet Mick Rouse, their head of photography, at a local lake. Conditions looked good as I set up my standard deadbaiting rigs on two rods and a third rod with my 'self hooking' bolt rig. As we sat and waited, the front alarm of the bolt rig rod bleeped a couple of times and the rod bounced in the rests. Seconds later, the rod bounced again and then stopped. Over the next minute or so this happened several times before the alarm suddenly screamed out in true 'carp run' style, and the 'baitrunner' whirred away frantically. Now it was time to tighten to the fish. There was no need to strike – it was on!

I bent into the pike, and it was clearly a reasonable fish. Mick was already prepared with his chest waders on as he wanted to get into the water to try for some shots from interesting and unusual angles. The pike approached and I had a quick glimpse of it, and it looked to be about 14 lb. Suddenly things started to happen very quickly, as they often do in these situations, and both of us needed to work together to try for a spectacular shot of the pike being netted.

I had already warned Mick that the gravel slope he was standing on, up to his waist in water, would shift very easily under his feet, and it dropped away sharply to 12 feet or more! I could see from the corner of my eye that Mick was struggling to keep his footing, but he was determined to capture the moment as the pike came between him and the net. In the split second that we had to get the shot, I realised the fish was much bigger than I first thought, in fact it was a 21 pounder! Mick was frantically firing off the camera as he knew that he would only get one chance, and like a true professional pushed himself to the limit to do so.

Then the unexpected happened. The pike swirled in the net and then tail walked straight out of it again, hitting Mick full on in the chest while he held his multi thousand pound camera high in the air, resulting in him losing his balance and starting his feet sliding down the shifting gravel slope. Whilst still playing the pike with my right hand, I managed to grab hold of Mick's clothing with my left hand, now up to my knees in water and getting a good soaking myself. I hung onto him very tightly as he gingerly regained his footing and somehow he managed to inch his way back up the slope, camera aloft and swearing like a trooper. In fact, we both were! When Mick checked his images, he was at least thankful that he had got the picture he wanted, but more thankful that he had lived to work another day!

Much of my work involves performing in front of the camera, whether to provide stills for magazines or footage for DVD and television films. I also produce my own photos for features, usually with the help of Jan, and even though this is done more within my comfort zone, we still have to come up with the goods. Deadlines still have to be met, but at least I have the opportunity to make several attempts at it until I achieve a satisfactory result. The worst scenario is when I have to work alone and forced to use my camera on a tripod to get photos, and that really can be a struggle. When you have regular writing contracts, it is wise, in fact essential, to plan ahead and build up a large library of suitable pictures to draw from. Currently, my photo library contains around 20,000 images, and I frequently have to supply material on request to sponsors, magazines and websites. Providing they are suitable in terms of subject and quality, such material makes you very useful to the tackle trade and media, and I take pictures of anything that could be useful, especially atmospheric and action shots. Thank goodness for digital photography which has brought my photographic costs down dramatically!

'MUCH OF MY WORK INVOLVES PERFORMING INFRONT OF THE CAMERA...'

'...He will usually want the rod silhouetted...' Pic: Dave Kelbrick

Most pictures will only have a limited shelf life as they can soon become dated and unusable. When sponsors change, for example, pictures with their logos and products may no longer be of any use, and neither are pictures where I am using discontinued products. Most pictures get used eventually through careful planning and provide a useful part of my income.

For the reasons mentioned, pro anglers rarely have days where they can indulge themselves with pure pleasure fishing sessions. They are always aware that the fish they catch can be very useful and valuable, and spend a lot of time 'fishing for pictures' at venues that they would rather not fish by choice. I would never complain though, the job is a pleasure in itself, and even with such restraints and restrictions, it's still very satisfying.

Catching for someone else's camera is very different to taking your own pictures, as a great deal of pressure is removed when they take on the technical responsibility for them. There is a downside however as you spend less time fishing and more time presenting to the camera, but catching in a tight time framework becomes easier as you become more experienced.

Producing photographs or film footage is pretty straightforward, provided that a few sensible rules are followed. You need to think in terms of the 'end result' and that will mean considering how things look from the cameraman's view. If playing a fish for example, he will usually want the rod silhouetted against the sky or water or a light background so that it stands out clearly, and you should always listen to his instructions. In fact, you should talk to each other constantly and do exactly as asked. For example, he may ask you to net the fish to your right, but keep it well out from the bank. This might not make sense to you and may appear a juggling act, but it's what he needs you to do to get the shot properly framed and the scene lit up correctly. Fortunately, digital cameras allow greater numbers of pictures to be taken at no extra cost, and without having to change films. Post processing software can be used to further enhance or correct pictures if they are not perfect straight from the camera.

When producing films or photos, you have to forget your own agenda! Just imagine that you are playing a big fish that you want to get in the landing net as it looks rather special, but the cameraman wants you to hold it back while he wipes water from his lens. You just have to be philosophical about it and if it comes off the hook, as several have for me, so be it. To ensure that the cameraman gets the correct shots, it's also necessary to slow everything right down and it's nothing like the normal pleasure or experience of playing a fish. Although there is a risk of loosing the fish, it is at least less stressful for them as they are brought much more gently to the net when filming. Netting and lifting the fish to the unhooking mat more slowly and methodically than usual so that pictures can be taken, is also less stressful to the fish and compensates in some way towards the fact that they tend to be out of the water slightly longer when making a film.

Trophy shots let a lot of anglers down. First of all, I wouldn't even bother to photograph a pike unless it was in pristine condition. It doesn't matter how big a fish is, if it has scales missing and split fins, no one will be impressed. On the other hand, some of the best pictures I have seen have been of quite small pike because of their wonderful colours, markings and condition. It's also vital to present the pike to the camera effectively. Many anglers spoil their photos by just not holding the fish properly, often at awkward angles and generally looking uncomfortable with it. To make things worse, some don't clean off leaves and bits of grass which can be very distracting. It's vital to show off the best assets of the fish and for me, where pike are concerned, it's their teeth and you have to learn how to hold the pike so that its jaw drops open and exposes them in the most impressive way.

And finally, you have to smile! Oh what a difference this makes. Tidy yourself up, take the fag out of your mouth and try and look like you should feel after the capture of a nice fish – elated! The worst shots, to me, are those where pan faced anglers look down at the fish and not at the camera, with a look that I'd reserve for a funeral!

There are plenty of other little tricks I have learnt to use, like

'IT'S ALSO VITAL TO PRESENT THE PIKE TO THE CAMERA EFFECTIVELY.'

wearing smart and colourful clothing. As anglers, we do tend to wear dull, drab clothing, but if you want to make your pictures stand out, a splash of colour will make all the difference. I tend to wear brightly coloured fleeces underneath my waterproofs, but just the addition of a bright scarf or hat can give the picture the boost it needs.

You'll notice that I'll comment now and again about the importance of being determined to get the job done. After all, even if you are a professional, you will not be engaged by anyone if you have a reputation for being unreliable. Reliability has to be one of your most important attributes, not just being reliable to turn up and have a go, but to have a reputation for coming up with the goods. Believe me that can be very difficult to achieve on a regular basis unless you pay vital attention to preparation. The camera crew's time is very expensive and cannot be wasted.

Catching pike for the camera in extremely cold weather, for example, can never be guaranteed, but sometimes in order to meet deadlines I have no choice and have to do it, and I'll use every trick in the book to ensure that I do not let anyone down. One way I improve my chances is to bait an area the evening beforehand with small pieces of deadbait and mashed fish so as to make the swim attractive to pike, but not over feed any pike that may come in to investigate so that they are not hungry the next morning.

Quite recently I was booked to do a deadbaiting feature on a large gravel pit which was obviously going to be a 'grueller' due to the low water temperature. I nipped across on the evening before and baited three areas with fish chunks. When the photographer and reporter arrived the next morning, I took them to the swims I had baited in different parts of the lake. I blanked in two of them, but the third one was full of pike and I took two 'doubles' and a couple of 'jacks' from it in a very short time. Once we were on the fish, the job was done very quickly.

On another occasion, I had to catch a river pike in extremely low water conditions, with the margins just starting to ice up. I knew this one might beat me, so I went the day before and fished a section of river to get a feel for where there might be a few pike holed up. While fishing a small wobbled deadbait, working it very slowly in the cold clear water, I attracted a 'mid double' to the bait and it sauntered from beneath a marginal watercress bed and nipped onto it. Before she could swallow it, I teased it away from her and she melted away back under the weed, and now I knew exactly where she was!

In such cold conditions I didn't expect her to move very far, if at all, and the next morning I kept the knowledge of her location to myself as a bit of insurance while I fished a few other swims first. They drew blanks, although not unexpectedly, so I moved to the swim where I had seen the big pike. I told the photographer to keep really quiet as I would be dropping my float fished deadbait right next to the bank in just two feet of water. Nothing happened for five minutes so I just lifted the bait slightly to give it the smallest movement and I saw her head appear and grab it. A 'mid double' was landed, photos were taken and we were on our way home before mid day. Another job done! Catching so easily for the camera on a regular basis must seem to be either through skill or the luck of the devil. It is neither and is simply down to thorough preparation and determination.

Making films is very different to magazine photo shoots, as here you will need presenting skills. I have never had any illusions that I have such skills, but I seem to have got away with it, having made almost 100 TV programmes and a dozen or more DVD appearances. I think that enthusiasm, not being afraid to have a go, and being able to catch fish, has made up for what I lack in presentation expertise. It's certainly a case of the more you do, the better you become as your confidence builds.

Most angling films have a fairly high technical content which I'm very comfortable with, but I quickly found that it's not a good idea to 'second guess' what the angling public want to watch. When I made my first films I took the technical side of it very seriously, and if you are not careful, such detailed content can become very long winded and boring. Of course this aspect is important but it needs to be presented in digestible bites and in a way that the viewer feels comfortable with. I have since found that most viewers do not like being talked down to by professionals either, and prefer a delivery with a certain amount of humour. DVD's do tend to be more technically biased than TV films as they are usually offered with education in mind, so television has to be approached differently, with a mix of fishing and banter. In fact, most anglers I meet tell me they like the entertainment more than the technical aspect. It has worked for me and I'm looking forward to producing more TV programmes once the economic climate allows investment again. As I always say, never change a winning formula!

Producing photo's and films relies upon many things coming together. First and foremost, you must pick the right venues or it will never work. Even if you pick a good venue you can never prepare for the unexpected, such as two seals suddenly appearing in your swim, as happened when we tried to make a Fox DVD on the Norfolk Cut Off Channel! You also need the basic angling skills and correct tackle, and then have to work methodically to a plan. Unfortunately, the fish rarely respond to timetables, and you cannot easily predict where or when they will be caught. As filming time is limited this can be quite worrying, but I always ensure I have something up my sleeve to get us out of trouble. It's important to remember that films are about providing entertainment and information and do not necessarily need to be factual. If they were so, they would often end up being very boring and not get across the points intended. The skilled anglers used to present these films are simply showing how to go about catching the sort of fish that they are used to catching. It is of no relevance whether the film is fabricated or in real time. In fact, if the commercial element had not been properly considered, the films that many have enjoyed would simply never have been made.

Filming '*Fishing in the Dark*' for Clean River Video Productions many years ago was an extreme example of how films sometimes need to be made within an economic and common sense framework. The essence of the film was how to catch pike and zander on a fenland drain in the dark, something I have done on endless occasions. To do so with any clarity would be impossible without adequate lighting and this was to be provided in the form of floodlights and a portable generator. In a margin swim on a small fenland drain, it was obvious that the bright lights and presence of the crew would ensure that I caught nothing at all! In order to make the film, we had to act out and replicate a typical night's fishing. This meant that the fish would have to be provided from another swim, away from the noise and lights.

'ON ANOTHER OCCASION, I HAD TO CATCH A RIVER PIKE...'

'Mick and Matt in Ireland filming The Greater Rod Race.

It was really very straightforward. Jan fished in the swim above me, away from the bright lights that were focused on me, and used identical tackle to mine. She hooked a couple of pike and a zander in the darkness of her swim, as and when required, and walked them into my swim. All I had to do was demonstrate landing, netting and unhooking them!

Fortunately, the vast majority of fish shown in my films have been captured in real time for the camera, such as the Linear St John's fishery record pike of 28 lb 2 oz, which I caught when making the '*Better Pike Fishing*' video for Angling Times and the 27 lb 12 oz pike which I caught in my appearance in one of Nev Fickling's videos.

There's never been an agenda to my filming or, in fact, any of my media work. All I have done is taken advantage of offers that have come my way. Many I've turned down as well, which have not suited me in one way or another. Opportunities to fish in very hot places or at sea I've declined as I suffer badly from heat and from sea sickness. Other offers have come at the wrong time and I've put my family life first after making earlier mistakes which have made me realise what my priorities are. I've done more than enough though to satisfy me and to pay my bills!

CHAPTER 25

Into The Future

'...THERE IS SOMETHING MAGICAL ABOUT THE WHOLE BUSINESS OF PIKE FISHING WHICH TIME HAS NOT EXTINGUISHED.'

As this book goes to print, I will have been fishing for pike for over forty years! After all that time, I can honestly say that I still feel that there is something magical about the whole business of pike fishing which time has not extinguished. There's no sense or logic in going pike fishing. You are called to it, and for me, it's been with a passion that has driven me on regardless of the pain or problems it has caused. I have been repaid though with rewards which are personal and have left me feeling so good, on so many occasions. They have often come at the most unexpected of times and in the most unexpected of ways.

At the moment I am planning my retirement, but this will still see me pike fishing within my financial means and physical ability. I approach this period of my life with mixed feelings. For sure, I will fish at a steadier pace, maybe not catch as many pike as I'm used to, but I will obtain sufficient satisfaction by now having a better appreciation of the value and meaning of my catches. Fortunately, I'm past the stage where I compare my catches with those of others. It was a pointless exercise, a human failing, and I realise now that the guy who seems to be doing much better might not be as contented as you think he is. What you catch, and how you feel about it, might seem to go hand in hand, but I have found that they don't, and satisfaction comes in many different forms. It's all in the mind and available to anyone who seeks it.

On the other hand, I might miss the heady chase from the days when I looked at things completely differently, sharply focused on catching pike at a rate which was totally out of proportion and perspective. It did have a certain vitality about it which age has taken away. Nevertheless, I have no choice now, cunning and careful planning will have to make up for my lost drive and stamina, not to mention my dwindling bank balance!

Finding waters with pike which are not being exploited by others gets more difficult with each passing season. I accept that angling writers like me have played our part in creating this situation, but I don't regret sharing my enthusiasm if it's encouraged others and led them to enjoy pike fishing as much as I have. It's an unfortunate fact that we live in a very small country, and there is not enough water to sustain good fishing for the growing numbers of anglers now interested in pike fishing. The challenge of the future will be in how we manage this situation. Thankfully we have organisations like the Pike Anglers Club of Great Britain (PAC), the Irish Pike Society (IPS) and the Pike Anglers Alliance for Scotland (PAAS) keeping an eye on things for the benefit of all pike anglers, whether members or not.

I am often asked why I have never had any involvement with the PAC beyond being an ordinary member. The answer is quite straight forward – I wouldn't have been any good at it! Being able to catch pike is one thing, angling politics are quite another and I take my hat off to those who have strived to tackle and solve the many problems which, if not dealt with, would have led to pike anglers being far more restricted than they are. I feel that my contribution, for what it has been worth, is to have encouraged pike anglers to fish in a responsible way and handle pike more safely. I still think we can go a lot further down this road, and as pike fishing becomes more popular we will probably have to police ourselves before others do it for us.

It may not go down well in some circles, but I think we will eventually have to consider restricting the number of rods we fish with, restrict the use and size of treble hooks on lures and bait rigs, and impose close seasons at appropriate times to limit fishing for vulnerable pike. Each suggestion opens up a can of worms and protests galore. I would have protested myself a few years ago, but time has shown me the sense in taking measures to protect the future.

At the moment we are allowed to fish in the UK with up to four rods, provided that we hold two Environment Agency rod licences. If applied with a little commonsense, I cannot see a problem with using four. I will do so when bait fishing on very hard waters where a single run in a day is quite a rare occasion. I will also start by fishing with four rods when assessing a new water to try and find pike holding areas, or to experiment with different baits. When I am getting runs though, I determine how many rods are practical. Sometimes I will drop down to three rods, and quite often down to two. My ideal water is where one rod is sufficient because the sport is just so good!

Lure fishing is a little different, as you would have to be pretty adept to cast with more than one rod at the same time. You can troll more than one rod of course, but here I limit myself to the number of rods which keeps me in control.

The type and size of hooks used on lures is a topic that will cause endless debate. As stated elsewhere in the book, I wish I didn't have to use trebles, but most lures need them for efficient hooking. I especially don't like to use lures with large trebles or those with combinations of huge singles and correspondingly large trebles, although I will admit to having done so before I turned against them, and nowadays I try and use smaller lures if possible. Many larger lures were never designed with pike in

I WON'T BE GOING SO MUCH IN THE COLD!

mind anyway, but because of their availability and effectiveness have eventually found their way into our hands, and they can, and often do, cause a lot of pike damage. Some pike anglers will undoubtedly argue against this, and if they can prove their case, then I must have been doing something very wrong when I used them! As part of my work in the tackle trade I have had to test such lures for my sponsors, and indeed I have followed fashion and used lures with large hooks from other manufacturers, and very effective at catching pike many of them were too. The damage that they caused to pike's teeth and gills though, always took the edge off the captures, often leaving me feeling very uneasy. Any angler who might disagree with me is well within his rights to carry on using them if he feels comfortable with them. I no longer do.

There will also be many arguments against the use of single hooks for bait fishing. I have already stated my case. They are not a universal remedy, but from my own point of view, I know that I will always consider whether a single hook rig is appropriate when I go pike fishing. When I use them, I am convinced that I reduce the risk of damage to pike. You may disagree with this, but my view is based upon catching hundreds of pike on singles whether jigs, spinnerbaits, flies or baits. I can only advise you to keep an open mind and base your own decision on practice, and not theory.

Looking much further into the future, we may see pike fishing banned altogether. I would never have imagined fox hunting would be banned – but it is. Although it's a much watered down version of the sport, huntsmen can still enjoy the 'thrill of the chase' by drag hunting, where the dogs are following a scent trail rather than a live fox. I can imagine how the hunters resent their traditional sport being reduced to nothing more than a lively hack. We may one day see pike fishing watered down in a similar way, maybe using hookless rigs with Velcro coated baits which catch in their teeth, which we use to tease them into the net. You may laugh, but remember you read it here first!

Restricting the times of the year when I fish for pike has made me feel better with regard to damaging them through exhaustion. On my own lake, which I leased for over ten years, I did not allow myself to fish from mid May till mid October. The water temperature was always too high in this period and would have resulted in hard fighting, but exhausted pike. On another lake, in another part of the country, local conditions may well be very different and such a restriction unnecessary or perhaps requiring a little modification. This is the problem with making 'blanket rules', and I think it's much more sensible for fishery managers to set their own localised rules to protect their pike stocks, adjusting them when required to fall into line with changes in local conditions. Problems would still arise however on public waters where fishing was unrestricted, as they also would on large or remote waters where such regulations would be very difficult to police. Policing would be too expensive anyway. Ten years ago, I would never have dreamed that my local waters could have been emptied of pike by anglers from a different culture who see nothing wrong with taking them for food – despite the law!

Otters are proving to be a major problem too as pike feature highly in their diet. I love otters and I love fishing, but someone must stand up and point out the obvious. Otters are being released by the few to cause mayhem for the many. Even worse, otters are being killed covertly on a large scale to protect anglers and angling business interests – I have more than enough evidence to know this to be true. Surely it is wrong to force otters onto a conveyer belt to death by trying to fit them into an environment which is no longer suitable or safe for them. My personal view of course! I cannot do anything other than live within the limitations that fish killing and otter predation will bring to my future pike fishing plans.

By the time this book is on sale I will be approaching retirement age, and no matter how much of an optimist I might be, I know my best days are behind me. This will not prevent me from still having plans and ambitions, but I do know that I will have my limitations too. Provided my health continues and my finances permit, I have plenty of pike fishing projects rattling around in my mind. If I'm honest, I'm not really content to allow my past achievements to be sufficient, I'm hoping I'll always have further dreams and ambitions because I see the journey as being just as important as arriving.

I have always enjoyed catching pike of all sizes, but as my time starts to run out I will devote more of it to catching bigger pike. Catching a 30 lb pike provides me with an unbelievable feeling of elation. Every time I catch one, I know how rare such a fish is and the dedication that's been involved in it's capture, and I always feel that it could be my last one. The last 30 pounder I caught filled me with all the emotion that the first and subsequent captures did, and I hope to feel that way a few more times before I throw the towel in!

The last 'thirty' I caught may well have been my final one, but I have plans which, if they come together, could see me opening the dusty bottle of champagne which Jan always threatens to get out when I catch a real monster. I have three waters in mind which I plan to tackle soon, each of which could produce a pike of considerably over 30 lbs. One is a water I have been tackling for ages without success, and I now feel it owes me one! The other two are very likely to hold a 'big thirty' due to their low pike density and abundant large prey fish stocks. On one of them, a new water to me which I have only fished once before, some very big pike have been found dead in recent years, and although not weighed, have been described in such a way that leaves me with little doubt. The other water I fished many years ago, and although I only caught a few pike from it, one of them was over twenty seven pounds. Since then it has been rarely fished by anyone else, and although it has not thrown up anything of note, a pike has been seen that left the observer quite staggered by its bulk. Sounds like my sort of challenge, but will my old bones be up to fishing in the cold weather!?

Pic: Matt Rand

I'M PLANNING TO DO A LOT MORE LURE FISHING.

None of these waters are easy to get access to, and if they were I might have caught some of their bigger pike years ago. They have been on the 'back burner' for a very long time while I have been working on relations with the owners to obtain better access. Even with access there are technical problems due to weed growth, and on two of them, restrictions will be imposed regarding where I will be able to fish within the lakes. There are still a few dreams that might come true, but in my later years this is all that they may remain.

Waters which offer a good chance of a 30 lb pike are few and far between, and usually require both time and money to track them down and fish them on a regular enough basis to catch one. I have always worked to a fairly tight budget, which means that most of my intensive projects for big pike are locally based to reduce travelling expenses. As I enter retirement, I will finally have the time I want, but sadly not the money!

Most of today's successful 'big pike catchers' fish almost exclusively for them, only tackling the waters that have them in a very single minded and focused way. Although I don't exclusively tackle such waters, I always have my eyes open for an opportunity of a big fish and I will drop everything for a while when I see it is viable, and that's how I intend to carry on for as long as I can. With more time on my hands, I might be able to make more sense of things which have mystified me in the past like understanding more about how pike behaviour is affected by moon phases and the weather, and whether we can go any further in stimulating pike to feed with bait additives. There's still plenty to go at!

Much of my time will be spent enjoying fishing in favourite places, where simply going fishing there is enough. A lot of this time will be spent on the fenland rivers as I never tire of exploring these ever changing venues, where fish movement and location provide plenty of interest on every visit. I will still do a lot of boat fishing, perhaps not so much in my smaller boats where the wind can wear me down and make even a young man's bones ache after a day in the cold. I'll probably do most of my boat

PIC: MICK ROUSE

'I HAVE ALWAYS ENJOYED CATCHING PIKE OF ALL SIZES...'

I ENJOY MEETING THE PUBLIC AT EVENTS LIKE TACKLEFEST.

fishing from my Orkney, and I really look forward to days when the weather is mild and the sun is on my back. If it's cold or windy, or I need a rest from casting a lure or fly, I'll get nicely snug in my chair in the cuddy and get a couple of deadbaits out, my floats perfectly positioned so that I can see them with ease. Whether the end result is a big pike, a big bag of pike or just exploring new water, I will thoroughly enjoy every minute, and these special moments of contentment will be as precious as the pike I catch. Even on days when the boat is battered by wind and rain, I can still experience this feeling as long as I'm warm and dry. Every run will be savoured and never taken for granted and the comfort gained from simple food and a makeshift shelter will remind me of the importance of my basic needs. Fortunately I live in an area rich in gravel pit stillwaters too, where there is also plenty of bank fishing to go at. I have found that nothing stands still with these waters, and each one needs to be monitored regularly in case something interesting arises.

Will reaching retirement age mean the end of my business? In the current uncertain times it's difficult to predict where any business is going but I need something to keep me occupied and I could never simply take it easy and watch the world go by. In recent months I have been surprised to find myself working as a consultant for Rapala. Their recent acquisition of Dynamite baits, my current sponsor, has suddenly opened up a new and unexpected chapter for me during the writing of this book. I'm really looking forward to using and promoting their lures and the continued involvement in the tackle trade. It goes way beyond the job and provides a chance to deepen my knowledge of lure fishing while topping up my income. I'll look forward to the ongoing camaraderie through my business projects and the continued contact with the public through events such as Go Fishing and Tacklefest. There's still as lot to look forward to and enjoy for as long as I can keep up!

Outside of pike fishing I have plenty of other fishing interests too. I enjoy working with my hands and making or building things, and one day, I might even get a better tune out of my guitar if I practice more. My son Daniel now has a degree in music and plays guitar himself so I no longer have any excuses!

There's other fishing too of course. In April and May I have my trout syndicate waters to enjoy and with each passing season, as I get better at it, I love to catch trout on the fly. In the early summer I would not miss my float fishing for tench, followed by river fishing for barbel when the conditions are suitable. Throughout the summer months I will be targeting catfish and through the winter, in between my pike fishing sessions, I will be targeting zander, chub and perch. There's still a lot of fishing that holds my interest as well as pike fishing, and with plenty of time on my hands during my retirement, I'm really looking forward to it as much as I ever did.

As I draw on my memories of a lifetime, I know it is easy to forget how things used to be and how I felt, so writing it all down will help me to remember the life I have thoroughly enjoyed. I only hope that in this book I have conveyed to you what it felt like to be a fanatical pike fisherman, and the anticipation, excitement and drama it has provided me with. I hope to some extent that it has given an insight into my life and reflects a flavour and historical record of the times I've lived in. I have tried to go a little further and capture the way it has affected my senses and the wide range of emotions it has evoked in me.

To really understand this though, you must become a pike fisherman yourself. You will have to get out in the wind, the rain, the frost and the snow and feel the effect of the elements on your body, and smell the atmosphere, sometimes cold and damp and sometimes warm and refreshing. Only then will you have a chance to feel as I have. Only then, will you know what I have been trying to say. I wish you good piking!!

EAGLE
FOX
GALAXY

GOOD PIKING!!

Glossary

TERMS USED BY PIKE ANGLERS:

I hope that this book is read by experienced and novice pike anglers alike, or even those curious enough to want to browse through it. To some, many of the terms used might be unfamiliar so I have selected a small glossary of popular terms used by pike anglers today. I would also point out that I have used Imperial units of weight and measure in the book in places where they are still commonly used by modern pike anglers, even though metrication has been in force in the UK for many decades. I hope this will help you to follow chapters more clearly and also give you an insight into the pike anglers 'lingo'!

'JACK' – a small pike of just a few pounds in weight.

'DOUBLE' – a pike weighing over 10 lb.

'TWENTY' – a pike weighing over 20 lb.

'THIRTY' – a pike weighing over 30 lb.

'BLANK' – a day when nothing is caught.

'RUN' or **'TAKE'** – when a bite occurs as a pike takes the bait.

'I'M AWAY' – I've got a bite.

'CHIN' – lift a pike by the gill cover.

'BUNG' – a pike float.

'BAITRUNNER' – a reel with a free spool mechanism which allows line to be taken freely.

'BACK WINDING' - playing a fish with the anti-reverse mechanism on the reel disengaged so that the handle may be turned backwards to give line.

Right: Catching pike for photographs for the Fox Predator tackle catalogue in 2004 with fellow consultant Dave Kelbrick on Esthwaite Water in the Lake District. Happy days!